MAKE 'EM LAUGH

Other Books by Steve Allen

Bop Fables (1955)

Fourteen for Tonight (1955)

The Funny Men (1956)

Wry on the Rocks (1956)

The Girls on the Tenth Floor (1958)

The Question Man (1959)

Mark It and Strike It (1960)

Not All Your Laughter, Not All Your Tears (1962)

Letter to a Conservative (1965)

The Ground Is our Table (1966)

Bigger Than a Breadbox (1967)

A Flash of Swallows (1969)

The Wake (1972)

Princess Snip-Snip and the Puppykittens (1973)

Curses! (1973)

What to Say When It Rains (1974)

Schmock!-Schmock! (1975)

Meeting of Minds, Vol. I (1978)

Chopped-Up Chinese (1978)

Ripoff: The Corruption That Plagues America (1979)

Meeting of Minds, Vol. II (1979)

Explaining China (1980)

Funny People (1981)

The Talk Show Murders (1982)

Beloved Son: A Story of the Jesus Cults (1982)

More Funny People (1982)

How to Make a Speech (1986)

How to Be Funny (1987)

Murder on the Glitter Box (1989)

Passionate Nonsmokers' Bill of Rights (with Bill Adler, Jr.) (1989)

"Dumbth": And 81 Ways to Make Americans Smarter (1989)

Meeting of Minds, Vol. III (1989)

Meeting of Minds, Vol. IV (1989)

The Public Hating: A Collection of Short Stories (1990)

Murder in Manhattan (1990)

Steve Allen on the Bible, Religion and Morality (1990)

Murder in Vegas (1991)

Hi-Ho, Steverino: My Adventures in the Wonderful Wacky World of TV (1992)

How To Be Funny (rerelease) (1992)

The Murder Game (1993)

More Steve Allen on the Bible, Religion & Morality (1993)

MAKE 'EM LAUGH

STEVE ALLEN

Prometheus Books • *Buffalo, New York*

Published 1993 by Prometheus Books

97 96 95 94 93   5 4 3 2 1

Library of Congress Cataloging-in-Publication Data

Allen, Steve, 1921–
   Make 'em laugh / Steve Allen.
   Includes bibliographical references.
   ISBN 0-87975-837-6 (cloth)
   1. Wit and humor—Authorship. 2. Comedy—Authorship. 3. Comic,
The. I. Title.
PN6149.A88A46   1993
808.7—dc20   92-20700
                                                            CIP

Printed in the United States of America on acid-free paper.

To all the members of my family, who somehow manage to keep me entertained enough to take on the task of entertaining others.

Of all the comedians I have ever met, Steve Allen is not only the most literate, but also the most moral. He not only talks about society's problems, but he *does* things about them. He's a good person, without being all sugar and showbiz, and I really dig him for that.

—Lenny Bruce
from *How To Talk Dirty and Influence People*

Contents

Acknowledgments

Once again I express my thanks to Cristina Gutierrez, who for several years has had the questionable pleasure of listening to the dictated tapes of my manuscripts and transcribing the almost endless pages that result.

Oddly enough, I don't recall ever having heard her chuckle about anything she was reading.

I am also grateful once again to Karen Hicks, who provides helpful editorial suggestions and supervises my work projects from the first-draft to the published stage.

Thirdly, Mark Hall of Prometheus Books has once again been helpful and supportive, as has publisher Paul Kurtz.

And, finally, I am grateful to the universe itself, that great mysterious creation which, by its sometimes tragic imperfections, provides enough raw material to keep all the world's humorists busy enough.

Introduction

Although my first volume on the art of comedy—*How To Be Funny*—ran to over three hundred pages, it became clear during the later phases of that manuscript's construction that there was no way to avoid the cliché about having "barely scratched the surface." While it is at least theoretically possible to gather together all human knowledge, as of a given date, about certain sciences—not to mention less complex subjects—such a total summation would be literally out of the question as regards humor. The root reason is that the entire business of funniness, covering both the transmission and the reception of it, is much more a matter of attitude and reaction than it is a collection of things, facts, and laws.

When we are very young, and hence inevitably naive, we tend to think that there is nothing particularly mysterious or even difficult about understanding funniness. A certain small minority of individuals, we observe, are funny. The rest of us laugh at them. What's so difficult about that?

When we have become more experienced and, one hopes, at least somewhat more knowledgeable, we begin to perceive that part of the difficulty lies in arriving at any broad agreement as to the specific identities of those who are funny. Both formal research and a casual glance reveal that no comedian or literary humorist appeals to everyone. I personally find it difficult to accept that there could be anyone on earth insensitive to the comic abilities of Laurel and Hardy, Sid Caesar, Woody Allen, Mel Brooks, or Martin Short. But no matter who the comic entertainer is, there is always at least a minority prepared to say, "What's all the excitement about? He doesn't seem funny to me."

As those who have read volume 1 of my study will have grasped, the naysayers are just as "right" as the admirers. Perceived humor, like those

13

other forms of beauty to which Shakespeare directed our attention, is in the eye of the beholder. It is obvious enough that there is something tangible that is beheld, but no one ever laughed at a comedian simply because the word *comedian* was written on that part of his income tax form reserved for the identification of his profession. No one ever laughed at a joke simply because it appeared in a joke book. In my own case, as reactor to—as distinguished from dispenser of—humor, I observe that I am easily amused by approximately 90 percent of my professional peers; but it is a far more puzzling question as to why the other 10 percent do not strike me as funny. If they were simply the most inept practitioners of their craft, if they were professional failures, there would be no mystery about my reactions. Some of those at whom I find it almost impossible to laugh are, in fact, in that unhappy category. But most of them are not. They are not only successful professionals but are apparently richly enjoyed by millions of people who themselves would not appear to be mentally or aesthetically handicapped.

If I were unique in this regard, I would not have introduced the fact here. The point is that we all dissent from the majority view regarding certain comic entertainers. There are even clichés that refer to this phenomenon: *Well, there's no accounting for taste. That's what makes horse races.* And so on. An appreciation of this insight is fundamental to understanding the relatively elusive nature of humor.

It does not follow from this that the student of funniness is fated to wander forever in a confusing maze. Comedy, like all other disciplines, does have its practical, nuts-and-bolts aspects; it is primarily these on which readers will be asked to concentrate.

I must point out here, too, that analytical knowledge about humor does not detract from and may actually enhance its enjoyment. An analogy with magic tricks does not hold up. Once you know how a trick is done, you can no longer be startled, surprised, or mystified by it, although you may still be impressed by the finesse and technique of the practitioner. But as regards humor, I am aware of no other class of people who enjoy a good joke more than professional comedy writers.

One should not be afraid, therefore, of learning the secrets of the magicians of comedy. You will still laugh. And the essential mystery will forever elude you.

I emphasize, too, that while this book teaches its own lessons, it is nevertheless designed as a companion to volume 1. Any reader serious enough to solicit instruction in the comic arts should therefore have copies of both books.

1

Thinking Funny

In the song "I Can Make You Laugh," which I wrote for a play about comedian Fatty Arbuckle of the 1920s, Fatty declares:

> I can break you up
> When you'd rather weep.
> I can wake you up
> When you're half asleep.
> Who'd have guessed
> That I'd be blessed
> This way?
> But I can make you laugh—all day.

Obviously that number is partly autobiographical in nature. But in those of us who have the mysterious ability to amuse others, it is usually the case that even before we were aware of our own abilities we had become practiced at laughing more than other children in our social circle.

Perhaps that is the way the gift first manifests itself, in simply being better able to either appreciate the comic elements of daily experience, or, presumably at a later stage, to say something funny about them.

I still do not fully understand, however, what makes me laugh. But laugh I do, all the time, at all kinds of things. I laugh at my sons and grandchildren. I laugh at our dog. I laugh at my wife, Jayne.

Sometimes I just laugh generally, sitting and thinking. In fact, this sometimes happens on television shows. I'm not always conscious of it when it occurs, but if I watch the program later I'll see it. Perhaps someone to whom I'm speaking will say something not funny in itself, but that makes

15

me think of a line, which I may not bother to express because it's too obvious, too dumb, or I assume the audience has already anticipated the point, or wouldn't get it.

For example, someone might say, "Tonight we're going to have more fun than all-get-out," and I just laugh, without bothering to say, "And if you don't think so, you can all get out," or something of the sort. It seems so obvious what can be done with the phrase, that I skip doing it. But the slight flicker of a smile crosses my face at just the thought.

It often seems that, for whatever strange reasons, comedians, in addition to their formal performances, have more comic experiences in real life than other people do. It may be so. An instance that comes to mind is of something that happened several years ago when I was working in Las Vegas. My son Bill and I happened to be in the coffee shop at Caesar's Palace, enjoying an early dinner. Suddenly I heard a page on the restaurant's public address system: "Mr. Steve Allen, Mr. Steve Allen. Answer the courtesy phone, please." So I went over to the cashier and said, "I'm Mr. Allen."

"Oh, are you?" the cashier said.

"Yes," I said. "The reason I'm identifying myself is that I was just paged. Which phone am I to pick up?"

The woman pointed to a phone. When I picked it up, an operator said, "Hello."

"Hello," I said. "This is Steve Allen."

"Hello, Mr. Allen," the operator replied. "How are you?"

"I'm fine," I said. "How are you?"

"Just fine."

"Well, now that we've established our mutual good health," I said, "perhaps I should mention that I'm responding to having just been paged."

"I didn't page you, sir."

"I believe you on that score. I assume, therefore, that somebody else paged me."

"Let me check," the woman said.

A moment later I heard the voice of another operator. "Mr. Steve Allen?"

"Yes," I said. "This is Steve Allen."

"It's six o'clock, sir," the voice said cheerfully.

"Your judgment on that point conforms to my own," I said, consulting my watch. "But I don't understand why you're telling me what time it is."

"Well, sir," she said, sounding just a bit miffed, "you did leave a wake-up call."

"No," I said. "As a matter of fact, I did *not* leave a wake-up call. But even if I had, I rarely sleep in the coffee shop."

"Sir," the woman said, her tone growing colder. "I'm quite sure you left a wake-up call. I have it right here in my records."

"I don't wish to sound difficult," I said. "But I can personally assure you that I left no such call. There is the possibility, however, that *Mrs. Allen* left such a call. Why don't you ring our room and ask her?"

"I already rang your room, sir. Nobody answered. That's why we paged you in the coffee shop."

This inane conversation went on at considerably greater length. The answer to the mystery, of course, was what I had suggested. Jayne had indeed left the call, but because she sleeps with ear plugs, had not responded to the operator's first ring-up.

One puzzling thing about spontaneous humor is that many events are funny only in retrospect. My attempt, one day in New York, to buy an unusual birthday present for my first wife, Dorothy, illustrates the point. While I wasn't ad-libbing jokes per se, merely holding a conversation with the store owner, looking back it is easy to see humor in our exchange, partly because it was embarrassing.

The idea for Dorothy's gift came to me as I was window-shopping on Madison Avenue and happened to pause in front of a shop that sold embroidered fancywork. My attention was drawn to a display of colorful silk scarves on which could be stitched the name of the recipient.

If the proprietor was willing to sew the name *Mabel* or *Irving* on one of the scarves, I reasoned, then he could be induced to embroider a message of any sort. So I decided to ask him to inscribe on one of his largest kerchiefs a series of phrases and baby-talk sentences that our children had uttered at one time or another. I knew that Dorothy would recognize these and be amused.

For example, one day when Steve Jr. was about three years old he asked for a piece of lunch meat, pronouncing it *wunch meat*. When I handed him a slice from the refrigerator, he declined it, saying, "It's not steern."

"It's not what?"

"Steern."

"What is steern?" I asked.

"Steern," he repeated, annoyed that I could be so dense. "Steern wunch meat."

By putting an assortment of wunch—er, lunch—meats on a platter in front of him, I dissolved the impasse for the moment, but for a long time we weren't able to find out what the word *steern* meant. For at least two more years Steve occasionally demanded steern wunch meat. One afternoon, when we were out driving, I tried the question again.

"Stevie," I said, "what is steern wunch meat?"

"It's wunch meat," he explained, "that's *round,* like a steern wheel."

But to get back to the silk kerchief for my wife—I decided that one of the phrases to be stitched on it was *steern wunch meat.* Another was *What am I fink I'm twynin' to do?*, which David, our then youngest, began saying at age two-and-a-half, after Dorothy, catching him in a minor prank, snapped, "David, what do you think you're trying to do?"

Still another phrase was *Jiggers, the kleeps!,* which had been Brian's way of warning me, when he was three, that a police car was approaching from the rear. Then there was *binkie* (Steve's word for bacon), *maynage* (Brian's word for mayonnaise), *waymuns* (Steve's word for raisins), *Ninan* (David's word for Brian), *stop dat waffin'* (Steve's attempt to say "stop that laughing"), and a couple of other phrases I have now forgotten.

Running these words over in my mind, I approached the shopkeeper and told him I wanted to buy one of the large blue scarves displayed in the window.

"Certainly, sir. And with what name would you like it inscribed?"

"Well, no name, actually," I said. "I mean, instead of a name I would like to have several other, er, *things* written on the scarf."

"I'm quite sure we can arrange that," he said. "Just what did you want to include?"

"The first thing is *steern wunch meat.*"

I'm sure he *did* bat an eyelash. "What was that again?"

"It's a little phrase one of my children, er, that is, it's sort of a personal thing that would be difficult to explain. But just put down *steern wunch meat* to start with."

"How do you spell *steern?*" he asked imperturbably.

I told him, and he wrote it down.

"The next word," I said, "is *binkie.*"

"Binkie?" He wasn't smiling.

"Yes. With an *ie* on the end."

"Very well," he said. "You understand, of course, that we charge by the letter?"

"That's quite all right. The next word is *waymuns*—W-A-Y-M-U-N-S. It stands for—well, never mind what it stands for, just put it down."

"Certainly, sir," he said, repeating the word softly to himself as he wrote it out.

"*Stop dat waffin'.*"

"I beg your pardon?"

"That's the next thing I want on the scarf. *Stop dat waffin'.*"

To the man's credit, he never waffed once. Nor did I. We were both extremely businesslike, he out of puzzlement, I out of embarrassment.

"And last," I said, "please stitch in the phrase *What am I fink I'm twynin' to do?*"

Again, not funny at the time it occurred, disconcerting, in fact. But amusing in retrospect.

Perhaps comedy performers and writers just pay closer attention to such comic experiences, but are there also attitudes, emotional states, or ways of thinking that are conducive to funniness for anyone?

People who think in rigid, habituated ways have stock responses to common questions, respond to almost all inquiries in their capacities as Communists, Nazis, conservatives, Catholics, or whatever, will become funnier by working to think *less* dogmatically. Political or religious fanatics are often recognizable by their inability to relax socially and be playful.

As regards techniques to break down rigid ways of thinking, first of all, just by being willing, by fervently wishing to be more playful, you've taken a large step in the right direction. Now you can explore *ways* of loosening up habituated thought patterns.

One way I've invented is called the Phrase Game. While one may play the game alone, it's more fun if two or three people are involved. The rules are simple. Anybody starts by citing a common saying. Let's try, oh, *You've come a long way, baby.*

Now what I have to do is say another phrase that starts with the last word of yours: "Baby talk."

Talk show.

Show me the way to go home.

Home cooking.

Cooking with gas.

At this point, if the next player cannot think of a phrase that starts with the word *gas*, he or she loses a point and you start another round.

You can include additional factors, such as an obligation to come up with a phrase within fifteen seconds, keeping score, and so forth. But the game itself shouldn't be taken too seriously, since the point of it is to make us think in digressive and not necessarily rational ways.

Another recommendation is to talk more often with very young children. It's impossible to converse with a three- or four-year-old in a totally serious, adult, square way. With children we tend to talk baby-talk. The ability to speak baby-talk, by the way, is a sign of mental and emotional health.

Another way to learn to have more fun is to attend a lecture such as that given by my oldest son, Dr. Steve Allen, Jr.—my-son-the-doctor, as they say. He's always had a sharp sense of humor and in recent years has done a good deal of comedic lecturing. In teaching audiences how to deal with stress by juggling, he passes out tennis balls, or brightly colored silk scarves. It's marvelous to see how he starts with a relatively uptight group of businessmen, let's say, and gradually converts them to a bunch of guys having a silly good time.

It's also helpful to watch other funny people perform. Go to a comedy club. Attend a comic play. But don't just sit there and laugh—envision yourself on that stage, playing a particular role, or doing a standup monologue. Whether you ever realize the fantasy or not isn't, at the first stage, important.

You might also try, in the privacy of your own home or in the company of close friends, playfully changing your personality. Speak with a heavy foreign accent. Imitate Richard Nixon or President Clinton. Pretend you're a southern sheriff. Or Mae West. Or Donald Duck. Buy a western hat and walk around the house like a cowboy. The point of all this, of course, is to draw yourself out of your accustomed groove.

It may seem odd to point this out in a book designed to teach you how to be funny, but the word *funny* is in itself a remarkably imprecise adjective. I have long felt that adjectives should be combined with a numerical factor, on a 1 to 100 scale, so that the pictures they draw for us might be more explicit. (Others, I've learned, have independently made the same recommendation.)

Two men saying "I'm hungry," for example, could be describing quite different emotional and physiological states. The situation becomes clearer if one says, "I'm about 5 percent hungry," and the other says, "I'm 100 percent hungry." We should provide food at once for the latter but not be required to move so fast to sustain the former.

Two women are described as *pretty*. From such slight evidence, we would conclude that they are approximately equally attractive. If, however, one of them is 60 percent pretty and the other 94 percent pretty, we will have no trouble knowing which we would enjoy looking at the more.

So, if we start by assuming—or at least expressing our individual opinions—that, say, Woody Allen is 98 percent funny, Steve Martin is 95 percent funny, Bob Hope is 85 percent funny, Andrew Dice Clay is 40 percent funny, and so on, then it might be that the reader is only about 20 percent funny. Once again, our aim is to enhance the funniness factor.

Interestingly, there are people who are essentially unfunny, except that in just one way they are wonderfully amusing. A classic instance would be ventriloquist Edgar Bergen. Edgar was a dear fellow with whom I had the pleasure of working on a number of occasions. I naturally didn't know him as well as his daughter Candice; her portrait of him in her autobiography is considerably less flattering. But the point is that Edgar himself seemed not only unfunny, but even on the dull side. He had a sort of cold, blank personality. But as soon as you put Charlie McCarthy on his knee something magical happened. In the role of Charlie, Edgar Bergen got laughs as big as did any comedian working in his day.

What was true of Bergen is true of ventriloquists generally. The same observation applies to impressionists. Rich Little is a great guy, a personal friend, and perhaps the best mimic of all time. But nobody ever says, "Let's go over to Rich's house just to have some laughs."

The same is true of Frank Gorshin, who can amuse when he speaks as Kirk Douglas, Burt Lancaster, or whoever, but does not appear to be funny as himself.

Marcel Marceau is funny with his body. Charlie Chaplin was not notably funny in speaking, but was wonderfully so physically. Buster Keaton did incredibly amusing things with his body. Stan Laurel had a great, natural clown's face and a wonderful knack for slapstick. People like Fred Allen, Oscar Levant, George S. Kaufman, Henry Morgan, and Dorothy Parker were born with the gift of wit. John Ritter is funny in a cute, acting context. Lily Tomlin and Whoopie Goldberg rarely attempt to amuse as themselves, but do so splendidly once they assume a character.

Back when Woody Allen was doing standup comedy he wrote the most marvelous jokes for himself. Almost all of them, however, were rooted in his character, the introspective, wimpy, New York intellectual. Don Rickles and Joan Rivers make us laugh by insulting us, or others. Billy Crystal does terrific characterizations. Bill Murray has a cute, relaxed, Irish comic sensibility. Harold Lloyd was strangely square in person but funny on-screen.

All these examples—and scores more that could be cited—establish that being funny is not just a matter of learning one skill or being limited to one approach.

I next recommend that students of humor brainwash themselves with the best expressions of the art by reading James Thurber, Robert Benchley, S. J. Perelman, Woody Allen, Max Shulman, Art Buchwald, Jim Murray, Dave Barry, Andy Rooney, Marvin Kitman, and Garrison Keillor, among others. But most readers will be more interested in performed humor—that found in nightclubs, films, and television—than in the written humor found in books.

Nevertheless, they still ought to read the books. And there's no reason they shouldn't develop a personal library of the classically funny films now available in videocassette form. In fact, I've compiled a list, not of every funny picture ever made, but a representative sampling, starting with the films of Charlie Chaplin.

Chaplin was there from the beginning. He almost invented the art of funny motion picture making. You might start with *The Goldrush,* which came out in 1925. Then there's *City Lights,* released in 1931, in which the Little Tramp falls in love with a blind flower girl. And, although I've never thought of *Monsieur Verdoux* (1947) as one of his best, it's still worth studying. It also features some funny moments by the delightful Martha Raye.

Limelight, released in 1952, is about an on-the-skids comedian who meets a dancer contemplating suicide. It doesn't sound as if it has naturally comic possibilities, but in Chaplin's hands something magical always happens to such story material. Other movies on the funny film list would include:

After the Fox (1966), Peter Sellers
Airplane (1980), all-star cast
Animal Crackers (1930), the Marx Brothers
Arthur (1981), Dudley Moore
The Bank Dick (1940), W. C. Fields
Being There (1979), Peter Sellers
Blazing Saddles (1974), Mel Brooks
Blockheads (1938), Laurel and Hardy
Born Yesterday (1950), Judy Holliday
A Chump at Oxford (1940), Laurel and Hardy
Dinner at 8 (1933), all-star cast
Dr. Strangelove (1964), Peter Sellers
Duck Soup (1933), the Marx Brothers
A Flask of Fields (1930–33), W. C. Fields
The General (1927), Buster Keaton
It Happened One Night (1934), Clark Gable, Claudette Colbert
Made for Each Other (1971), Renee Taylor, Joe Bologna
The Milky Way (1936), Harold Lloyd
My Little Chickadee (1940), W. C. Fields, Mae West
My Man Godfrey (1936), William Powell, Carole Lombard
A Night at the Opera (1935), the Marx Brothers
The Pink Panther (1964), Peter Sellers
The Producers (1968), Zero Mostel, Gene Wilder
A Shot in the Dark (1964), Peter Sellers
Some Like It Hot (1959), Marilyn Monroe, Jack Lemmon, Tony Curtis
Sons of the Desert (1933), Laurel and Hardy
Steamboat Bill, Jr. (1928), Buster Keaton

This Is Spinal Tap (1984), Michael McKean, Christopher Guest, Harry
     Shearer, Rob Reiner
Way Out West (1937), Laurel and Hardy

I would also include almost any film ever made by Robert Benchley,
including his minor roles in full-length features and solo work in his own
comedy shorts.

I recommend that the student of the art of comic film see every picture
Woody Allen ever made, with the exception of his serious work, such as
Interiors. Allen's films are among the best of recent comedy movies. It makes
sense to study the masters, not the producers of schlock, no matter what
field of professional endeavor one is interested in. If it comes to a choice
between Woody's pictures on the one hand and films like *Caddyshack* or
Animal House, or sex comedies aimed at the teenage and college freshman
audience on the other, it makes no sense to choose the inferior examples.

Here's a list of Woody's comedic films. You can buy or rent most of
them on videocassette; since they're frequently reshown in theaters or on
television, it's also not particularly difficult to track them down that way:

What's New Pussycat? (1965)
What's Up, Tiger Lily? (1966)
Take the Money and Run (1969)
Bananas (1971)
Play It Again, Sam (1972)
*Everything You Always Wanted to Know About Sex (But Were Afraid
     to Ask)* (1972)
Sleeper (1973)
Love and Death (1975)
The Front (1976)
Annie Hall (1977)
Manhattan (1979)
Stardust Memories (1980)
Midsummer Night's Sex Comedy (1982)
Zelig (1983)
Broadway Danny Rose (1984)
Purple Rose of Cairo (1985)
Hannah and Her Sisters (1986)
Radio Days (1987)
September (1987)
Another Woman (1988)

Crimes and Misdemeanors (1989)
Alice (1990)
Shadows and Fog (1992)
Husbands and Wives (1992)

*   *   *

There used to be an art form called the "comedy of manners." Why aren't comedies of manners made now in this country? The answer is simple. We no longer have manners to speak of. Oh, most of us have table manners, I suppose, but not much more. Emerson once referred to an original gentleman who, if manners had not existed, would have invented them. Do you meet many such today?

In the 1920s, '30s, and '40s our playwrights created what were called drawing-room comedies. Just as manners are now largely gone, so are drawing rooms. To the extent that there is anything properly identifiable as dignity in our society today, our present writers of comedy would be inclined to treat it as a proper object of ridicule.

What residue of good form remains in our society is, to a great extent, an inheritance from the seventeenth- and eighteenth-century phases of our history, which were chiefly English and Continental culturally. You see this sort of thing reflected, as I started to say, in the American theater. In the thirties and forties there were leading men and women, even in motion pictures, who had a marvelous social grace, a certain genteel charm. This was by no means simply a matter of being born into the upper classes since few, if any, popular Broadway or film actors of that period were more than middle class in origin, and some not even that. But they must have admired the social qualities of the gentleman because they learned how to not just copy them but to absorb them and regulate their own social behavior on the basis of such standards.

But doesn't theater have to reflect the entire spectrum of society? It did not in past centuries, but since the advent of more realistic drama, the egalitarian tendencies in society have naturally been reflected in the theater, too. That's all right with me. You would hardly have hired Sir Cedric Hardwicke to play a plumber or a cowboy, and no one expected to see Dame May Whitty playing a prostitute from Chicago, or a waitress in a Brooklyn diner. But today we do not have the William Powells, the Ronald Colemans, the Cary Grants, and the Melvyn Douglases. Today we have Sylvester Stallone, Prince, and people like the late John Belushi.

❖   ❖   ❖

Whether the motivation for studying this book is to make conversations sparkle, become the life of the party, add humor to speeches, write funnier letters—whatever—readers will concern themselves with jokes. So let's return to the subject of joke construction formulas detailed in chapter 3 of *How To Be Funny*. Construction devices are important. In general, the straight line of a joke sets up a premise, an expectation. Then the funny ending—the punch line—in a sense contradicts the original assumption by refusing to follow what had seemed a reasonable train of thought. Many jokes involve that simple matter of leaping outside what had appeared to be the rules of the game at the moment. The following formulas are described more fully in *How To Be Funny*.

The Play-on-Words Formula

The oft-quoted line incorrectly attributed to Robert Benchley (after being caught in a rainstorm)—"I've got to get out of these wet clothes and into a dry martini"—is an example of a play on words that has rightly become a classic of its genre. A key technique involves *manipulating words that sound the same but which have more than one meaning*. You frame the joke around the alternate definition of a word, or phrase, that has been either stated or implied.

Another thing you can do is to break the key word apart. If someone asks about my attire, for example, and I'm wearing a seersucker suit, I might say something like, "Really, Sears will sell it to any sucker who comes along."

Another way to play on words is to create a word-picture by purposely misusing the intended definition. A classic example of this type of joke is Henny Youngman's famous "Take my wife—please." It's a wonderful play on two separate meanings of the verb *take*.

A variation of this homonymic play on words is one in which you essentially substitute a similar sounding word or phrase for another. A marvelously effective illustration of this device comes from the 1940s. I can't recall its specific origin, but in the scene, a comic character is smitten by a young woman's beauty:

COMIC CHARACTER: You bewitch me, absolutely bewitch me.

WOMAN (*walking away*): I'll be wit'cha in a minute.

There are more facets to the wordplay approach. Sometimes you can even do jokes using just parts of words—prefixes, suffixes, or, for that matter, any important syllable at all. The "seersucker" joke already mentioned is an example.

One of my own techniques involves the splitting up of a compound word, changing its meaning and adding the phrase "and you know how painful that can be" at the end. I spontaneously created this device while doing radio comedy in the 1940s. *Hornswoggle* was the first word subjected to it. "And if you've ever had your horn swoggled, you know how painful that can be."

"Well, I'll be dad-blasted. And if you've ever seen your dad blasted, you know how painful that can be."

"We were going down the road lickety-split. And if you've ever had your lickety split, you know how painful that can be."

"Women all over the country are furious about the Tailhook incident. And if you've ever had your tail hooked, you'll understand how they feel about the matter."

Recently, when I was being interviewed by Eddie Schwartz of Chicago's radio station WLUP, someone mentioned the name of comedienne Paula Poundstone. "And if you've ever had your stones pounded, you know how painful that can be."

Another wordplay device I sometimes employ involves *discarding the obvious key word* in a sentence or question and giving an answer that might be perfectly reasonable if the concentration were on another word. For instance, say Jayne asks me, "Did you eat pork for dinner last night?" I might answer, "Yes. I considered smoking it, but eating it seemed more reasonable."

There is also the *literalizatio. device*. It involves simply interpreting an idiom literally and providing a response based on that mistaken interpretation.

EDGAR BERGEN: I laughed till my sides split.

CHARLIE MCCARTHY: Well, a little Band-Aid will take care of that.

While it is common to denigrate word play as a category of humor the fact is that there can be inferior and superior examples of the type. The similarity in sound between two words once provided me with an extremely effective response to a question that had been put to me by someone in an audience during my Question Cards routine. The question arose because of the fact that I had had to call on the services of a not especially talented hairdresser while doing a series of comedy concert appearances on the road.

Consequently, I was not terribly surprised to see that someone had written the question, "Is that your own hair—?"

My first response was to take a purposely goofy look down at the rest of my body and say, "Is *what* my own hair?"

That part worked, but then I read the rest and more important part of the question: "—or are you wearing a hairpiece?"

My response was as follows: "You know, it's interesting, but I've been in show business for over forty years and for practically all of that time no such question has ever been put to me. But I think I know what gave rise to it here: there was an article recently in the *National Enquirer* on this general subject. Parenthetically, I was very honored to be mentioned in that story. Now you might be thinking—how could it possibly be an honor to be referred to in an article about hairpieces? The answer is that the other nine gentlemen referred to in the story were all superstars—John Wayne, Frank Sinatra, Burt Reynolds, Liberace—they were all people of that calibre. Consequently, as I say, I was honored to be listed among them. Now the title of the article just happened to be 'The Ten Worst Hairpieces in Show Business.'

"Let me say, by way of explanation, that if the *New York Times* said that I had a hairpiece it would be reasonable to believe the report, even if it later turned out to be factually incorrect. The assumption of its accuracy would be reasonable because, as you know, the *Times* has a superb reputation for factual reporting. The *Enquirer*, by way of contrast, has no such reputation. In fact, they are so careless with the truth that almost every year they are successfully sued by someone who feels he's been maligned or libeled. But even if they lost, say, $20 million a year on such lawsuits, the fact that they may make a couple of hundred million a year simply means that they can claim the losses as a tax deduction so that it's not a serious problem for them."

The audience was listening to this analytical and intentionally noncomic rationale with respectful attention, apparently having assumed that as regards this particular question I was not going to do a joke but simply give a frank answer to the question about my hairdo.

"Now sometimes," I continued, "if false information about you gets into print you're at a total loss as to how such a story ever got started in the first place. In other situations, however, there may be some small grain of fact which is then misinterpreted and distorted. So, to finally resolve this question—the fact is that I do *not* have a hairpiece. What I *do* have is—*herpes*."

During the laughter, I kept adding elements to the rationale, such as, "And the two words, you see, *sound* very much alike, so it was understandable that someone who might have overheard a conversation about this, perhaps in a bar someplace, would get the wrong impression."

The laugh was so big that I've reused the response in a few additional instances when the same question has come up.

The Reverse Formula

This involves saying the exact opposite of what is expected. The natives of India, for example, have a simple joke that may not amuse you, but it contains the proper mechanical elements: The tiger and the rabbit had a fight. The rabbit won.

The Exaggeration Formula

Exaggeration formula jokes call for more ingenuity than the types mentioned above, for the obvious reason that not every exaggeration is automatically a joke. One of the best jokes ever written was Fred Allen's line about a scarecrow that was so scary the crows not only stopped stealing corn, they brought back corn they had stolen two years earlier. That's a brilliant, even poetic exaggeration.

The Implication Formula

Many jokes involve making a more-or-less obvious point, but managing not to state it directly. A good illustration is the following exchange that took place between Art Linkletter and a seven-year-old boy he interviewed on one of his shows years ago.

ART: Were you born in California?
BOY: No, we moved here from Kansas City four months ago.
ART: Why did you move to Los Angeles?
BOY: My daddy wanted to see if he liked it.

ART: How *does* he like it?
BOY: We're moving back next week.

Naturally the child's line got a tremendous reaction.

What excites the reasoning part of the listener's brain is the slight connective jump it must make between the last statement of the joke, or exchange, as rendered, and the implicit *meaning* of that line.

The "I'm Not So Dumb" Formula

Application of this formula involves three steps. First you refer to a common but somewhat stupid belief. Second, you confidently assert that you, personally, are too intelligent to believe any such thing. Third, you confess to some other equally inane opinion. One time, in referring to dumb things that very young people accept, I said:

Of course, on the other side of the ledger, there were certain common beliefs about sex that I never fell for, even though a lot of my friends did. For example, I never did believe that nonsense about Chinese girls. (*pause*) Japanese girls, yes. But not Chinese girls.

Another technique is to summarize quickly the facts of a familiar case and then reject the obvious conclusion and suggest an alternative that is, or seems to be, dictated by common sense.

I remember the time, years ago, when a friend of mine, a songwriter, was having trouble coming up with just the right title for one of his numbers. His first was "Tea for Five," but that didn't sound right. Then he tried "Tea for Four," but the publishers wouldn't accept that one either. He thought of "Tea for Three." But something about it didn't seem quite right. And then last, of course, he had the perfect solution. He wrote a song called . . . "Honeysuckle Rose."

One of Victor Borge's writers once used the same formula:

I was trying to invent a soft drink, but I had trouble deciding on the right name for it. First I called it 4-Up, but nobody was interested. Then I tried the name 5-up, and that didn't work either. I also wasted a lot of time trying to promote a drink called 6-Up, but then suddenly I had the name that I'd been looking for—*Pepsi Cola*.

The Visualization Formula

The construction of a joke can be an exercise of the visual imagination. Consider:

QUESTION: Have you ever tried sniffing glue?
ANSWER: Yes, I once did try to sniff glue. But all that happened was my nostrils got stuck together.

The important thing to remember when using any of these formulas is that whatever can happen along these lines should, of course, come naturally and not be forced.

2

A Brief History of American Comedy

In some ways, one of the great differences between the humor of today and that of fifty years ago is that now humor for the most part is performed whereas the earlier material was meant to be read. The humorists of the 1920s admired writers like Mark Twain, Artemus Ward, and Josh Billings of the previous century. Some of them knew of Oscar Wilde. The new literary entertainers of the 1930s included Irvin S. Cobb, Stephen Leacock, Robert Benchley, Frank Sullivan, S. J. Perelman, Ring Lardner, and James Thurber.

But, as humorist Corey Ford has observed, with the advent of radio, and then television and the rise of the popular comedian, those who might have become humorists in their own right took to writing "comedy material" for the performers. Humor became more and more mass-production, assembly-line jokes and sketches. Today more comedy is being written, and more comedians are standing up in front of audiences, than ever before.

Interest in comedy in the United States was by the mid-1980s at an unprecedented high point, although there had earlier been other peaks on the humor market chart, each stimulated by technological innovation. In the 1920s, for example, although vaudeville comedy continued its brisk development, the introduction of silent films produced a worldwide wave of interest in such gifted practitioners of the comic arts as Charlie Chaplin, Buster Keaton, Harold Lloyd, Laurel and Hardy, Fatty Arbuckle, the Keystone Cops, Harry Langdon, Charlie Chase, and Ben Turpin. Then, in the 1930s, the sudden explosion in radio ownership concentrated attention on Eddie Cantor, Amos 'n Andy, Stoopnagle and Budd, Fred Allen, Ed Wynn, Jack Benny, Fibber McGee and Molly, Fanny Brice, Lum and Abner, Garry Moore, Ransom Sherman, Bob Hope, Edgar Bergen and Charlie McCarthy, and

George Burns and Gracie Allen, almost all of whom had come from vaudeville.

The next wave of popularity resulted from the introduction of television. Throughout the decade of the 1950s, there was scarcely an American TV owner who did not watch and enjoy Milton Berle, Arthur Godfrey, Jerry Lester, Martha Raye, Pinky Lee, Jackie Gleason, Art Carney, Lucille Ball, Red Buttons, Jan Murray, Jack Carter, Larry Storch, Herb Shriner, Wally Cox, George Gobel, Jack E. Leonard, Phil Silvers, Ernie Kovacs, Jimmy Durante, Red Skelton, and your obedient servant. The 1950s were, to be sure, a golden age for television comedy.

But nothing lasts forever, least of all in television. For the next thirty years big-time comedy—which is to say sketch and standup monologue comedy requiring the services of full-time professional comedians—was notable chiefly by its rarity on TV. There were, obviously enough, the happy exceptions. The Smothers Brothers had their run, as did the "Laugh-In" show. I worked one primetime season on ABC (1961), another on CBS (1967), but did comedy chiefly within the talk-show format, for a total of twelve years. Some of the giants of the 1950s—Gleason, Caesar, Skelton, Berle—were rarely seen.

Television still had comedy, of course, little thirty-minute playlets which by no means required the services of professional comedy specialists and which, in fact, rarely employed the most gifted comic artists. By and large, the situation comedy stars of the 1950s, '60s, and '70s were simply charming, likable people who, because they could seem "believable" in playing light comedy, were well-suited to this now-dominant form. In this connection one thinks of Robert Young, Gale Storm, Bob Cummings, Donna Reed, William Bendix, Barbara Eden, Fred MacMurray, Valerie Harper, Cloris Leachman, Bea Arthur, Mary Tyler Moore, Carroll O'Connor, and Jean Stapleton. Professional comedians Don Adams, Bob Newhart, and Redd Foxx did star in successful situation series but were far outnumbered. Tim Conway and Don Rickles, though certainly talented, did not succeed in the form, despite repeated attempts.

Oddly enough, the situation was not unprecedented. The film industry had undergone the same change in moving from the period of the great screen comedians into the "situation comedies" of the 1930s and 1940s, the films that starred such ingratiating performers as Cary Grant, Carole Lombard, Clark Gable, Irene Dunne, Frederick March, Jimmy Stewart, Myrna Loy, and William Powell.

The 1960s brought us the hippie culture. What was fascinating about the youthful rebels of the 1960s is that, whatever else they were, they were not purposely funny. The decade produced some lively journalism, some interesting art, a great deal of vigorous music, some fascinating wardrobe, and some approaches to social problems that were at least innovative. It seemed, however, to have little interest in humor in any formal sense. Perhaps the rest of us require the services of professional humorists because our lives seem essentially serious, if not tragic. It may be that if you spent so much time wandering through strawberry fields, smoking pot, attending love-ins, dropping out, and goofing off, you would not have the emotional need for the escape valve that humor represents to the generally more puritanical human race. It is interesting, in this respect, that the conservative groundswell of the 1970s and '80s brought with it a new wave of comedians, liberals all.

In the late sixties there were a few young comics who pretended to be hippie comics, but in my view they were people who weren't funny enough to succeed along traditional routes and therefore let their hair grow and forsook their old tuxedos for Nehru jackets and granny glasses. I found them no funnier in the new clothes than they had been in the old.

Since the 1960s, there has been a continuing leftward swing of the pendulum in American humor. Why can't rightists manage a counterswing? Probably because, with some happy exceptions, they tend to be conservative socially as well as politically. They laugh, of course, but the list of things they are prepared to be amused by is shorter than that which titillates the rest of us.

The relative absence of right-wing humor returns us to the question as to what function humor itself serves.

One of its uses is to criticize and hence modify or improve society. Although conservatives sometimes are paranoid in feeling that they are in a tiny minority and largely without influence, the fact is that American society is itself largely conservative, if not always strictly so in the political sense. Unlike Europe, we do not have Communists, socialists, or radicals of any type in the White House, in Congress, or, despite the views of the far right, running our governmental departments and bureaucracies. Consequently, when a comedian does jokes about congressmen, senators, governors, presidents, the Pentagon, the CIA, the FBI, the Catholic church, or whatever, he is almost invariably attacking an essentially conservative institution. Even comedians such as Bob Hope, who are themselves politically rightist, do such jokes, apparently without always realizing the philosophical thrust of what they are doing. Johnny Carson is not a particularly political entertainer, but because he jokes about items in the news, much of his humor seems to have a liberal bias.

Another factor is that there is in Protestantism a puritan, Calvinistic, narrow-minded extreme. It is that element of Christianity that traditionally has frowned on gambling, dancing, drinking, going to movie theaters, playing cards, listening to popular music, and casual mingling between the sexes. In the last century, sad to say, people of this stripe supported slavery and the subjugation of women, largely because they thought it was ordained by God because it was found in the scriptural record.

There's a great deal more that might be said about this, but even these few observations help explain why the conservatives are unlikely to produce a counterhumor, despite the fact that the right loathes much of modern comedy because, as noted, it attacks persons and institutions they hold dear. One can hardly imagine a right-wing Lenny Bruce, Mort Sahl, or Richard Pryor.

One fascinating development of recent decades has been the rise of the black comedian. I wrote an article in 1957 pointing out that our society would not then permit the emergence of black comics who were the equivalent of Bob Hope, much less any who were like Lenny Bruce or Mort Sahl. While there were a number of funny black performers in earlier times, they generally portrayed eccentric maids, Pullman porters, butlers, or stablehands. I did not mean to suggest that somewhere out behind a barn there were youthful Dick Gregorys, Bill Cosbys, or Eddie Murphys doing witty monologues for underground black audiences. My point was that blacks in America had not yet come to the point of social evolution at which the development of philosophical comedians could be expected of their culture. What produced the present rich crop of black comics was nothing less than the Negro social revolution.

One of the reasons we have struck such a rich vein of black comedy is that humor has often risen from a climate of rebellion. Many professional funny people are Jewish; another group well-represented in the field has been the Irish. Both cultures have a tradition of restless submission to dominant authorities. The yearning for freedom and relative control of one's own destiny can be a powerful mainspring supplying energy to those who have the mysterious comic gift. It is no wonder, therefore, that we have seen so many black comedians in America in the 1980s and '90s.

White America for years salved its guilty racist conscience, to an extent, by its true adulation of certain gifted black entertainers. Somehow a man felt less like a bigot if he could say—and mean it—"I sure love to see Bill Robinson dance," "That Lena Horne really is beautiful," or "Nobody writes prettier music than Duke Ellington." It is important to understand that blacks are not living out their revolution in a vacuum—an obvious impossibility;

white Americans are participants in the same drama, and our sophistication regarding the confrontation between the races is keeping pace with that of blacks. Whites have now become civilized enough to *grant* the black freedom to indulge in biting social commentary. This is much to the good, because black comedians can accelerate the education of American whites that is necessary to our advancement toward fuller social justice for everyone.

But what of the question: Are certain ethnic groups funnier than others? I believe they are. The Jews are the funniest ethnic group on earth. This does not mean that all Jews are funny, any more than we mean that all Italians are musical when we say that the Italians have a particular love for music. In the American context over the last century, the Irish and blacks, too, have produced a good deal of humor.

In a discussion of Jewish humor on TV, critic Joel Siegel of "Good Morning America" asked, "Why don't we see Jews playing Jews on TV? Why did the character of 'Rhoda' stop being Jewish when she got her own show?" It's a fair question. Television and film executives are often themselves Jewish, so it is odd that they would prefer to cast gentiles in the role of Jews (I have been cast in Jewish roles in three instances), or somehow downplay the Jewishness in comic characters.

The first time I heard about this sort of thing, it related to Warner Brothers' film studio in the 1930s and 1940s. Although Jack Warner himself was Jewish, he and other studio executives would almost invariably cast gentiles in Jewish roles, and preferred that Jewish actors, if hired, change their names. The reasons are many and are rooted in Jewish history. I've written a bitter comic story titled "The Day the Jews Disappeared," in which I state what has long been my belief, that it never made sense for gentiles to treat Jews as though they were inferior, when precisely the opposite is the case. Intellectually and culturally, Jews are a superior people. I had, in fact, never even mingled with such large numbers of highly intelligent people until I entered Hyde Park in my third year of high school in Chicago, where the student body was largely Jewish.

Jews have traditionally been better educated, their family life has been more stable, and statistically they have been happily underrepresented as regards wife-beating, drunkenness, abandonment of family, and barroom brawling. Although Jews represent only about 3 percent of the American population, they have received 27 percent of the Nobel Prizes awarded to American scientists.

But as I say, when the reality is that they are truly superior—even morally—their treatment at the hands of non-Jews over several thousands of years has naturally instilled in them a perfectly understandable degree of wariness and defensiveness. Consequently, even though they may personally be thrilled at the great success of Admiral Rickover, Benny Goodman, George Gershwin, Irving Berlin, etc., it is usually left to gentiles to publicly identify such citizens as Jews. Jews see America, quite rightly, as a gentile environment; and to the extent that they have flourished here as a people, they have done so at the sufferance of the not-forever-trustworthy gentile majorities. It is this, I think, that is behind the reluctance of some Jewish theatrical executives to seem "pushy," to use a word common in anti-Semitic language.

Exactly what happened to bring about today's comedy revolution? By the late 1970s, it had become apparent to the public, if not to network executives, that comedy was enjoying a sort of underground revival. At first in major cities, and then in smaller communities, nightclubs sprang up featuring comedy entertainment, generally by newcomers. The Comedy Store, the Improv, the Laff Stop, Catch a Rising Star, the Comedy Womb and similar establishments were opened simply because scores of new comics were emerging, there was a youthful audience waiting to hear them, and neither the traditional nightclubs nor television were prepared to accommodate the expanding market.

By 1980, the new comedy explosion had become evident even to the densest of television programmers. Comedians' pictures appeared on the covers of national magazines, zany films were again important at the box office, funny record albums sold in the millions, and comedy concerts were consistently sold out. NBC's "Saturday Night Live" was the first indication that at least one network recognized the new phenomenon. It was significant that at more or less the same time, the last of the old-style comedy shows—"The Carol Burnett Show"—was going off the air. Carol herself was just as funny the day her program ended as she was the day it started. The program's declining ratings showed nothing more mysterious than the fact that no television show stays on forever.

So what explains the sudden emergence of hundreds of new comics after the long dearth? The dominant factor seems to be those people in the twenty-five to thirty-five age bracket who have some natural tendency to be witty or zany or eccentric and who have enjoyed the benefits of years of brainwashing by television comedy in one form or another. We would hardly be surprised if, having put great emphasis on welding for thirty years, our society were now producing a large number of gifted young welders. So the funnier of the young people, having watched this particular art form for literally all of their lives, had, largely unconsciously, absorbed the tricks of the trade.

Statistically, however, this is a more remarkable societal phenomenon than the reader might assume. Comedy has always been an extremely rare art. As of 1960 there may have been as few as three hundred professional comedians in the entire human population. Granted that creative artists are always in the minority, the fact remains that the rarest of all have been comedians. Against this background, then, the recent mushrooming of new comics is unprecedented.

Another reason for the proliferation of comedians may stem, in part, from the fact that of all the arts, two—singing and comedy—appear to the observer to be the easiest to perform. This naturally does not apply to truly extraordinary instances, such as operatic singing, the film performances of Peter Sellers, a television sketch by Sid Caesar, or a pantomime by Marcel Marceau. But in watching the bulk of vocal or comic performances, many people have the I-could-do-that reaction.

There is, after all, an apparent effortlessness to Steve Martin's having worn the old novelty shop arrow-through-the-head and acting like a jerk; the nervous little mannerisms of Don Knotts; the blank-faced, relaxed befuddlement of Tim Conway; the cue-card reading of Johnny Carson's monologues; the memorization of a few dozen marvelous and utterly disconnected jokes by Henny Youngman or Rodney Dangerfield; or the drunken meanderings of Dean Martin or Foster Brooks.

As for singing, one does not necessarily imagine that one could do what Barbra Streisand or Mel Torme do, but since the emergence of Bing Crosby in the 1920s millions of Americans have simply opened their mouths in showers, automobiles, on the street, or at the beach under some sort of hazy, goofy impression that what came out when they sang the latest popular hit wasn't really all that far from what Bing and later Frank Sinatra and Dinah Shore and all those other lucky people were paid so much money to do.

As for singing, it seems that the popular confidence is not all that misplaced. Most of those who become successful singers are, by and large, simply lucky freaks of nature. The genetic accidents accounting for their physical structure happen to give them a certain combination of vocal chord tissue that produces a sound interpreted by others as pleasant. They have then only to put this entirely natural noise together with contributions by a gifted composer, lyricist, arranger, and professional musicians to create a harmonious and pleasing whole.

Presently, almost every young person in America seems to entertain the fantasy of being a rock singer. And with good reason. The singers with most rock groups are, in fact, lucky shmucks, the majority of whom are getting away with the sort of artificial screaming, shouting and black-imitating currently in vogue rather than doing true singing of the traditional sort.

But most comedians are not just lucky amateurs. The illusion of ease, naturalness and simplicity is mostly that—an illusion. Almost anybody can sing, but statistically very few are qualified to become professional comedy entertainers.

If the reader thinks that he or she nevertheless might be among the fortunate minority, know that at least it won't be necessary to go to a great amount of trouble to discover whether one's confidence is unfounded. Becoming a good clarinetist or violinist requires years of painstaking practice. But you can actually start a career as a comedian with a remarkably modest investment of time and effort.

3

Ad-Libbing Your Way Out of Tight Spots

The knack for ad-libbing is invaluable for talking oneself out of a tight spot. There's a great deal of that, oddly enough, in comic fiction. Witness the famous "road" pictures starring Bing Crosby and Bob Hope, as well as more modern instances such as some of the comedies of Burt Reynolds and Clint Eastwood, or the "Moonlighting" TV series. The writers of such scripts seem guided by the principle that a funny answer turneth away wrath.

In reality, when one is not supported by comedy writers, it is of course more difficult to be funny in the face of danger. Even so, that approach to the problem, however imperfect, should by no means be overlooked. Many comedians and comedy writers have shared the childhood experience of learning to joke to protect themselves from neighborhood bullies when challenge or physical defense were not among the sensible options.

In moments of fear or outright panic, even those who have some gift for the creation of jokes are likely to be so distracted that their spontaneous abilities are impaired. But something about forcing a playful attitude at such moments can be effective. Even the worst monsters are not totally without a spark of humanity, although they often, in their own minds, dehumanize their victims as a way of rationalizing their crimes. We see this in times of war, when governments deliberately dehumanize entire populations, sometimes hundreds of millions of people, to lessen the guilt of attacking and slaughtering them. It is easier to kill people conceived of as the yellow peril, primitive savages, or dirty Communists, than if the victims are seen for what they really are—fellow human beings. Consequently, anything a victim can do to ingratiate himself with a would-be attacker, including smiling or joking, could be a perfectly rational form of self-defense, even though one may be feeling a combination of anger and fear as the social drama is acted out.

Ad-libbing is also effective in other "tricky" situations. I've managed to use it several times when affairs at which I was performing didn't go as planned. One occasion dates back to 1951, after I had begun to do a daily comedy show for CBS television. I got a call from someone asking me to do a benefit performance at a club for underprivileged children somewhere in New York, the Lower East Side, I think.

When I got to the gig, I discovered that the audience consisted entirely of tough-looking nine- and ten-year-old boys. The first thing that struck me was that very few of them would have the slightest idea who I was, since many of them, in those days, were too poor to have TV sets, and even if they did, were unlikely to have become familiar with me in just my few months in New York.

Obviously a comedian cannot simply launch into his regular act or patter in front of an audience of children. Fortunately, I had by then discovered that in situations of this general sort the best thing to do is get a question-and-answer exchange going, since, if the audience themselves bring up a subject, they will obviously be interested in whatever is said about it.

But it took quite some time to get anybody to ask the first question. Finally, one little guy, a pint-sized version of a Dead End Kid, put up his hand.

"Yes," I said, pointing to him. "The young man right over there."

Standing up without a trace of shyness, the boy said, in a voice already raspy and tough, "Hey, are you Superman?"

Inasmuch as my resemblance to the fictional cartoon character, Clark Kent, had often been remarked upon I was not totally surprised by the question. But I also realized at once that if I said I was *not* Clark Kent I would be of even less interest to the boys.

"Yes, I am Clark Kent," I said with calm assurance.

At that, a smattering of applause broke out. I do not mean to suggest that the boys present were so mentally deficient that they thought I could possibly be a living embodiment of a cartoon character, but by that time the adventures of Superman were already being acted out in a filmed series. The boys did, however, seem unclear as to whether I was the actor who *played* Clark Kent in the *Superman* series, or the real article.

I was prepared for another question on a totally different subject, but the same inquisitor remained on his feet. "If you're really Superman," he said, "let's see ya do somethin' strong."

Fortunately, as a pianist I was aware that the large angled piece of wood at the front of all grand pianos is detachable, something the average person would have no reason to know.

"Very well," I said. Striding to the piano, I pretended to rip the music rack section off with a mighty heave, after which I held it above my head with one hand.

Tremendous applause.

My little friend, however, was still not entirely convinced. Either that, or he enjoyed seeing mayhem. "Do somethin' else strong," he called out.

For a moment I was at a loss, but then a solution occurred to me. "Sure," I said. "No problem." At that I picked up the mike stand, placed it across my knee and pretended I was going to tie it into a pretzel shape. After making a fierce face to effect expending some muscular effort, I glanced into the wings, as if someone there was attracting my attention.

"What?" I said to the imaginary person. At that I walked stage right, still carrying the microphone stand as if it weighed only an ounce, and faked half a conversation.

"Oh, really?" I said. "Well, then I'd better not do it."

Turning to the audience, I said, "The fellow back here says this is the club's only microphone and if I tie it up in a knot you guys won't be able to hear any more of the shows they put on here."

This produced a smattering of applause, presumably for my nice-guy attitude. But my questioner still would not let me off the hook.

"If you're really Superman," he said, looking at me shrewdly, like an old mafioso, "let's see you fly around the room."

"No problem," I answered, after which I realized I had damned well better figure out—and fast—some method of becoming airborne. Four factors were evident: (1) the stage was a bit higher than normal, (2) there was a center aisle between the rows of seats, (3) I was in good physical condition, and (4) the stage was rather deep-set. Taking advantage of all this, I stepped quickly upstage, turned to face the audience, stretched out my arms as if to fly, and ran forward as fast as I could, executing a high, looping broad jump, which carried me out to about the sixth row, where I landed in the aisle, not all that steadily.

The only reason I can think of for the tremendous burst of applause that greeted this ungainly move was that the boys had really wanted very much to believe that I was Superman. Not all of them were convinced, but there's no question that some of them were.

Another time when the ability to ad-lib my way out of a tight spot proved useful happened when I first went from New York to Los Angeles in 1960. Members of the Democratic party, knowing of my serious interest in a number of social issues, began to approach me about the possibility of running for office. The House of Representatives, the Senate and the governorship were brought up during such conversations. From one point of view, this may sound absurd, but there were those who thought it equally absurd when the first rumors about Ronald Reagan getting into politics were circulated.

In fact, that reminds me of a joke David Steinberg told: "When I see the commercial with the actor who says 'I'm not a doctor but I play one on television,' I think of Ronald Reagan. 'I'm not a president but I play one on television.' "

In any event, my clever answer was then what it is now, "No thank you." But an unusual situation came up in 1965 when Congressman James Roosevelt retired, leaving ten months of his sixth term unfilled, a fact that called for a special election. At that, some party people came back to me and said, "We know you've already said you're not interested in a political career, but we'd like to talk to you about this situation anyway because it's so unusual. The twenty-sixth district here in town is overwhelmingly liberal, and there would be little possibility of your being defeated. Secondly, you'd only have to serve ten months in Congress. After that you could decide to remain there or return to your regular work."

I found this approach interesting, and agreed to enter the race, campaigning for several weeks and enjoying every minute of it. Eventually I was ruled ineligible on the election law technicality that I was not registered as a member of the Democratic party but as an independent. But the campaigning, making speeches, shaking hands, all of that was quite stimulating.

The one part of it that I thought before the fact might be difficult was answering questions from the floor. It turned out that my fears were groundless. Responding to questions was a good deal more pleasurable than making speeches, although it naturally required doing one's homework. I still recall the first such instance. It was at a meeting of a Jewish organization in the Fairfax district of Los Angeles. The speech was well received, after which the chairman announced that I would entertain questions. An elderly woman rose and put to me what is possibly the most difficult question of the century, so far as finding a simple resolution is concerned: "Do you think you could actually help resolve the difficult problems in the Middle East?"

"Absolutely," I said. "I know exactly what ought to be done there."

This brought the audience up short; an attentive silence enveloped the room. Remember, we were discussing the most intractable political and foreign policy problem of the world. I paused for just a moment as the audience pondered the fact that I had just said I knew precisely what should be done. "But," I added, "who could get the Israelis and Arabs to *listen* to me?"

Hearty laughter.

Obviously, from one point of view, I had given the audience a fast shuffle. But the joke was another way of saying that, while any interested arbitrator might be able to recommend a fair solution in the Middle East, it might be quite impossible to get both parties to accept it because of the heat of emotions involved in the conflict.

Another time quick thinking helped me land on my feet came when I was a guest on the late Oscar Levant's TV program in Los Angeles, in the 1950s, plugging my just-published book *The Funny Men*. The book praised all its subjects highly, with the one exception of the late Eddie Cantor. Oscar, just for the sake of argument, took up the case for the opposition. At one point he said, "Did you interview Eddie before you wrote this chapter on him?"

"No, I didn't," I said.

"Well then," said Levant, "how could you possibly feel qualified to write about Cantor if you don't know him that well?"

"Oscar," I said, "are you taking it as a principle that one must interview a subject before writing about him?"

"Yes I am," he answered.

"Well," I said, "in that case, you've just put Jim Bishop out of business."

The line got a big laugh, although it would be unlikely to today, simply because in the early fifties Bishop had written two best-selling biographies: *The Day Christ Died* and *The Day Lincoln Was Shot*.

Let me stress that in using humor to get out of a difficult spot you should evaluate the audience first. If it is a stern school principal, three dour relatives of the woman you're dating, or a no-nonsense prospective employer, you should keep a tight rein on your gift for comedy. On the other hand, if the situation is more relaxed, if the authority figures themselves seem genial or good-natured, then they might react quite favorably to some joke or witticism.

Have there been occasions where I've felt embarrassed after ad-libbing a joke? Oh, yes. I remember one time a few years ago when I was a guest on the "Tonight Show." Steve Martin was hosting. I was introduced after actress Cloris Leachman was to have completed her turn. But she was continuing to babble on about some producer she had met, saying, "I'm so excited! He came up and offered me two jobs!" I injected, "Yeah, a nose job and a chin job." Though the line got a laugh, I immediately regretted saying it. Thank goodness Cloris knew it was all in fun; as a young woman she had been a beauty contest winner.

The instantaneous creation of jokes requires more than knowledge, or even mastery, of the several technical formulas already discussed. Some degree of common sense is also important. When I was entertaining in Orange, Texas, recently, for example, someone in the audience asked, "Who is your favorite comedy team of all time?"

I said, "Gosh, that's a pretty tough question because there have been so many good ones. Though if I had to be specific I would say the Dallas Cowboys because I—" At that point there was no possibility of continuing the line because the laughter was so deafening. The instruction here, of course, is not that you should give the answer "Dallas Cowboys" whenever the question comes up. The reason the name of that particular team worked well in this instance is that Orange is a community not far from Houston. I therefore assumed that the local loyalties, so far as professional football was concerned, would be with Houston, a long-time rival of Dallas.

But even given that factor, the line would not have worked if Dallas had just won the Super Bowl. The team a comedian might mention would have to have just lost a crucial game, perhaps through ineptitude, or have had a generally poor season. Of course the root factor of the joke is that the word *team* has at least two separate meanings.

Fairly often, props—food or other items that may be in my general vicinity—give me ideas for funny lines. Back in the 1940s, I used to walk up and down the aisles of radio studios interviewing members of the audience while holding a hand-microphone. One day it occurred to me that as I strode up the aisle, I looked like a priest holding a device with which, in Catholic churches, holy water is sprinkled on people sitting in pews. So I spontaneously made a gesture, with the microphone, as if sprinkling holy water on the audience.

Only those familiar with Catholic ritual knew what was funny about the move, but there were enough of them present that it got a good laugh. I still do the business from time to time, and it's been borrowed by a number of other comedians over the years as well.

Another time I remember somebody sending me a box of Silly Putty through the mail. I played with it on camera during my talk show, rolling it into a ball, twisting it around. Then I put it on the front of my desk and totally forgot about it. But Silly Putty cannot be so treated. It doesn't stay in one shape: It begins to flow, like liquid, though very slowly.

I soon noticed that the audience was laughing in strange places, places that as an entertainer I knew were not appropriate. So I said, "What the hell are you laughing at?"

They shouted, "Look at the front of your desk."

The Silly Putty had flattened out to about a foot-and-a-half in length and was oozing down the desk. When the director got a shot of it, I said, "Oh, now I see what you're laughing at, Rona Barrett's tongue."

In the fall of 1985 I filled in as host for Merv Griffin on two of his talk shows. Merv had suddenly been taken ill so I was given only a few hours' notice to appear. My opening monologue, based on ideas dictated while driving to the theater, plus on-air ad-libbing, went like this:

Hi folks. Thank you very much.

This is a hamburger. It's not a comedy prop. A woman just came up and thrust it in my hand, and that's how it is. I propose to eat it during the show because I'm starving. This is not a comedy routine. I'm just sharing a little reality with you.

When they called today about this, they said, "Do you want food?" I said, "Yes." It's just now arrived.

Anyway, good evening, ladies and germs. Look what you laughed at. Comedians always say this. I think Milton Berle was the first one—(*public address system comes on*) Ah! There we are. Now we can all hear each other.

As I say, Milton Berle was the first person to say "ladies and germs," but tonight I *mean* it because (*cough*)—Oh, boy! Now you know what I'm talking about, right? I have not been in contact with very many ladies today but lots of germs.

As a matter of fact, it's ridiculous that I am replacing Merv on the grounds that he is sick, because I am much sicker than Merv is.

Merv's always sick. I said to him years ago, "Merv, you're sick. You know that?"

He didn't take umbrage.

How many of you know what the word *umbrage* means? Would you just put a hand up? That's what I thought. It was a five-hundred-dollar question. Sorry, you're too late, sir.

Anyway, Merv—(*spits something accidentally*) Oops! That was a peanut.

I don't entertain. I just let you watch me live for about an hour. That was really a *piece* of a peanut. If it was the whole peanut you'd get sick looking at me.

But I finally said, "Where's my cheeseburger?" and they said, "Here's a peanut," so I ate that. And it came out. I guess now that I've got the burger, I didn't need the peanut anymore anyway.

Anyway, Merv called me about an hour ago. He said, "I've lost my voice." He really did. I said, "You've lost your voice?" He said, "Yes." And I said, "Then through what portion of your anatomy are you communicating with me at this time?"

And he laughed, good-natured slob that he is.

Well, actually, it was not Merv who called me, because—figure it out—if he'd lost his voice, he couldn't be calling me.

But the producers had been looking high and low for Merv's voice, and *they* called me. I'm not kidding. They did look high and low. But nary a trace—Do you know any other comedian who uses words like *nary*? None at all. That's right. That's why they're all in Vegas making a million tonight, and I'm stuck here. But that's all right.

Anyway, the producers were really looking high and low for Merv's voice. One of them was high, the other was low.

And neither of them could find it. So I finally listened to this nonsense, and I said to them, "Get lost."

They were so desperate one of them actually did get lost. And the other went and looked for *him*. That's why there was no warm-up for the show tonight. But that's all right.

Anyway, they thought they'd invented a new game called hide-and-seek.

(*to man in front row*) Where are you from? I'm sorry, sir, your time is up.

That was a hundred-dollar question. You have to pay attention!

I'm just warming you up because it wasn't done earlier; later our guests are gonna come out here and expect laughs.

I'm already secure. I don't need laughs. (*cough*) I just need a hospital. But they said Merv is under the weather, and I said, "So am I. And there isn't room under there for both of us."

And they said, "But the show must go on."

I said, "I don't care. My pants must come off. Really, I'm not joking with you. I'm sick as a dog."

They said, "We'll order dinner for you."

I said, "Fine."

They got me Gravy Train.

See, now you're laughing at garbage! The good stuff went right over your heads. But that's alright. We'll arrive at an understanding in a few minutes.

I said, "I'm really not kidding. I just got up out of a sick bed to answer the phone." They said, "A sick bed?" I said, "Yes, it's a Chippendale. And if you've ever had a chip in your dale, you'll know . . ."

Do any of you have *any* idea what I'm talking about? I don't. So that makes two of us.

Oh, there were some question cards here. They're under a glass of—Is this a glass of water? Is that some superstition of Merv's? You put cards under water and they turn into something else?

Some of you folks wrote questions. They thought of this at the last minute, too, so there was no time to get your names and addresses and your thumbprint and all that.

Be that as it may, where is Bill Sweeney? (*man waves*)

Hi, Bill, nice to have you with us. He writes, "Steve, what's it like being married to a beautiful woman like Jayne Meadows?"

It's interesting that what you actually wrote was "beautiful women like Jayne Meadows." Did you know you wrote that? That's what it's like! No—there's a lot to Jayne. No, no, no. I didn't mean it that way. I mean there's a lot to her. She's very versatile. She's in Northville, Michigan, right now, making a speech about great women of history.

(*man yells out*) I'm from Michigan!

You're from Michigan?

Yes.

Who cares? (*laughter*) No, I just said that to see if something would wake you people up, and look what did it—rudeness. Comic brilliance went right over your head, but at rudeness you laughed right away. That's terrible.

Audiences are conditioned now to insults in humor, instead of jokes, or situation-comedy shows. Is that your face, or did you block a kick? That's what you laugh at.

Bad cess to you. And bad cess to the Roto-Rooter man, now that I think of it. (*man laughs*) Thank you, sir, but what is your opinion against that of thousands? One man down here is hysterical.

Jane Sweeney. Hi, Jane. Oh, you're with the gentleman from Michigan. Nice to have you with us. She writes, "Where do you live, Mr. Allen? Do you have a place on the ocean?"

Yes, I have a place on the ocean. It's called a raft. That's a silly answer, but the question wasn't too great either.

I live in Santa Monica. I don't *want* to live in Santa Monica, although it's a lovely community. But I had to get out of my other house. It was burned about a year ago. It was in all the papers. They were burning, too.

"How long have you and Jayne been married?" We've had twenty-four happy years. (*applause*) We've been married thirty-six, but . . . (*laughter*) You laugh at old stuff. We'll get to some more of those a little bit later.

I think I'll sing now. Who's to stop me? I'm six-foot-three, I weigh two hundred pounds, Merv is home in bed sick, so who's going to stop me?

❋   ❋   ❋

All comedians have a special fondness for jokes they can use again and again, and always count on. Unfortunately, some lines, either pre-written or ad-libbed, have a relatively short shelf-life. That is particularly true of jokes about whatever is on the front page of the newspaper as of a given moment, whatever Dan Rather or Tom Brokaw mentioned on last night's news. Johnny Carson's writers, for example, daily searched the papers for stories on which they could base timely lines. The same is true of the fellows who provide jokes for Bob Hope and Jay Leno.

I've never concentrated much on timely humor of that particular sort. But there have been many instances where lines worked wonderfully well, in an ad-lib context, and yet, because of the seemingly ever-accelerating way the planet revolves, the jokes may never be used again.

One instance that comes to mind happened in 1985 when Ronald Reagan made a personal visit to the Bitburg cemetery in West Germany, where numbers of former Nazi soldiers were buried. He was subjected to a great deal of criticism at the time, and rightly so.

A few days after the visit I was working at the Bottom Line, a comedy club in Greenwich Village in New York. Somebody on one of the audience question cards asked, "What do you think of Reagan's visit to Bitburg?"

"To tell you the truth," I quipped, "I don't think it's the biggest deal in the world. What I've always had more trouble with is his visit to Washington."

It got a big laugh, accompanied by applause and foot-stomping, but represented a one-time-only triumph.

Another one-time-only joke: When I performed in Greensboro, North Carolina, early in 1986, it just so happened that the rock singer Prince was doing a concert in town that same night. So when somebody asked, "Is it true that you and Prince are here to do a musical comedy together?" I said, "Yes. As soon as I finish paying this year's taxes, we're going to do a musical version of *The Prince and the Pauper*." I would be unlikely to ever be able to use that specific answer again.

One of the strangest questions I've ever had asked came from someone named Charlie Dobbs: "What is a double lip lock?" To begin with, I haven't the slightest idea, even now, what a double lip lock actually is, although it sounds as if it might have something to do with plumbing or piping equipment. But oddly enough, it wasn't hard to answer. I just said, "As I recall, a double lip lock is the only way you can wrestle Martha Raye to the ground."

From the people who knew what I was talking about that got not only a laugh but applause. Unfortunately, only about 30 percent of the audience knew what I was talking about. Many young people, of course, know who Martha Raye is, but a surprising number of them think of her as that pleasant woman who does the denture commercials. We old-timers remember when all the comedians in the business, including Martha herself, did jokes about her allegedly big mouth.

Actually, her mouth is not all that big, any more than Bob Hope's nose, in physical reality, has a funny shape. But the public will buy anything if you keep joking about it, just as Hitler discovered they will believe any sort of vicious lie if a government keeps repeating it long enough.

So, as we review the components of the answer to the question, I was aware, from the days I did comedy-announcing on the wrestling matches in Los Angeles back in the late 1940s, that certain wrestling holds are called *locks*. There is a wrist-lock, leg-lock, arm-lock and so forth. If you put all those factors together, at least it becomes possible to see what the point of the quick answer was.

Another question I was once asked that is unlikely that I'll ever hear again came from a Kelly Odem from "State College": "What did you say into that little black tape recorder at the main seating of dinner?" That came at the first show one night, right after dinner, when I was entertaining on the cruise ship SS *Royale*. Perhaps I should explain that I do all my writing by tape recorder, not by typewriter or word processor, and I am literally speaking into the machine at all hours of the day, wherever I happen to be.

So on the ship, particularly after Jayne got off to resume a lecture tour, I was dining alone and, quite seriously, getting a lot of dictation work done during dinner.

But what did I say to Kelly Odem? I saw his question about ten minutes before I went on, and it gave me a crazy idea. I picked up my tape recorder and dictated a brief announcement into it. I was taking a bit of a chance, because ordinarily I just give some sort of funny answer to a question and then move to the next card. Fortunately, the experiment worked very well. After reading the question aloud, I said, "You know, Mr. Odem raises an interesting question. I dictate so many things during the average day that I can't remember at what specific time I dictated what material. At the moment I haven't done a great deal of dictation since the dinner hour, so I'll tell you what—(*I took the recorder out of my pocket*)—why don't I just turn the machine on right now and hold it up to the mike, and we'll all find out what it was that I was dictating during dinner."

The audience suddenly fell very quiet because they thought I was being sincere, and they did indeed seem curious to know what I had dictated.

I touched the play button and the audience heard the following announcement:

> Attention all security personnel. This is Steve Allen sending out a 5-19. At this moment I am being stared at by a suspicious individual named Kelly Odem. Concerning his background, I know only that he attends state college. Please note that this unauthorized surveillance must stop immediately. During the next twenty-four hours either Kelly Odem is thrown off the ship, or I jump overboard myself, since I cannot put up with one more minute of his hideous harassment.

The people reacted to the announcement as if I had done some sort of magic trick. Half the audience was really laughing; the other half was smiling and staring, I suppose wondering how the hell I could have a quick, ready answer to Odem's question on the tape recorder.

I then said, "Ladies and gentlemen, I must confess something. You thought you just heard an announcement played from this tape recorder. Actually, this machine is *not* a tape recorder. It is an electric shaver." At that point I held up the little black box like a shaver and pretended to be shaving my whiskers with it. "I just made the announcement now, but because my lips did not move, you were all fooled into thinking you were hearing it come from this device I hold in my hand."

By this time the audience didn't know what the hell to believe, although they were still laughing.

Here are a few other instances of lines I undoubtedly will be unable to use again:

> Q: Have you ever whipped a chihuahua with a curtain rod?

> A: What a bizarre question. Of course not. As a matter of fact, I'm not "into" violence of any kind. Although, come to think of it, my father always said, "Spare the rod and spoil the child." Of course, he used to pack a rod.

> Q: I'm actually from Limerick, Ireland. Please finish this limerick:
>
> > *There once was a merry young floozy,*
> > *At the Playboy she got pretty boozey.*
> > *She drank by the gallon,*
> > *Then cornered Steve Allen,*

> A: *And at midnight he gave her a doozie.*

On the flip side of the "one-time-only" question, it's perfectly reasonable, within the rules of the game we've already established, to give the same answer in a second instance if the identical question comes up. But there are also times when the same question requires different answers.

For example, on two separate nights, on the SS *Royale*, I got the question, "What is your net worth?" The first time I said, "Well, ever since the swordfish practically cut it in half, it's not worth a hell of a lot. Three, four dollars maybe. And at that, I'd have to find a fisherman who was interested in salvage."

In the second instance, I said, "Let me see, if I can recall the price of the whole set. . . . The tennis rackets cost $39.50 a piece, the balls were $2.75, and I think the *net* was worth about $69.50."

Sometimes people in the audience, thinking perhaps that they are helping me, or contributing to the fun, will ask a question that itself is funny. I'm rarely able to use such questions, because the joke of them is basically over once they are stated. No funny response is called for. And some of them, too, are so old and dumb that you can't use them for that reason. Examples would be: "Why does the chicken cross the road?" "Why does a fireman wear red suspenders?" "How do you get down off an elephant?"

I was once able to make use of one such question, however, simply because I received a question card from a man named Chuck Wood. I ignored the question, read his name aloud and then said, "Ladies and gentlemen, this is the man made famous by the immortal question, "How much wood would a Chuck Wood chuck if a Chuck Wood could chuck wood?"

There is another category of inane questions, however, that I am often able to get some mileage out of. The questions are so odd that I'm not sure whether the people posing them are intentionally trying to be funny or are on the eccentric side. An example was a question put to me recently while on a working cruise to the Bahamas, "Have you ever eaten a boiled peanut?"

In using a question of that sort, of course, you must put some sort of preamble to it, or set it in a framework. "Ladies and gentlemen, here's a question just received from the 'Twilight Zone.' "

Or, "You know, most people would think that this question-answer session is nothing more than fun and games. But it's encouraging to note that some really thoughtful and concerned citizens have matters of more profound importance on their minds, as well they might in these troubled times."

With a lead-in of that general sort, an off-the-wall question will get a much bigger laugh, even before you get around to a funny answer. In any event, the approach in this instance involved pretending to take the question perfectly seriously, as if it were indeed worthy of respect. "Well," I said. "As it happens, I *have* had occasion to eat a boiled peanut. Actually I didn't eat it all at once. I kept slicing off tiny pieces. Stretched the little mother out for about a week, as I recall."

After getting a laugh of that sort, you can then switch back into a more realistic mode, perhaps adding some quick Jonathan Winters eye-rolling-to-the-ceiling business, as if to say, "Boy, what a weird question."

What this example illustrates is the possibility of not just getting one but several laughs relating to a single original question. In this same instance, I noticed that the hometown of the person was Fitzgerald, Georgia. So I said, "Given that Ms. Clark is from Georgia and that peanuts are an important crop in that particular state, I ask—Is there any connection between those two facts?"

When Ms. Clark called out "No," that was another good laugh. The only way I could top it was to crumple up her card and throw it on the floor, as if disgusted with the whole business.

Another useful technique is to pretend to agree with the philosophical thrust of the question, if it has one, but then to say something more or less the opposite of what would be expected if there were, in fact, such agreement. Sharon Boccuzzo, of Lynn, Massachusetts, asked, "Why do so many of today's comedians feel they must use filth and profanity?" I paused for a moment, made a solemn face, nodded, and said, "It beats the crap outta me, Sharon."

I wouldn't have used that sort of answer if I were entertaining the members of a religious organization, speaking to an audience of children, or working on television. But in a nightclub setting, using the key word *crap* is considered a mild offense by today's standards.

An extremely important point is that when someone brings up a subject of that sort, something with meat on its bones, you can use it as a springboard to go off into several jokes, or even a monologue that you already have in your repertoire that relates to the subject. There's a joke from the sixties, for example, that would work well in this sort of context. "You know, in the old days on television you could never use words of that sort. We couldn't use any words having to do with sex. But today, people are *doing* these actual things on TV, never mind the words."

Do I ever get questions that are rude or impertinent? Yes, but I love to use them. The audience immediately perceives the emotional awkwardness of the situation. On the *Royale*, for example, a fellow passenger who had noticed that I wasn't at my accustomed table in the dining room asked,

"Why weren't you at dinner tonight?"

The question was harmless enough, but I pretended to be offended by it, as if my privacy had been invaded. "None of your business," I said. "Why didn't you shower this evening?" as if to say, "If we're going to trade impertinent questions, Mac, I'll give as good as I get."

Lines of that sort work well because they're not at all a matter of standard joke construction or wordplay but seem to have an emotional or dramatic component.

The very next question, from Bill Nichol of Holiday, Florida, implied that I had been hiding out while on shipboard. He said, "Where have you been all during this trip?"

"I've been running all over the ship looking for *you*, Bill."

Another of those pointed, nosy, possibly embarrassing questions came from a Linda Broadwater: "Do you fool around?"

"No," I said. "When I do that sort of thing, I'm in deadly earnest."

There are reasons that line worked well. First of all, the subject matter was sensitive. Secondly, it dealt with sex, always one of the easiest topics with which to get laughs. Thirdly, I instantly chose to concentrate on the word *fool*. Once that decision had been made, I simply had to make some quick statement of any opposite line of reasoning to get the laugh.

4

Delivering Funny Speeches and Emceeing

I was in sixth grade the first time I was required to speak in front of an audience. I had terrible stage fright and felt quite ill, in fact, by the time I had to give my little talk to students in another class across the hall. But public speaking, as I point out in my book *How to Make a Speech*, fortunately was never an ordeal again, once it had become a reality.

During my fifty-year career I have given some five hundred speeches. Generally the audience is a special group of one sort or another—people of the same profession or organization for example. To help them relax I typically use humor at the top of my speech. Generally these remarks, based on observations made shortly before being introduced, are ad-libbed. However, in some instances, I employ openings that have worked well in the past. For example, under certain circumstances, I use one standard opening in which I deliberately start out with a serious attitude, feigning a discussion of profound philosophical questions. The laughter usually begins before the end of the first paragraph and steadily builds:

Hegel (close to Schopenhauer's chosen field in the philosophy of history) inveighed—as this audience is very well aware. . . . But he made his famous distinction between the finite volitions of men and the astuteness of the essential idea which, while working through men, obviously nevertheless often directs their wills to ends that they do not fully anticipate nor adequately apprehend, even after they occur.

Nietzsche takes his clue from these, distinguishing between the finite, empirical will of men and the apparent dichotomy earlier suggested by

Maimonedes—Wait a minute! This is a speech I'm supposed to give *tomorrow* night!

Apart from using humor in speeches on the lecture circuit, I also do a great deal of emceeing at a wide variety of fundraising benefit dinners. While I am generally invited to emcee because I bring not only laughs but a certain measure of dignity to the proceedings, I recognize that my being invited to participate in such events is related to my ability to ad-lib. Although there are situations where I prepare a number of jokes beforehand, I often arrive at the banquet hall with only the noncomic introductions or announcements required of the master of ceremonies and routinely provided by the host organization.

But as soon as I reach my chair on the dais, I begin making notes about things that strike me as at least moderately amusing. It can be an observation about the room, the lighting, the public address equipment, problems with parking I might have noticed or experienced, the salad dressing, the philosophical rationale of the event, whatever. Although most people have little or no conscious understanding of humor, they nevertheless have a sense of how to react to it. And they laugh in a special way at something they know is a true ad-lib. Consequently, a spontaneous witticism might not actually be as strong a joke as something prepared, but, in most situations, the ad-lib will get the bigger laugh, simply because it is spontaneous.

In *How to Make a Speech*, I talk about how and when to use humor when speaking in public, so rather than repeat those observations here, I'll refer the reader to that book for detailed information. As a confidence-builder, however, I will point out that only a fraction of 1 percent of the human race ever has occasion to speak publicly, and among those who do make the attempt the great majority are incredibly inept.

But the situation is even worse than this. It would not be surprising if people were inadequate at something they rarely had the opportunity to do. No one, for example, would expect to play tennis well, regardless of other athletic gifts, unless he or she played the game frequently. The same would apply to golfing, playing bridge, pulling teeth, or any human activity more complicated than chewing gum. But the fact is that even the great majority of those who are often called upon to speak in public—business executives, teachers, political figures—are truly awful at it.

No one who has gone through twelve years of grade school and four of college would deny that few teachers have special rhetorical gifts. Even some world-famed scholars who think and write brilliantly are dull on the lecture platform. Oddly enough, even most U.S. presidents are poor speakers.

Not long after Jimmy Carter had been elected his inadequacies at delivering either extemporaneous or prepared remarks became clear. Mr. Carter does communicate with sincerity and decency when he speaks; his personal goodness is apparent, and there is certainly nothing of the old-style political windbag about him. But, those old windbags had something. They at least knew the tricks of the speaker's trade.

As compared with Carter, Ted Kennedy—like Jack, Bobby, and reportedly Joe before him—has the knack of electrifying audiences. A few years ago I served as master of ceremonies at a big Democratic party celebration in L.A. Present were the then new governor, Jerry Brown, Mayor Tom Bradley, Sen. Alan Cranston, and other party dignitaries. Judged as orators they ranged from terrible to fair. Then I introduced Ted Kennedy. In less than ten seconds he had the rapt attention of everyone in the auditorium. A minute later he had them cheering. In more recent years, unfortunately, Sen. Kennedy has been somewhat less effective at the podium.

Ronald Reagan, because of his long training as a radio announcer and film actor, is also an effective speaker.

In *How to Make a Speech* I recommend that lecturers do not deliver precisely the same talk to any two groups but that they always make certain changes and modifications on the basis of the makeup of their audiences. The same applies to comedians. Most do *not* change to conform to their audience's expectations. Bob Hope is always the same on stage, which is certainly to make no criticism of him. George Burns is always his adorable and funny self. Red Buttons always does those terrific never-had-a-dinner jokes, wherever he works. Nevertheless, I would advise young comedians, or just plain folks who want to be more amusing, to give the most careful possible thought to those factors that distinguish individual audiences. Is a given audience largely Jewish? Catholic? Humanist? Young, old, liberal, conservative? I not only make it my business to be aware of such factors, I make use of them in constructing a given show.

I'm not recommending that an entertainer be a chameleon, changing totally to accommodate separate audiences, but if I'm working in a jazz club in New York City, for example, I would not do the same act that I would when performing at a Jewish retirement center in Florida.

Even purely physical factors—props, clothing—can be altered to advantage. Again, I'm not talking about traveling on the road with forty-seven different kinds of wardrobe. I'm simply saying that when a comedian is deciding how to dress for a performance the makeup of his audience is a factor that should be considered. The simple tuxedo, which was the comedian's uniform for about fifty years, is not appropriate for most of today's comedy clubs, rock concerts, or college campus appearances, where casual attire makes more sense. When George Carlin converted himself, rather quickly quite a few years ago, from a more or less conventional, though always very funny, comedian into a hipper comic of the Lenny Bruce sort, he made a complete wardrobe change. He's now a middle-aged man who dresses young, and he's right to do so. If he walked out on stage in a Johnny Carson suit or a Milton Berle tuxedo he just wouldn't seem like the George Carlin we all know and love.

Speaking of appropriate attire, I once did a routine when hosting a cable television special in Los Angeles from the Improv, one of the first of the new-wave comedy clubs. In any event, when I walked out on stage, my outfit consisted of Levi's, a bright Hawaiian shirt, an old-fashioned Art Carney–type black vest, and jogging shoes. The outfit struck people funny right away because no one expects a comedian of my age and general type to dress like that. I said,

> You know, ladies and gentlemen, I'm wearing this outfit simply because we're not working out of the NBC studios tonight but here at the Improv, which is a hip, funky place. And this is the way most young comedians dress who work in joints like this. I wouldn't want you to think, however, that they originated this kind of clothing. I had an uncle who, forty years ago, was dressing like this. Of course he was a bum. . . .

But let's get to the speaker's address itself. In *How to Make a Speech* I devote an entire chapter to comedian Pat Harrington, Jr.'s address in accepting an award given him by the Christian Brothers. It's an excellent example of a humorous talk. Although it has a lot of funny lines in it, it's not a collection of one-liners, which many professional comedians resort to in a situation of that type. Pat wrote the speech himself and obviously gave careful thought to it. Every line is directly relevant to the story of his professional experience, the situation of the banquet, and the award ceremonies.

The speech indeed reflects the fact that Pat is a witty, quick-minded man. Years before he enjoyed success as the character of Schneider in *One Day at a Time* he was a member of our stock comedy group on the old Sunday night show. I suggest you refer to his talk in *How to Make a Speech*.

The following is a short speech I gave at a Friar's Club dinner for Bill Harbach and Nick Vanoff on January 30, 1965. Tony Martin was master of ceremonies for the evening's entertainment, which included comedy by Mel Brooks, Carl Reiner, Bill "Jose Jimenez" Dana, George Burns, and Corbett

Monica. I was introduced as "a man who had the good sense to buy Polaroid at twelve."

Thank you, Tony, and good evening, ladies and gentlemen.

Yes, as you've been told, I did buy Polaroid at twelve. Unfortunately I *sold* it when I was fourteen, like an idiot.

But I'm extremely happy to be here this evening to pay my respects to two such close friends. We worked together for so many years and I have benefited greatly by their support. In fact, I've often gotten credit for things that they were responsible for. It was Nick Vanoff, for example, who actually discovered Andy Williams and Carol Burnett.

He discovered them in the back seat of a parked car.

But these two men are successful today, and they deserve their success. You can always tell, of course, when people have that certain something. I am reminded of the day, almost fifteen years ago, when two young men came to me just bursting with good ideas. They had great energy, a lot of ability. I knew they were going places. I'm talking about Panama and Frank. What happened to Harbach and Vanoff after that meeting. I have no idea. . . .

But—seriously—it's wonderful to see these two fellows working together so effectively when they come from such different backgrounds. Think of it. These two young men, one of whom is from the wrong side of the tracks, the other of whom *owns* the tracks . . .

Now of course you all know that Bill's father is the great American songwriter Otto Harbach. But what some of you may not know is that Nick's father was the great *Macedonian* songwriter Otto Vanoff.

You all know about the wonderful songs written by Bill's father, but let me tell you about Nick's father.

Bill's father wrote "The Indian Love Call." Nick's father wrote "The Armenian Love Call."

Bill's father wrote "Smoke Gets in Your Eyes." Nick's father wrote "Smoke Gets in Your Nose." And he wrote it first!

Bill's father wrote "You Do Something to Me." Nick's father wrote "I'll Do Something to You."

Bill's father wrote "The Touch of Your Hand." Nick's father wrote "Your Feet Are Like Ice."

Bill's father wrote "Rosemarie." Nick's father wrote "Morey Amsterdam."

Jayne and I have known Bill since his early days as a young fledgling actor, when the two of them worked at M-G-M. In fact, that was Bill's professional name in those days, Fledgling Young. He didn't want to make it on his father's reputation. But his story is inspiring. He came to Hollywood, ladies and gentlemen, without a penny in his pocket. But with fifty thousand dollars in his briefcase.

Now I know that's an old joke. But Bill is no spring chicken himself.

You know, when I met these fellows they had already done great things in the early days of television. In New York, Bill had produced the "Jean Martin Show, "The Nick Kenny Show," and the "Late Weather Report with Nancy Berg." These were milestones, ladies and gentlemen.

And at this same time, in Hollywood, Nick was producing the "N.T.G. Bathing Beauty Parade," Peter Potter's Platter Parade," and the "Roller Derby." Remember that great program, "You Asked for It?" Well, Nick was doing a horror show called "It Asked for You."

But it's a wonderful tribute, not only to these two men, but to our American way of life, that a wealthy young man from Park Avenue could work side by side for all these years with a poor Macedonian *immigrant*. But Bill is very graceful about his wealth. And so is his lovely wife, Faye. I remember seeing her with their first child several years ago as they sat in the back seat of a limousine on Park Avenue. The little girl was just a year and a half old at the time. I said, "Can she walk?" and Faye said, "Thank God she'll never have to!"

Today Bill and Faye have *two* children, and, like their parents, they're not at all spoiled by being so rich. Last Christmas their oldest little girl walked up to Santa Claus and said, "What can I do for you?"

But seriously—Faye and Bill live a very simple life. They don't keep servants. They *hire* a lot of them, but they don't keep them.

And once again I say "but seriously," and this time I mean it, when I express my pleasure at being here this evening to be part of this program that is meant to convey the admiration and deep affection all of us feel for Bill Harbach and Nick Vanoff.

Now let's turn our attention to the art of emceeing events. Serving as toastmaster calls for a combination of two factors: 1) the ability to make up jokes, and 2) the power of observation. You can't do jokes about things if you don't first *notice* those things. So, as suggested above, get in the habit of paying attention to your surroundings in any situation in which you are going to perform. Developing a keen awareness of everything around you at all times is an advantage in any area of comedy but nowhere more so than when you are emceeing.

Can *any* comedian serve as master of ceremonies? By no means. Oh, any comedian can *do* it, but many will not do it well. The reason has nothing whatever to do with the degree of funniness or wit the comedian possesses. Some of the funniest comedians in the business are never asked to serve as host of a benefit or roast program simply because they are not well-suited to that narrow task. You really can't be funnier than Jonathan Winters or Robin Williams, but to my knowledge they have never been asked to officiate at a public function. They are, it might be said, too funny for such an assignment.

Obviously, it's fortunate if an emcee is witty since he can then take advantage of things that may happen during the course of a formal evening's program. But many comedians who rarely do true ad-libbing can nevertheless remember hundreds of old jokes and know which ones to use, on short notice, in certain situations. But I'm not talking about that. I'm talking about a certain quality of authority, a certain measure of stature—even dignity— that the best masters of ceremonies have.

One thing a toastmaster should be able to do, especially when officiating at a public function (as distinguished from a television talk or comedy show), is to have some sense of when *not* to be funny—a feeling for those moments which are best handled in a noncomic vein. In recent years there have been some instances of top-drawer people selected to serve as hosts or co-hosts of the most important televised awards ceremonies—Oscars, Emmys, and Grammys. The comedians were at a particular peak of popularity at the moment and, after all, how many years could the academy go on inviting Bob Hope to officiate? But even if Bob is, let's arbitrarily assume, not as funny as, say, Robin Williams or Tim Allen, he has one quality they lack: the air of authority.

In the case of Robin particularly—and I'm his biggest fan—he seems literally unable to play anything at all straight, so lavish is his comic gift. His mind is wonderfully creative and strikingly fast, but there are certain moments, however few, when a straightforward, noncomic announcement is better than the world's funniest joke. Perhaps in time that realization will dawn on those who seem to feel that if they have not had a laugh in the last ten seconds they're in trouble.

And then, of course, there are other comedians, including some of the most brilliant—Sid Caesar, for example—who make no sense as a host or MC simply because they cannot say "good evening." They are funny only in the context of certain kinds of monologues or sketches.

An interesting problem that arises for those who perform as master of ceremonies is how to handle eating *and* hosting at a dinner event. When David Letterman introduced me on the TV Academy's Hall of Fame 1986 telecast, Jayne and I invited him to have dinner with us before the show. He sent a message back that he very much appreciated the invitation and looked forward to seeing us both, but that he would feel quite uncomfortable eating and mingling with people before he had to go on. David is not alone in this discomfort.

When serving as toastmaster of a dinner event, however, one is frequently expected to attend the dinner portion of the evening. As with any other performance, a good part of the work will have been done *before* you take your place on the dais, but there are always last-minute notes to make or study. In my case, it's question cards and jokes triggered by my immediate observations. So what do I do? Generally, as soon as I am seated, I move the bread-and-butter plate, water glass and other impedimenta to clear off a working surface. Then I get right to work, even before making small talk with whomever is seated to my right or left. By the time dinner is actually served, I am able to enjoy the meal, occasionally jotting down additional jokes or observations as they occur to me.

MCs, of course, must be prepared for things that can go wrong. It is common to encounter spotlights that aren't turned on, reading lamps on the lectern that aren't plugged in, and microphones that don't work. But if you ad-lib, such problems can work to your advantage. Unfortunately, this is not always so, as the following story, repeated from *How to Make a Speech*, demonstrates.

When Things Go Wrong

I recall the time several years ago that officers of UNICO, an Italian-American organization, decided to arrange an important banquet in Los Angeles to honor the great songwriter Harry Warren, composer of such hits as "I Only Have Eyes for You," "You're Getting to Be a Habit with Me," "42nd Street," "You're My Everything," "The Lullaby of Broadway," "Jeepers Creepers," and "Chattanooga Choo Choo."

I was first alerted to the forthcoming event when I received a call from my good friend Gus Bivona, a clarinetist and bandleader. He had just been hired to provide the orchestra for the affair.

"The whole thing will be to honor Harry Warren," Gus said, "and some of the UNICO guys said that because you're a composer yourself, and you love good music, you'd be right to emcee the show."

"I'd love to," I said, and asked to be provided with further details.

A few days later a letter arrived, giving the names of speakers, entertainers, and local dignitaries who would be participating. I was asked if I could recommend any suitable entertainment. The only idea that occurred to me was to book my dear friends, comedians Bill Dana and Pat Harrington, Jr. The reason these particular names came to mind—as opposed to, for example, those of Louis Nye and Don Knotts, who also worked on my television show at the time—was that a few weeks earlier Bill and Pat had done a comedy record album for a company in which I had a financial interest. The funniest routine on the album was Pat Harrington's portrayal of a character called Guido Panzini, who, it was alleged, had been first mate of the ill-fated *Andrea Doria,* the Italian liner that had been involved in an accident at sea some months earlier. It may be recalled that some members of the Italian crew had not exactly distinguished themselves when, instead of shepherding the women and children into the ship's lifeboats, they first made certain of their own security. As I recall, only a few men out of a large crew were guilty of such conduct, but as is often the case it was the negative part of the story which made an impression on the public consciousness.

In retrospect, it was easy to see that recommending to Pat and Bill that they do the *Andrea Doria* bit at an all-Italian dinner was not the wisest suggestion I ever made. It occurred to me, however, because when one is putting a show together, preexisting comedy routines or monologues that have some relation to the subject matter at hand are often the first straws at which one clutches. If one were booking attractions for a football banquet, for example, it would be natural to ask Andy Griffith to do his famous football monologue, to ask Don Adams if he would do his funny routine about football cheers, or to ask Tim Conway if he would perform his marvelous comedy interview in which he plays a harebrained road manager for a professional team.

In this case my reasoning was simple. It's an Italian dinner; let's see, who do I know who does an Italian routine?

The banquet was held in the large ballroom of the then-new and glamorous Beverly Hilton Hotel in Beverly Hills, California. As I mingled with the crowd during the cocktail hour, I began to pick up comments that indicated there might be some confusion about the evening. A number of people were overheard to ask just who Harry Warren was, and two or three who knew him fairly well still seemed puzzled that he had been chosen to be the guest of honor at such an illustrious outing; they thought he was Jewish.

Eventually the audience assumed dinner places and the waiters began to serve a sumptuous meal. The first indication that the evening had already taken a peculiar turn was when it suddenly occurred to me that the dinner serenade I had been listening to for perhaps a quarter of an hour consisted, not of Harry Warren's music, but of my own.

During the orchestra's first intermission I excused myself from the head table and sauntered over to Gus, who was just stepping off the bandstand.

"Thanks a million for playing my tunes, man," I said, "but do you plan to play anything by Harry Warren?"

"Well," he said, "Not during the dinner hour. I just brought charts of those twelve songs of yours that we did in the new album. To tell you the truth, I didn't give the thing much thought."

Bivona had indeed recorded a dozen of my songs a few weeks earlier, the arrangements having been done by Henry Mancini and Skip Martin, an arranger for the Les Brown orchestra. Gus and I both assumed, of course, that during the formal entertainment later in the evening heavy emphasis would be put on Warren's music. I returned to the head table, and for the next forty-five minutes or so continued to enjoy the orchestra's melodious and spirited renditions of my own compositions. The exclusive playing of them must, I suppose, have greatly puzzled Harry Warren, who had been assured that every part of the evening's festivities was intended as a tribute to him that was not only well deserved, but for which the poor man had been waiting during some thirty years of general obscurity.

At last the dinner had been served, the waiters had removed the dishes, and it was time to get to the program itself.

When one serves as a master of ceremonies for an affair of this sort, one is provded with cards on which are typed introductions to the various program participants. The order in which the various ladies and gentlemen appear, either to speak or to entertain, is predetermined; the introductions therefore are rendered in the appropriate order. The first gentleman I was called upon to introduce was a Catholic priest. His name escapes me, but he was pastor at a local church, perhaps the one attended by Mr. Warren, who—contrary to common assumption, even in the music business—was not Jewish but Italian Catholic.

The priest was seated about a dozen chairs to my left, and when I introduced him I naturally assumed that he would take over my microphone at the center of the head table, offer the customary brief invocation, and return to his seat. To this day I haven't the slightest idea why he kept on walking when he reached the podium. He did not stop until, a good two minutes later, he reached a microphone at the far side of the room—in right field, so to speak—in front of the orchestra, on a small dance floor. Two thousand pairs of eyes followed his peculiar journey through the room, which he accomplished by curving around tables, bumping a shoulder or two, and all in all having a bit of difficulty wending his way to the distant mike.

Eventually he reached it and, one assumes, muttered a suitable prayer. I say "assumes," because the microphone was not turned on, nor is there any reason it should have been; the audio engineer had expected that the good father would speak into the mike designated for his use. No one in the room, with the possible exception of a few people standing very close to him, will ever know what he said. There would be no evidence that he said anything at all except that his lips were observed to move. His prayer made such a faint impression on the audience that I would not be surprised to learn that God himself, no doubt being otherwise occupied at the time, overlooked it.

And, of course, after the pastor had finished his mumbled remarks, all guests—still standing respectfully—had then to wait while he retraced his long, rambling course back to his chair. A number of witty comments occurred to me, but I held my tongue.

When the priest had returned to his starting place, I made the traditional announcement, "And now, ladies and gentlemen, the national anthem." At this point dazzling spotlights, properly enough, focused on an American flag behind the dais down to my right. As it happened, a short, thin gentleman named Ned Washington, himself the lyricist of a number of fine popular songs over the years, was standing directly in front of the flag. Washington had no idea, however, that Old Glory was behind him. All he knew was that he alone, out of two thousand people, was suddenly illuminated by two of the brightest spotlights he had ever seen. His face, as he tried to fathom why this might be so, was a study. He blinked, smiled, looked from side to side in embarrassment, frowned, looked at me, raised his eyebrows, and blinked once more into the lights. Most of us, of course, were singing, but a number of people, observing Washington's puzzlement, blew a few notes, and there was a bit of elbowing and giggling, I regret to say, during the singing of the anthem.

Pat Harrington has recalled, "I was next to Ned and also partly blinded by the spot on the flag. I estimate the flag and stand at five feet, three inches, and Ned is about five feet, five inches, so he covered it completely. He hadn't been paying attention to the announcement and stood up perfunctorily when everyone else did. When the spot hit the flag—or him—he froze, thinking he had been singled out for some momentary praise. When he heard the first words of the anthem coming up from the crowd, he sidemouthed to me, 'I didn't write this.' "

I then formally welcomed the audience and opened the evening with a few jokes.

Another tip-off that things were not going to go well came after I had introduced the first of several civic dignitaries representing, respectively, the county and city of Los Angeles and the state of California. Two of these gentlemen, in fulsomely praising Mr. Warren, and asserting the enormous respect in which he was held by millions of Californians, referred to him quite distinctly as Harry Warner.

The first time this happened the audience gasped, then laughed. I leaped to my feet, stepped briefly to the microphone, and said, "No, no, Mr. Simpkins. The dinner for Harry *Warner* is taking place in the ballroom on the *other* side of the lobby."

This saved the moment, in a sense, although I'm sure it did not relieve the speaker's embarrassment. It seemed to put him, in fact, in something of a panic, so that a moment or two later he concluded his remarks by saying, "And therefore it gives me great pleasure indeed to present this handsome plaque, from the people of Los Angeles and the mayor personally, to that great American composer Harry *Warner.*"

It was the coliseum roar of laughter that greeted the second gaffe that probably unsettled the nerves of the following speaker. I can think of no other explanation as to why he would get up and commit exactly the same offense, but he did.

It was then time to introduce the first entertainer of the evening, a young gentleman of whom I had never heard before, nor since. His name was Joe Vina. I said something to the effect that it was remarkable how many of America's greatest singers over the years were Italian and that I had every confidence that young Joe Vina was going to join the distinguished company of Frank Sinatra, Dean Martin, Enrico Caruso, Perry Como, Russ Columbo, et al.

Just as I was about to call for the usual "nice big hand" for Vina, my eyes drifted to the orchestra. Far from being on the qui vive, instruments poised, the musicians were lounging about in their chairs. Most of them were not holding instruments at all, and were clearly in a state of nonattention. While I had no idea what the explanation of this mysterious circumstance might be, neither did I have the luxury of speculating about it, so I simply introduced Vina. He promptly ran out, smiled broadly, waited until the applause died down, spread his arms wide as if he were to leap off a rocky cliff on the west coast of Mexico, and then—believe it or not—just stood there with his mouth open, not making a sound.

Two thousand people stared at this puzzling spectacle for a few seconds. My eyes went again to Bivona and his orchestra, none of whom yet gave any indication that they were expected to accompany Mr. Vina. In an instant I solved the mystery and rose to my feet.

"Joe," I said, "by the fact that the orchestra hasn't snapped to attention may I assume that you had planned to do a record-synch?"

"Yes," Mr. Allen," he called out gratefully. "They're supposed to play my record now."

"Well, thank you, Joe," I said. "I guess whoever the engineer is now knows what he's supposed to do, so don't you worry about a thing, Joe. We're all with you, and I'm sure we'll enjoy hearing your recording, whatever it turns out to be. We'll also be impressed, I'm sure, by your singing live right along with it, if that's part of your plan."

Inasmuch as I had already made it clear that we were gathered for the purpose of honoring Harry Warren and his truly incredible contributions to American music, it was naturally assumed that whatever number Vina had recorded was one written by Harry. No such luck, of course. The record finally started—much too loud, as I recall. Vina had a bit of trouble synchronizing his motions with it, but finally he and the record were on the same track. The number had a faintly Italian flavor, as I recall, but naturally fell strangely on the ears of Harry Warren, who no doubt also had assumed that Vina was there to accord him the honor of performing one of his songs.

After Vina had retired from the stage-dance floor, I introduced a young lad named Pat Healy who, it was anticipated, would regale us with not one, but a medley of songs by Harry Warren. The spotlight illuminated the location where it was reasonable to look for Miss Healy, but she did not appear. I jumped up again to the dais mike and began a verbal search for the missing singer. The light roamed around a bit while again Bivona and the orchestra sat with the same degree of interest and curiosity as the audience, not preparing to play their instruments but simply craning their necks to locate Miss Healy. She was finally found, oddly enough, lost in thought, seated at a nearby table, from which dreamily—and unsteadily—she arose and moved to the microphone.

I never had the pleasure of getting to know Miss Healy well, so to this day I do not know whether she had a few drinks too many or whether she simply had one of those loose, off-the-cuff personalities that, a few years later, was to become associated with the hippy demeanor.

"Oh, wow," she said, running a hand through her already disordered hair. "I'm not really dressed for the occasion and I'm sorry to say I-I—haven't prepared a particular song. In fact, I don't know what to sing at *all.*"

Two thousand jaws dropped.

I looked at Harry Warren and groaned inwardly.

"Please, God," I said to myself. "Whatever the hell she sings let it be something written by this great composer."

"Well," Miss Healy continued, "I mean, I didn't bring any arrangements with me—as a matter of fact, I don't *have* arrangements of anything written by Mr. Warren, so maybe the piano player and the drummer and I can, you know just *fake* a little something here, to pay our respects to Harry—er—Warren."

Miss Healy's approach might have been defensible if she had not the slightest warning that she was about to be called upon, but to my knowledge she had had a good many days' warning.

"What would you folks like to hear?" she said, not very wisely.

Somebody called out, "How about 'Lullaby of Broadway'?" one of Warren's great standards.

"All right," she said, at which she turned to the drummer and indicated, by languidly waving her hand, at what tempo she wanted to do the number.

As anyone over twenty will know, "Lullaby of Broadway" is one of the best up-tempo numbers written, very much on a par with the best of Gershwin, Porter, or Berlin. It is peppy, original, harmonically complex, and yet eminently singable. Nevertheless, although you may find it hard to believe, Miss Healy indicated to the drummer and pianist a tempo that would have been more suitable for "Someone to Watch over Me." Perhaps the word *lullaby* had confused her.

The musicians had no alternative but to play an introduction in her snail-like tempo. She sang—not precisely on key, either—"Come . . . on . . . along . . . and . . . listen . . . tooo . . . the . . . lull . . . ah . . . by . . . of . . . Broad . . . way."

Mercifully, considering possible alternatives, she proceeded at once to forget the rest of the lyrics and then said, "Oh, God, I forget the words. Mr. Warren, can you ever *forgive* me?"

We all know the answer to that question.

"God," she said, "I'm so sorry. This is really embarrassing. I'll tell you what—I'll make up for it, Mr. Warren, by doing *another* one of your great songs. This is one my *mother* used to sing to me. Actually my mother should be here tonight, because she was a lot better singer than I am. She was really *great*, my mother was. Let's see, now . . . what was it I was going to sing, anyway? Harry Warren, please *help* me!"

By this time the audience had lost control and was laughing. It was not actually a cruel laughter and was not really directed at Miss Healy herself. The object of the laughter was simply the astounding incongruity of the situation. On the one hand was one of America's greatest composers, and on the other incredible long-playing chaos that was supposed to have been a tribute to him.

I stepped to the microphone and said, "Well, Miss Healy, just relax. Perhaps a little later in the evening the full lyrics to some Harry Warren songs might occur to you."

She left the floor and, I would not be surprised to learn, show business.

I felt that since the audience was already laughing this might be a suitable time to introduce Pat Harrington and Bill Dana.

"Ladies and gentlemen," I said, "we are very honored to have with us tonight a gentleman who is the cultural attaché to the United States from the Italian government. He has recently come here from Rome, and I know that you will want to hear his comments on this marvelous evening staged under the auspices of UNICO."

At this stage in his career Bill Dana had not yet made his great splash on our TV show as the lovable Mexican character Jose Jimenez. He had worked chiefly, to this date, as a comedy writer. He had one of those swarthy Mediterranean faces that could pass for Jewish, Greek, Spanish, or—in this instance—Italian.

Bill, as the Italian diplomat, stepped to the mike, thanked me, and said, "Good-a evening, ladies and a-gentlemen. I'm glad to introduce-a to you tonight-a a man who was a survivor of the crash at sea between-a the *Andrea Doria* and-a the *Stockholm*. He's-a here with-a me now."

Pat stepped to the mike.

"Sir, did you come over with the *Andrea Doria*?"

"Ala-most," Pat said.

"And what-a was your-a particular job?"

"My name is Guido Panzini. I'm Italian."

"Well, that's okay. Now, tell-a me, Mr. Panzini, what-a was your job-a on the *Andrea Doria*?"

"I was the general officer. We had-a young-a ladies on board. My job was to—"

"No, no. I mean-a, what was your *position*?"

"Are-a you kidding?"

The audience was laughing heartily.

"No, seriously, Officer Panzini, I want to ask-a you about the accident. When did you first-a realize you were on a collision course?"

"Well, it was when Captain Calamai asked a question—and-a somebody answered in Swedish."

"I see. And what was the first thing out of Captain Calamai's mouth?"

"When he realized what had happened?"

"Yes."

"His lunch."

"No, what I mean is . . . what was the first thing he *said*?"

He said a beautiful, quaint old Italian expression."

"What was it?"

"*Ma canso care mia fino—*"

"And what does that mean?"

"It means *What did we hit down there?* At least, that is what it means in one dialect. In another dialect it means *Abandon ship!*"

"Talk about abandoning ship," Bill said, "There were a few rumors that the *crew* actually saw fit-a to abandon ship first."

"Well, that's only a *rumor*."

"Is it true?"

Yes, it's a *true* rumor. But you must understand-a the reason-a why it was that way. The passengers, they was-a too busy to get off the ship. They all went downstairs to take snap-a shots of the accident, you know? Meanwhile, *we* got off the boat. I was way up on the bridge. I don't-a want to boast or anything, but I made it to the first life-a boat in 9.6. It's-a incredible. I finished-a second."

"Who finished-a first?"

"Captain Calamai did. He made it in 9.4."

Pat and Bill had gotten about this far into the routine when a remarkable thing happened. Far down to the left on the dais, perhaps a dozen seats or so away from the lectern, a short dark-complexioned man suddenly stood up and began walking toward us. At first I did not notice

him, but then I saw that the people in the audience were no longer looking at Pat or Bill but were following a moving object to our left. When
I turned to see what it might be, I observed a fellow whose face was
red with fury and whose brows were knotted in a fierce scowl. During
the three or four seconds before he reached the lectern my mental computer began to range over a number of possible explanations for the intrusion.

The man stomped angrily past us, muttering furiously under his breath
in what, as I recall, was half-Italian and half-English. The only phrase I
remember clearly was "You think-a it's-a funny, eh?"

Continuing his rightward progress, he approached a middle-aged
woman seated far down to the other side, grabbed her by the wrist, pulled
her to her feet, and, one assumes, said to her, "We're getting the hell out
of here right now."

By this time, Pat and Bill had, understandably enough, fallen into stupefied silence. The three of us joined the audience in simply staring at
this peculiar demonstration, which now continued as the man and woman
—he still furious, she looking puzzled and embarrassed—came back toward us. I thought that perhaps this time he might explain to us what
was going on, and then it occurred to me that he might be a physician
who had to leave to attend some emergency.

No such luck.

Pat Harrington recalls, "The guy stopped on the way back—with wife
in tow—shouldered in between Bill and me, and said, 'This is not funny.
People died, men were killed—This was a bad thing and you should not
laugh.' He left, and when he got perhaps twenty feet away—still pulling
his wife—Bill said, 'Boy, you know, you give a guy one line—one small
line—and he thinks he's the whole act.'

"It got a laugh. I, of course, was frozen; the *Doria* was my piece,
and for it to provoke this kind of reaction meant an unpardonable lack
of sensitivity on my part. Bill was trying to pull us out, I was stricken
with onrushing guilt, and you, as I recall, were misting your fingernails."

The intruder now continued off to the left and then through a dozen
or so tables, whose puzzled occupants stared at him open-mouthed.

The single oddest event in this whole crazy night occurred now. The
lighting man was responsible for it. Apparently, observing from his distant
perch at the other end of the great hall that three popular television comedians named Dana, Harrington, and Allen were at the lectern, he must
have assumed that the stranger and his woman companion were part of
the act. Accordingly, he had hit the man with a brilliant spotlight as soon
as he had started to walk, and he and his assistant then continued to il-
luminate the two strangers, with *separate* spots, as they departed. This left
Bill, Pat, and me in relative darkness, a factor for which we were at the
moment profoundly grateful.

While the audience's attention was still focused on the man and his hapless wife I leaned over to one of the UNICO executives at the dais and said, "Who the hell were those people?"

"I'm sorry to tell you," the man said, "that he is what you said Bill Dana was. He's connected with the Italian embassy—either here or in Washington, I'm not sure which."

The mystery about the man's anger was thereby explained. Although jokes about the *Andrea Doria* were funny to Americans, even those of Italian descent, to a representative of the Italian government the humor was not so readily apparent, particularly since some of the funniest jokes dealt with the cowardice of a few of the ship's crew.

It was, of course, out of the question for Bill and Pat to continue with the routine. Bill turned to me—speaking now without an accent—and said, "Steve, Pat and I would like to thank you very much for getting us into this thing tonight. Believe me, we'll remember this for a long time."

In a daze myself, I rose, thanked the fellows for being "good sports," whatever that meant, and explained, in case there were any other native Italians in the room, that there had been no intention to malign the Italian people nor to transgress the bounds of good taste in any way.

The next of several performers on the progarm—not a single one of them celebrities, by the way—where were Frank Sinatra, Dean Martin, and Vic Damone?—was a young chap named Johnny Holiday. He is a fine singer, but I do think it would have been more appropriate if the dais had been graced by Tony Bennett, Buddy Greco, or Perry Como, not to mention an Italian comedian or two. But no, the singers were all totally unknown to the public and, with the exception of the luckless Mr. Vina, mostly non-Italian.

As for Mr. Holiday, the world would little note nor long remember what number he performed at this point, with the assistance of Gus Bivona and the orchestra, for the reason that the entire room was in noisy consternation over the dramatic walkout of the Italian diplomat and his wife.

A sotto-voce explanation of the incident started out from the dais, and as of five or six minutes later had reached the back of the room. This was accompanied, of course, by a rushing wave of whispers, hoarse cries, laughter, and catcalls. At any given moment hundreds of people were saying, "Who was that? What the hell's going on?" while those who had already absorbed the news were explaining the situation.

This inevitable wave of primitive communication did serve the purpose of apprising the audience of the benumbing state of affairs, but of course made it impossible to hear the song that was, all during this time, being sung by the unfortunate Holiday. If I am any judge of horseflesh, he too was singing something not written by Harry Warren; but, as I say, we will never know. Both music and lyrics were totally drowned out from start to finish.

Frequently, when audiences get even a little out of hand, the master of ceremonies takes over the microphone and either pleasantly or sharply calls for order. In this case I could not even do that much, since Holiday was singing—or reciting the Gettysburg Address, for all the evidence there was to the contrary.

At staggeringly long last, the evening drew to a close. The president of UNICO himself stepped to the lectern to make a presentation of the Italian-American group's most prestigious honor, called the Columbus Award. In presenting it to the gentleman he said, "It gives me great pleasure to present this handsome plaque to Harry Warner—er, *Warren*—because we are very proud of what he has accomplished in the world of music. And therefore, on behalf of UNICO, I present him the Columbus Award. Although it's not Columbus Day now, it will be next year."

More hysterical laughter.

I would not be surprised to learn that at least one of the handsome plaques that the guest of honor received that night is inscribed in bronze to Harry Warner.

One more thing: A couple of weeks later Gus Bivona and the members of the orchestra received their checks for playing at the event.

They bounced.

What about acting as emcee on, say, a TV show or in a nightclub? Is that something to which the new comic should aspire? I say, "Why not?" It's always better to be able to do two things—or for that matter 749 things—than to be competent at just one. There are many opportunities in the field of comedy that are open to comics who can serve as hosts or emcees. In fact, sometimes a performer who isn't actually hysterically funny can find employment simply because he or she is the only one available at the moment who can speak in English sentences, ad-lib pleasantries, or smoothly introduce other performers and acts.

There's not even any necessary connection with humor here. Some emcees are funny, some are not. Preparing or qualifying for that sort of duty is, in certain ways, like learning to be a public speaker of any sort.

For many people, speaking in front of an audience, even at a relatively small gathering, is really a nerve-wracking prospect. Whether your personal intention is to become a professional comedian or merely a more entertaining after-dinner speaker, you will eventually have to come face to face with the problem of stage fright.

While I deal with this subject at greater length in *How to Make a Speech*, I'll include here some good news and some bad news. The good news is that you will get over the problem. The bad news—and actually it's not all that bad—is that it will take some time to work through the matter. There's no sense trying to talk yourself out of it, any more than you can talk yourself out of any other neurotic fear. But all the public speakers in the world were nervous when they started, and so were all comedians and actors.

What about ad-libbing at least part of a speech? Can one prepare at all? Yes. Again, start by building on the information that is available to you at the moment. By way of illustration, here are some remarks I made in Norfolk, Virginia, several years ago, at the opening of that city's enormous Scope Auditorium. Part of the speech consisted of lines that occurred to me while I was studying a promotional brochure about the auditorium in the few minutes before I went on; part was ad-libbed. (It should be noted here that "Norfolk's Mace" is a large, medieval-looking staff that is the city's symbol.) A voice on the PA system introduced me: "And now . . . Mr. Steve Allen."

Good evening, ladies and gentlemen. I don't know whose voice it was who just introduced me, but I'd like to thank the gentleman for that very flattering introduction. (*laughter*)

I hope I have the opportunity to return the favor sometime. (*laughter*)

But I must say that it has been a most enjoyable experience visiting your wonderful city. The warm welcome started the moment I got off the plane this morning, when Mayor Martin ran up and presented me with Norfolk's Mace.

I just wish he hadn't sprayed it directly into my eyes. (*laughter*)

It was also most gratifying when I came into the auditorium this evening to see a group of hippies giving me the peace sign. . . . one finger at a time. (*laughter*)

Although the existence of Scope is naturally of enormous importance here in Norfolk, I had heard nothing about it, three thousand miles away in Los Angeles, until just recently. In fact, when I first received the invitation from Scope, I thought I was being booked to appear at a mouthwash convention. (*laughter*)

This place is really fabulous, and it's not even finished yet. They plan to have not just great entertainment here, but sometimes four and five shows going on in different areas simultaneously. Even tonight they have this wonderful *Spirit of America* musical in this room, there's a rock band rehearsing in Chrysler Hall, there's a Latin combo in the Little Hall, you can hear taped music in the parking lot, and they have entertainment going on in the restaurant.

Would you believe I went into the men's room a few minutes ago? . . . (*laughter*) They've got a six-piece band working in there. (*laughter*)

Don't laugh . . . they were getting a standing ovation. . . . (*laughter*)

And wait till you *see* this great *Spirit of America* show. It's really something. You'll see literally hundreds of fighting men. . . . You'll see British soldiers pitted against American Colonials. You'll see covered wagons racing to open the West. You'll see rugged cavalry men fighting off hostile Indians. You'll see Johnny Carson beaten senseless by Ed McMahon. (*laughter*) You'll see Sen. Fulbright answering an obscene phone call from Martha Mitchell. (*laughter*)

And—if you'll refer to your programs—you'll notice that it says, "to top it all off, there'll be spectacular fireworks following the show."

It wasn't planned that way, but we've been having a little trouble with the electrical system. (*laughter*)

Speaking of the printed program, I do hope you've studied it carefully, because it gives you such fascinating information about this fabulous Scope project. Let me direct your attention to a few of the high spots.

"It might be said that Scope grew out of a basic need and a late-night phone call, from Mr. Lawrence M. Cox in Washington, D.C., to Mayor Roy B. Martin." Collect. (*laughter*)

Mr. Cox, then executive director of the Norfolk Redevelopment and Housing Authority, said it might be possible to include the construction of a new center in Norfolk in the 1965 Federal Housing and Urban Development Act. This has meant that the federal government, as part of Norfolk's overall urban renewal program, pays two-thirds of the final construction costs, whereas the city of Norfolk pays only one-third. How Harry Byrd [a conservative senator] justified this in his mind, I have no idea. (*laughter*)

The project was designed by the Williams and Tazewell Partnership of Norfolk, and this fabulous dome roof over our heads was the concept of the famed Italian architect, Señor Nervi . . . and when they got the bill, they saw why he was called nervy. (*laughter*) Just look at that roof. It doesn't have one visible inch of supporting structure, but it's perfectly safe and strong . . . I hope to God. (*laughter*)

No, seriously, it is very strong. But I do suggest that you do not all cough at once. . . . (*laughter*)

And if you will pay particular attention, after the show this evening, to the lower concourse, you will notice that the program advises us, "There are sunken gardens on either side of the lower entry." Think of it, ladies and gentlemen, sunken gardens. They didn't plan it that way, it's just that there was a little problem with the cement. (*laughter*) But whether those gardens sank or not, they're still beautiful.

The handsome restaurant and cocktail lounge seats 240 persons . . . and sleeps seventy-five. (*laughter*)

Next is a storage area and parking space for the Zamboni, the machine that keeps the surface of the skating rink ice smooth. Actually, that's not a machine . . . it's an old Italian guy named Zamboni. (*laughter*)

The rink, located in the arena floor here, has twenty-two miles of steel tubing buried in the concrete and will provide ice not only for professional hockey, but also for drinking. (*laughter*)

"Extensive landscaping enhances the brick paved plaza and is a focal point for a large reflecting pool, which is only three inches deep." Who the wise guy was who put the diving board at one end, we don't know. (*laughter*)

One of the world's most advanced electronic scoreboards will provide a dazzling display of lighted information. It is one of the nation's biggest . . . although the scores here won't be that big, I understand. (*laughter*)

But you will be able to see great sports events here. All the local athletes and coaches are thrilled. Particularly Johnny Wilson, new coach of the Wings hockey team. I was just reading in the program that Johnny was the winner of the Calder Cap. Apparently Calder himself decided not to wear it anymore. (*laughter*)

But Johnny is terrific. He earned the nickname "Iron Man" when he played 580 consecutive National Hockey League games. Unfortunately, he doesn't remember the last 107. (*laughter*)

The scoreboard was built by American Sign and Indicator Corporation of Spokane, Washington. There is just one little problem. They have to fly a guy in from three thousand miles away to change a lightbulb . . . (*laughter*)

"Individual temperature readings in the various areas can be monitored and adjusted," at a central control station, conveniently located in Birmingham, Alabama. (*laughter*)

And notice this announcement: "An emergency power system was designed to provide emergency lighting within eight seconds, should the primary source of power fail." So if everything suddenly goes dark here tonight, ladies and gentlemen, remember—you have exactly seven seconds to wild it up. (*laughter*)

Speaking of that sort of thing, I direct your attention to the forty very attractive young ladies who will serve as usherettes at the various sports and entertainment events here. As you will see by the program, the ensemble they wear is made of polyester double-knit and features navy hot-pants. Frankly I don't see what's so special about that. The Navy has had hot pants for years. (*laughter*)

One really unusual thing is that "the fashions were selected by Miss Sarah Higgenbotham, an interior designer for the Williams and Tazewell Partnership architectural firm." So far as I know, this is the first time that women's clothing has been designed by an architect. It's worked out pretty well, except for one little problem—the undergarments are made of cement.

Lastly, I suppose I should say a word about a point that has been the subject, I understand, of considerable controversy here in Norfolk during the last few years. There is just no denying the fact that the total cost of Scope itself, as the program tells you, was $28 million. If we include tips and bribes, it came to $49 million, but what the hell. (*laughter*)

At the first show last evening, I introduced quite a number of dignitaries. I think the number was 497. At the moment, the only dignitary present is your vice mayor, Mr. V. H. Nusbaum, Jr. It's interesting that you have a mayor for that, too. (*laughter*)

And now . . . on with the show.

You can see how I made use of the raw material at hand, in this case, statements in the printed brochure. Unfortunately, that address could never be used again, for the obvious reason. In fact, that's true of many of the routines I do, particularly at large public events, fundraising banquets. They are appropriate only to that occasion. One or two of the jokes may be quoted by columnists, but that's about it. The routines could never become part of any regular act.

Although any comedian who agrees to make an appearance at a public function will have a certain amount of prefabricated material he can do almost anywhere, again I recommend paying careful attention to the specific circumstances in each such instance, since invariably things will come to your attention about which you can joke. In the case of the following remarks, given at the dedication ceremony of Cedars-Sinai Hospital in Los Angeles, I had made a number of observations while waiting to go on that were helpful when I was finally introduced.

The event was staged not in an enclosure, but in the middle of a parking lot adjacent to new hospital construction. Secondly, I noticed that the program started quite late and seemed to be dragging on interminably. Third, I observed that several hard-hat construction workers on the fifth floor of the partially completed building had knocked off their work to see what our group was doing down below. I repeat here a point I've made a few times before: Although an audience can be fooled, they will usually have the ability to tell which jokes are truly ad-libbed and which are part of a stock repertoire. And audiences have a special appreciation for ad-lib humor that applies to the situation in which they find themselves. In any event, here are my remarks at the dedication ceremony:

Thank you very much, ladies and gentlemen. This microphone seems to be much too low for me, and there's apparently no way to raise it. . . . I never realized that height could be a problem.

Well, it has certainly been exciting to listen to all the previous speakers and to take part in so important an event.

I admit that I *was* a bit startled when, in his opening remarks, Mr. Weinberg said that there were going to be "quite a few speakers." I thought he said "quite a few *streakers*."

(*photographer at my knees suddenly shoots a flash picture*) It's always interesting when a photographer runs up and shoots a picture up your nostrils.

You may take all the pictures of that kind you want, sir, but I do want you to know that they will be of interest only to the eye-ear-nose-and-throat department of this hospital.

As you may have noticed, I've been sitting here on the platform—for quite a long time, come to think of it—and jotting down notes as they occurred to me. In fact, I've been sitting here so long that I now have enough material for a two-hour speech.

But having just written these observations, I confess I'm very anxious to hear them myself.

Seriously, it *is* an honor to be a part of these proceedings this morning because when this institution is completed it will attend to the medical needs of not only our local citizens but also our fighting men. The gas station owners. [This was during the shock of the first national gasoline shortage.]

Steve Broidy just referred to the fact that this morning culminates a ten-year effort. That is indeed the case. Think of it, my friends, ten long years, the last two of them spent listening to Mr. Broidy talk.

But I shouldn't complain; I'm lucky to be here at all. As you may have noticed, I drove in late because I was driving our *camper* rather than one of our cars, and I got lost a few blocks away from the place. I leaned out the window and said to a fellow standing on the sidewalk, "Where is Cedars-Sinai Hospital?" He said, "I'm sorry I can't help you; I'm a Christian Scientist."

I am not kidding. I really did have to drive the camper here this morning. My son's car was out of order so he drove Jayne's car to school. And Jayne took *my* car. So all that was left for me was either the camper or the motorcycle.

But I couldn't ride the motorcycle because I've just had my hair done.

But I must say a camper is a million laughs during a gasoline shortage.

But there it sits, right there in the parking lot. And after these proceedings are concluded this morning, ladies and gentlemen, if you'd just like to step over that way I'll be glad to take chest X-rays of all of you.

But in any event, I *am* here now and—like all of you—I've been here a good long time. In fact, we've been here so long that this lady in the red hat (*pointing to lady with a large flowery picture hat seated in the audience*) has taken *root*.

But this morning means a bit more to me than it might to some of you because I can remember back twenty-five years ago when a friend of mine was ill and told me he was going to Cedars of Lebanon. I went to visit him one day and discovered that there was no hospital—just *cedars*. He was sitting in the shade of one of them and making himself as comfortable as possible.

Actually, they no longer call this institution Cedars of Lebanon. It's now—as you know—called Cedars–Mt. Sinai. There still *is* a Cedars of Lebanon in Los Angeles, however. That is now the name of Danny Thomas's house.

Ordinarily, at functions of this sort, I am assigned the task of making a few introductions, but Mr. Broidy has already done that. In fact, this is the first public meeting I've attended where every single person in the *audience* was introduced. Since that's the case, I'd like to introduce a few bystanders over there beyond the ropes. I see several former bootleggers, some disbarred attorneys. I'm glad to recognize them.

But just look at the skeleton of this magnificent building behind us, my friends. Look at them up there. . . . (*pointing to the construction workers watching*) Looks like a Nixon commercial in the 1972 campaign.

Speaking of that, ladies and gentlemen, as I look at this audience this morning, I see a great many extremely wealthy people of the Beverly Hills area. I ask you people to just *think* of all the money you gave to Nixon in '72—secretly or otherwise. If you'd given it to Cedars-Sinai, this place would have been finished two years ago.

Mr. Weinberg, when he introduced Dr. Charles Aronburg, the mayor of Beverly Hills, commented that it seemed odd to him that a doctor should also serve as mayor. Personally, I think it's a marvelous idea; it might be just what we need to attend to all of our sick cities.

In this next illustration, the circumstances involved my having been invited to introduce Mayor Tom Bradley of Los Angeles at a fundraising auction and luncheon program at the Valley Beth Shalom Temple in February 1980. The raw materials of the situation were as follows:

1. The instructions I had been given about parking were unclear.

2. The luncheon was served much later than it should have been, as a result of which, by the time the audience of about a thousand left the dining hall and repaired to the sanctuary, the program started some forty-five minutes late, about ten minutes before two.

3. The host group had assured me that I would be able to leave by two, and on the basis of this assurance, my secretary had given 2:40 as the time for me to report to a private residence in the Westwood area where I was scheduled to film a television interview with Barbara Walters.

4. At about five minutes to two, I asked the woman who was to introduce me exactly where in the program Mayor Bradley and I were scheduled to speak. "At the end," she said.

I quickly explained to her that, for my own part, I would simply have to be put on earlier since otherwise not only Ms. Walters but a technical and production crew—all on hourly wages—would be kept waiting for over an hour. It was then agreed that I could get on a bit earlier, though not much.

5. A Dr. Lieber, distinguished theological scholar and administrator of the University of Judaism, I was told, would be speaking just before me, "from two to five minutes."

6. Earlier in the program there had been an address by a Rabbi Johnson.

At this point, you might briefly glance again at the preceding few paragraphs, and, as an exercise, ask what comedy capital, if any, could be made of such distressing particulars. My introductory remarks, in any case, went as follows:

Thank you, Mrs. Bernstein, for your flattering introduction.

It may have seemed arbitrary, a moment ago, ladies and gentlemen, that I put up my hand to stop your applause; but the fact is that I am in quite a serious predicament as regards time, and I simply didn't want to waste any of the precious seconds in meaningless bowing.

Then, too, I had not been made aware that you had two parking lots here. In any event, I entered what proved to be the wrong one and, of course, found it fully occupied. Since I was already late, I parked there anyway, then hurried into the building and presented a most helpful gentleman with my car keys, suggesting that he solve the problem, if he could. I am now able to report to you that my car has just been auctioned off. It raised $12,000 for this most worthy cause.

Seriously, the Jews—as this audience will be well aware—have a distinguished record of problem-solving, over long centuries and in many parts of the world. The Jews have successfully dealt with problems in the areas of theology, philosophy, politics . . . but not in parking.

As regards parking—if you don't mind my saying so—you've got a lot to learn.

I had originally agreed to address you quite late in the program, in which case I would have been happy to speak at length about the political virtues of my good friend, Mayor Bradley. Unfortunately, once it became clear that I was not going to be able to deliver my remarks until sometime in late September, I had to ask to be introduced earlier in the program because at this moment Barbara Walters is waiting for me in Westwood.

Another complicating factor is that I was told that the most notable characteristic of Dr. Leiber's remarks would be their brevity. But I suppose it was too much to expect that so distinguished a theological scholar, with an intimate knowledge of several thousand years of Jewish history, would be able to confine his attention to the modern age. And, to tell the truth, I was a bit distracted, while listening to Rabbi Leiber, by the fact that we had earlier been addressed by Rabbi Johnson. How a man named Johnson became a rabbi in the first place I do not understand, but that is perhaps neither here nor there.

My problem of the moment is that I'm *here*—and I'm supposed to be *there*. So I must excuse myself and go there now, otherwise we run the risk of having Barbara bring her camera crew here, and this whole program this afternoon may end up being investigated by her and Mike Wallace and subjected to national embarrassment on "60 Minutes."

Nothing that would put Voltaire to shame, but it does demonstrate how you can take the nuts and bolts of a given situation, particularly if there is *some element of trouble,* and use it as the basis for an at least moderately witty commentary.

Although I never reasoned my way through to the point, I've discovered from scores of predicaments over the years that the combination of the inherent embarrassment or awkwardness of the situation combined with a dignified, analytical approach invariably produces a result that audiences find amusing.

If you're a lecturer, there is a good likelihood that you'll be asked to respond to questions. In most cases this works out easily enough, since presumably if you know enough to deliver a speech on a given subject, you're well enough informed to provide additional information as required. But it's fairly common for someone in the audience to rise and, instead of asking a short question, launch into a long, somewhat meandering speech. Gary Apple, of the newsletter *Current Comedy,* suggests the following lines to use after hearing an exceedingly long question:

I'd ask you to repeat the question—but we only have the hall until Sunday.

Was that a question—or a miniseries?

Ladies and gentlemen, let me paraphrase that question—for those of you who might have dozed off halfway through it.

I couldn't have said it better myself. Shorter, yes. Better, no.

Sarcastic? Sure, but the questioner will have brought it on himself.

Another point that might be of help to fledgling comedians is that it is a definite drawback—whether you are trying to be amusing or merely fascinating—if directly in front of the speaker's lectern there is a large open space of the sort usually reserved for dancing. Whenever I can control this factor, I ask the host group simply to move tables and/or chairs up to the edge of the stage or speaker's platform. Otherwise you get the feeling, as you speak or entertain, that you are performing in a conventional theater, the first thirty rows of which are empty.

Injecting humor into an extemporaneous speech will add to its effectiveness and relax *you* at the same time. As an aid to help you think on your feet, you might enroll in a comedy improvisation workshop. Practicing to speak freely and in an entertaining manner before a small group can make you feel more at ease when the time comes to address an audience in a formal situation.

But whether your speech is prepared or ad-libbed, the inclusion of humor can be an important means to keep the audience's attention and get your message across, especially when dealing with a heavy topic. As comedy writer Gene Perret notes in his book *How to Hold Your Audience with Humor*:

> The mind can fall into a rhythm which lulls it to sleep. Your wit can be a splash of cold water that keeps your audience listening. . . . A serious talk needs splashes of lightheartedness.

5

Stand-Up Comedy: Writing Monologues

One might think that the combination of (1) people in a given audience who have been laughing at me over the past forty-five years, and (2) the success of the first ten or fifteen minutes of one of my concerts might mean that, on nights when things are going particularly well, an audience will laugh at almost anything I say, brilliant or not.

And that is sometimes true. To convert that point into how-to advice here, however, may sound comic in itself: All you have to do is to have good fortune as a comedian for the first forty years and after that it will all be easy!

The first time this insight occurred to me was one night in Hollywood a million years ago. I was about twenty-two, in town looking for work, and somebody gave me a ticket to see a "Command Performance" radio show. Bob Hope was the star that night and when he walked on stage he got a three-minute ovation, just for showing up. He hadn't done anything or said anything funny, and yet he was already a hit.

Comic author Larry Gelbart told me about something that happened when he was working as a writer for Hope in 1948. "We were in Blackpool, England," Gelbart recalled. "Bob was doing a benefit for a local orphanage that had been bombed during the war. I remember standing in the wings next to a young lady, and Bob did a joke, the last word of which was *motel*. I knew that there was no such thing in England at the time, and yet the woman laughed. I asked her why. 'Do you know what that word means?' I said. 'No,' she replied, 'but it's Bob.' "

Sometimes, too, things work so well during a comedian's first few minutes that it is possible to take control of the audience. When that happens, assuming you're competent at your craft, it's true that you'll get bigger laughs than somebody else doing the same jokes, all other things being equal.

Milton Berle has said that if he has an audience on a roll, he can get a laugh just by timing almost any innocuous phrase in a certain way so that it *sounds* like a joke, and he's right.

As a matter of fact, there are some performers whose jokes don't really have the *content* of wit, but who have the timing and structure of jokes down so well they still get laughs. I think of Debbie Reynolds and talk-show host Virginia Graham in this connection. I do not refer here to prepared routines or shows that Debbie and Virginia do. Debbie has a wonderfully enjoyable act and gives the customers a great deal for their money—singing, dancing, impressions, comedy. So does Virginia. What I'm talking about is ad-lib situations, either on talk shows or at parties. I cannot recall a quotable line that either of these charming ladies has ever said, yet I have seen audiences laugh at them because they sensed when something funny *should* be said, jumped in at just the right moment, and made a relevant and only vaguely amusing comment that the audience somehow accepted as a joke. Go figga, as we say.

There are rare instances when, while one part of my brain is creating a joke, another part evaluates what I've said and realizes I've just given the audience a fast shuffle.

This happened recently when I got a card from a woman in the audience named Oma Majesty. After reading her name aloud, I said, "Oma Majesty. That sounds like what Princess Di says in the middle of the night," at which I repeated the woman's name as if I were saying "Oh, my Majesty" in a vaguely erotic tone of voice.

But of course the joke did not make sense, strictly speaking, because what Princess Di would really say is, "Oh, *your* Majesty." Despite the breakdown in meaning or coherence, the audience nevertheless laughed.

Although it is true that eventually audiences give you credit for sheer survival, I wouldn't want anyone to think that you can walk on stage without anything else in your repertoire and have good luck for very long. The last word, then, is that while there are enormous advantages to having been around long enough to condition audiences to respond to you, there is no such thing as a guarantee of success at any time, for any performer, and for comedians least of all. Singers have the easiest way in the world to make a living, although I doubt if many of them appreciate the fact. A singer, as I've said, is basically some lucky man or woman blessed by what is really a freak of nature, the ability to make a pleasant sound when the mouth is opened and air is being forcefully expelled from the lungs.

It is much different for comedians. Even when the audience loves you,

you're still living from joke to joke, walking a tightrope. Nobody gives a circus acrobat a hell of a lot of credit if he walks forty-three feet across a tightrope and then, in his next step, falls off. It is the same for comics. They can be great the first seven minutes and then suddenly, with three weak jokes, be in trouble. And I don't just mean the moderately talented. Superstars, too, can lose control of an audience. They can even bomb totally. And do.

In another instance where I gave an audience a fast shuffle but got the laugh anyway, there was a card signed "Nancy, with Eastern Airlines." She wrote a deliberately "naughty" question, which I used because it would obviously get an "uh-oh" reaction: "Since Jayne isn't with you tonight, what are you doing after the show?"

There are quite a few directions you can go with a straight line like that, but my instant association was the phrase *the friendly skies* used in the popular television commercial. The second stage of the development of the joke was to use the formula that goes "I've heard of so-and-so, but this is ridiculous . . ."

I said, "I've heard of friendly skies, but this is ridiculous." The line indeed got a laugh, but half a second later it occurred to me that I'd made an error because the friendly skies are associated with United Airlines, not Eastern. But by the time some of the audience could have figured that out we were off and running with other questions.

Does the fact that a joke is delivered perfectly and adjudged excellent by a jury of experts guarantee it will get a big laugh? Believe it or not, it doesn't guarantee that it will get any laugh at all. At least not from every audience. Even when a joke is of good quality, there may be some one factor about it that is unintelligible to a specific audience. Consider, for example, one of the cliché lines comedians sometimes use when getting a microphone or other piece of stage equipment out of the way. Most of the old-time comics would simply stand at the microphone, at center stage, and deliver their lines without making any special use of the instrument. We would expect to see Bob Hope, Milton Berle, and Henny Youngman work in that way.

But slightly younger comics, including most of today's performers, will take the microphone off the stand and move about the stage with it. Oddly enough, this is also true of singers. In the old days, they remained in front of a microphone unless they were working sans amplification, as in a Broadway musical, and had to move about the stage.

(It has only just now struck me that the primary reason that the old-time vocalists remained in one position was that when microphones and audio systems were first introduced into nightclubs and theaters, the mikes were firmly attached to their stands so that performers were obliged to use them in exactly the same way they would in a radio studio.)

But to return to comedy, today's performers sometimes will do funny shtick with the mike or the wire, as when you lift the microphone off the stand and then decide to move the base to one side. You hold the stand up in the air, pretending for a moment to be undecided as to where to place it. Then, very quickly, you say, "I'd like to thank the Knights of Columbus for this award—" and, after the initial laugh, you can kick the joke along, so to speak, by saying such things as "I just hope I live up to it. I know what a great honor it implies," etc.

That line became cliché chiefly because it's a strong, reliable joke; whoever its unsung originator was, he or she deserves credit. But for the line to get a big laugh, there have to be enough Catholics in the audience who have heard of the *Knights of Columbus* (a Catholic fraternal organization). The line might not get a laugh at all in front of a largely Protestant, Jewish, or secular humanist group. In those cases, of course, you would delete the Knights-of-Columbus component and replace it with the Masons, the B'Nai Brith, or the American Humanist Association.

There are many instances of excellent jokes which, for various reasons, did not work at a specific moment. An example would be a line that occurred to me while I was entertaining aboard the SS *Royale*. The audience was red hot and everything was going wonderfully well. Nevertheless, the best joke of the night got almost no reaction except from members of the band, mostly jazz players, who became hysterical. I had noticed, after spending several days aboard the ship, that its crew and service personnel seemed to have been recruited entirely from the Third World. Among the people serving in the cabins, the dining rooms, the bars, and elsewhere, there were Algerians, Turks, Indonesians, Lebanese and so forth. At one point I said, "By the way, this ship has a very interesting crew—people from North Africa and the Middle East. You know, if terrorists took over this vessel right now, how would we know the difference?" Perhaps another reason the audience didn't laugh was that the subject was in fact of some concern to them.

Particularly when you're starting out, the right material can be crucial to your acceptance and success. If you are not a full-time comedy performer, or if you formerly worked for an extended period at some other trade, you might, for instance, want to do jokes about your previous occupation. An example would be:

I know I'm not getting many laughs tonight; but believe me, if I didn't get a single laugh all night long this would still be a better deal than what I was doing for a living last year. Any of you folks ever try to sell Bibles door to door?

There are so many opportunities for aspiring young comedians to make experimental test flights that even performers with severe handicaps have been given the opportunity. Kathy Buckley, an attractive young woman who is deaf and therefore has learned to speak only with great difficulty, does funny routines about her disability. Geri Jewell, who suffers from cerebral palsy, also makes a good living at comedy clubs and other venues all over the country.

In 1978 I went to see a blind comic named Alex Valdez perform. My son, Bill, later a network and studio executive but then a student at the University of Southern California, had produced a film about him. The day after I saw Valdez, I sent him this letter containing suggestions for routines I thought might be appropriate for him:

Dear Alex:

I must tell you again how much I enjoyed your performance at the Comedy Store the other night.

As I mentioned in the parking lot, I've thought of a few lines that might make sense for you. Needless to say, if they don't hit you, no problem.

1. There's one place where you're talking about what it's like for a blind guy to go to a baseball game, getting hit by the ball, etc. You might say, "Whenever a ball is coming, there's one thing people always yell. They always say, 'Heads up!' "

"So I'm sitting there and about fourteen people are sitting around me yelling 'Heads up!' I put my head *up*. The ball hit me right in the mouth."

Naturally, while saying the line, you raise your eyes toward the ceiling.

2. In another place, where you're talking about TV, you might say, "I dig TV. In fact, I have my own special name for it—*radio*."

3. There's not any *real* reason you should conclude your routine with a song, but if you are still at the stage of making experiments—just to see if certain kinds of things work out—by coincidence I wrote a number recently for a handicapped friend of mine. He gave me the title "Just Because We're Handicapped." It's being played at a Christmas party, in a few days, for a disabled group here in town. It's a simple, warm Bing Crosby–Irving Berlin sort of tune. If you do any singing, you would have to have an accompanist show you how the thing goes. Or I could make a vocal tape so you could listen to it.

Using it for a finish would be pure schmaltz and ordinarily might seem sort of un-hip, but I can assure you almost all audiences would enjoy it.

4. Something like this might work for you: "You know, when you're blind for many years, you really get adjusted to it. It comes to seem like—for you—the normal way of life. So in one sense, it's not really a hang-up at all. But when other people meet you, sometimes it's a hang-up for them. And people say really dumb things to you.

"A lot of people walk up and say, 'Hey, Alex, why don't you come over and *see* us sometime?' "

Then you do a quick, embarrassed expression while saying, "Oh, gee!"

"Or maybe it's a nice day out and somebody says to me, 'Hey, Alex, don't you really *love* to see weather like this?' . . . Oh, gee!"

5. After your "Justice is blind" line, you might want to add the following: "There are a *lot* of things that are blind. *Love* is blind. When a guy really gets *juiced,* bombed out on tequila or whatever, he says, 'Wow, I was really *blind* last night!' "

"And a lot of people are *color*-blind. I'm color blind, too. . . . Also *shape*-blind, *form*-blind."

6. "Or maybe rich people will walk by and some guy says, 'Hey, man, did you see the *diamond* that woman was wearing? Man, it'd knock your *eye* out.' . . . Whoops!"

7. "Or some guy in a bar will offer me a drink and say, 'Well, Alex, here's *lookin'* at ya.' . . . Whoops!"

8. Each place where you say *whoops,* it will help the laugh if you do a quick "take." Of course Bill explained to me last evening that inasmuch as you've never seen a take it isn't the easiest thing for you to do. I suggest a good way to show you how is to put your fingers on a guy's chin as he does one so that you can feel how the head is turned one way and then does a quick little double-flip back the other way. The lines will get laughs even without the takes, but with them—as I say—they generally pay off a little better.

9. There's also an *old* joke that you could adapt for your own purposes. I'm sure *you* would get a bigger laugh with it than it ordinarily elicits.

The original joke goes like this: "When I was a kid, I was a Boy Scout, but I kept getting into trouble. I remember one time I helped an old lady across the street. But she didn't take it very well. She didn't want to go."

You could do the line as such: "People are nice, though. They try to be helpful, they really do. Like earlier this evening I was standing out on Sunset Boulevard, and this guy helped me across the street. Unfortunately, I didn't want to *go* across the street."

10. "Speaking of crossing the street, people really say some dumb things to you here, too. Like one day I was going to cross at the corner of Hollywood and Vine. There was this guy standing next to me, so I said to him, 'Hey, Mac, is it okay if I cross the street here?'

"He said, 'Yeah, it's cool, but just be sure you walk between the white lines.' "

11. "Or if it's late at night, and a friend is staying too long, he might say something like, 'Well, Alex, I think I'll go home now and get a little *shut eye.*' . . . Damn!"

Again, note that the use of phrases like *damn* or *oh, gee,* or *whoops,* etc. are supposed to convey the sighted person's sudden embarrassment when he realizes he said something to a sightless person that would have a meaning other than the one intended.

12. There's another line you could use as part of the routine where you talk about driving on the freeway and getting stopped by the cops. As you may know, very often cops stop young guys driving a car to check them out. They shine a flashlight right in their eyes to see if their pupils are dilated, since that means they could be on something. You could do this routine where you seem to be playing the part of one cop talking to another. The line could go something like this:

"It would be pretty wild when they pull me over, if they wanted to check me out to see if I'm on anything. One guy shines his flashlight right in my face and says, 'Hey, Bob, check the pupils on *this* guy. His left eye shows he's on *speed* and his right eye looks like he's on *soy sauce.*' "

The point here is to use any silly word as applying to the *second* eye. It can be *soy sauce, Kool-aid,* or whatever.

13. "Or if a friend is arguing with you about something, he might say, 'Well now, Alex, I know you and I don't see eye to eye on this.' . . . Whoops!"

14. Another physical shtick that sighted people do when they catch themselves in a dumb mistake is to snap their fingers while saying *damn,* or *oh, shoot,* or whatever.

15. "Actually—although you may have never thought of this—there are a number of *advantages* to not being able to see. Like I happened to be in New York a few years ago when there was that big power blackout. I'm standing on Sixth Avenue and this dude on the street yells, 'Oh, oh, now we're *really* in trouble.' And I said to him, 'What do you mean, *we?*' "

16. "When I was a little kid, they used to show this very popular program on television called 'What's My Line?' Some famous celebrity would walk out on stage, and all the people on the panel had to wear these black masks and try to guess who the celebrity was. I used to think how great it would be to sit on the 'What's My Line?' panel and not have to bother with that mask."

17. Another thing you might do is have your friends tell you whenever some referee or umpire in a big important football or baseball game makes a really rotten call. In other words, he calls the guy out at home plate when the instant replay shows—with 40 million fans watching—that the

guy was actually safe. For four or five days after that kind of a goof, you could get a laugh where you talk about what you might like to do for a living—by saying, "I could always get a job as an umpire in Pittsburgh." Or "I could always get a job as a referee in the American League," or the NFL, or wherever the bad call was made.

18. You might also do a routine based on the titles of famous songs that have the word *eyes* in them. The routine could go something like this:

"You know when you don't see anything, your *hearing* becomes very acute. So if you think you dig music, all I can tell you is *I* enjoy it a lot more than you do because I can really *concentrate* on it. In fact, I like music so much I've been thinking of recording an album. But I can't record just any old tune the way a lot of singers can; I'd have to check it out. There might be a problem about the lyrics to some of the songs.

"I've been thinking of recording songs like 'I Only Have *Ears* for You,' 'Five Foot Two, *Nose* of Blue,' 'I'll Smell You In My Dreams,' and 'I'll Be Hearing You.' "

As you realize, the titles should not be *said*, but sung. The piano accompanist could lead you into the various phrases, although you would get a laugh even if you were working without a piano.

I hope some of these ideas are helpful to you, Alex.

❃   ❃   ❃

One of the things I sometimes object to with the under-40 comics—and some who are older than that—is that they often have a certain insensitivity to the make-up of their audience, though this says nothing about their talent. This is particularly true of comedians who do off-color material. It is by no means just a generational thing. There are deservedly successful comedians over sixty—Buddy Hackett, the late Redd Foxx, to name a couple—who "work dirty." But I attach importance to the fact that one of the fastest rising young comics of recent years is the clever Steven Wright. He creates his own material, he can pack any comedy club in the country, and he's especially popular with the young-adult segment of our society. But if he's ever done an off-color joke, I haven't heard it. His meteoric success is consistent with the old saying that if you're really funny, you don't have to be dirty.

Veteran jokewriter Harry Crane, speaking of his respect for Wright's jokes, says, "The jokes are so strong that you could send out a road company—almost anybody could read those great jokes and get laughs."

I think some of today's young comedians think that if you're really dirty, you don't have to be funny. Now *that's* funny! Let me see if I can think of some way to dirty it up. But seriously, audiences can be made to feel uncomfortable by vulgar material, particularly if it's delivered by a woman. I saw this once some years ago, and I've never forgotten the incident because of the hideous embarrassment that everyone present felt. The occasion was a fund-raising benefit for the National Organization for Women that took place in the Coconut Grove of the Ambassador Hotel in Los Angeles. Jayne and I were among a number of entertainers present. It's important to note first that the audience consisted almost entirely of people clustered generally toward the opposite end of the social spectrum from the Moral Majority. In other words, they were quite prepared to tolerate daring statements from speakers and entertainers. But at one point a comedienne got up and launched into a seven- or eight-minute monologue replete with a great deal of gutter language.

I can't recall the woman's name. She was blonde, blue-eyed, reasonably pretty; but she must have gone into instant shock about sixty seconds after getting on stage, because this generally sophisticated, permissive audience was not laughing at her. At all.

I chuckled it up for a few of her cleaner jokes because I hate to see a fellow comedy performer suffer, but the situation was so disastrous that helpful laughs from our table could not possibly have resolved the young woman's predicament.

Once the audience had somehow made the group decision to reject her material, they began doing something else equally horrendous, in terms of a performer's interests: they began to talk, clink glasses and silverware, and pay practically no attention to the poor woman during the last few minutes she was on. The woman finally reached the end of her routine, mumbled a quick thank you, and blessedly got off the stage.

About five minutes later, however, she walked back on stage, without being reintroduced, took over the microphone and said something along the following lines: "Ladies and gentlemen, somebody mentioned to me, a few minutes ago, that you were offended by some of the things I said up here. Well, I just want to say that I'm sorry. I didn't mean to do that. I meant the jokes and all that, but I have great respect for this organization, and I'm sorry if I caused you any embarrassment—"

The poor soul went on, in that vein, for another two or three minutes. People at nearby tables were actually groaning sympathetically, putting their hands over their eyes so as not to witness the self-immolation. It was terribly embarrassing. A long story, perhaps, but the point of it is that I don't think the same unhappy fate would have befallen a *male* comic who had gotten up and done precisely the same jokes.

*   *   *

Although some of my jokes can be pointed, as a general rule mine is not the humor of attack. But are there any formulas for creating outrageous or strongly critical humor? Yes, in the sense that many of the previously discussed formulas will work for various kinds of jokes. But in this case we would have to add another element, which is that the creator of the jokes or monologues would set out to be deliberately provocative. Lenny Bruce used to do that. There were times when he was as interested in outraging an audience as in amusing it. An example would be his comment on the Leopold and Loeb case, in which he suggested that maybe the two killers weren't so bad as they were cracked up to be "because Bobby Franks was a snot."

Franks, for those readers not familiar with the case, was a poor child killed by these two degenerates. Lenny, being brilliant, *must* have known that he was going to take a lot of heat for that kind of a line, but such material did serve to attract attention, which in turn set Bruce off from the run-of-the-mill nightclub comics of his generation. Such a line may be counted upon to anger almost 100 percent of those who will hear it. Other jokes of that bitter sort—they used to be called *sick*—may antagonize only a given segment of the overall audience. For example, when I engaged in a debate about British and American humor at Oxford University in May 1986, I said something to the effect that the British should be held responsible for the fact that their former colonies are not noted for their humor. The Jews, I said, in Israel or not, are funny. But there are not too many Palestinian comedians. "Arafat is not funny. *Chicken fat* is funny. But, on the other hand, any man who wears an Italian tablecloth for a hat . . ."

Obviously, such a joke would seem objectionable to members of the Palestine Liberation Organization, to Palestinians in general, perhaps to most Arabs.

Regarding insult, put-down, or cruel humor generally, can one *learn* to do what Don Rickles or the late Jack E. Leonard have done so well? Yes, the skill can be taught, although not to everyone. Don is personally a pleasant fellow to spend time with, and Jack was a real sweetheart. But both he and Don had not only a natural wit, but a dominating and almost threatening quality on stage. Because Jack was in the business before Don, he broke this particular ground. He started out doing something that almost all comedians who work in nightclubs have done at one time or another—that is, being critical, naturally in a comic way, about the circumstances under which they are working. All of us have suffered from miserable air-conditioning systems, poor lighting, lousy public address equipment, noisy drunks at ringside tables, a second-rate orchestra, or whatever. Some of the early comics developed the quite understandable habit of joking critically about these things. It was an easy step from that to doing jokes about the audience.

But if the reader really wants to learn to be funny in that way, he or she will first have to have that sort of personality. In other words, such an approach would not work for Don Knotts, Bob Newhart, Stephen Wright, or any other entertainer who works in a gentle, nonagressive manner.

Don learned a trick or two of the trade from Jack but eventually surpassed him as a practitioner of this art form. Not only does Don have natural gifts for firing a barrage of insult jokes, but he has consciously developed those abilities, going so far as to do research on popular entertainers he expects to visit his shows, as all of us do when we either perform in or visit Las Vegas. Don will often come to the clubs where the rest of us are working or visiting and plead with us to come see him. "I'd love it if you'd catch my show Friday night. Can you do it?"

He arranges with staff people of his casino to let him know when celebrities are in the audience and, by a combination of his forethought and knack for spontaneous humor, rakes one or another of us over the coals.

Some years ago, when Jayne, my mother—vaudeville comedienne Belle Montrose—and I performed at the Flamingo, Don somehow acquired the information that my mother had a drinking problem, which indeed she had. This became the basis of several minutes of the routine he did when we went to see him one night. My secretary at the time, Donna Zink, became furious at some things Don said about my mother and, for that matter, about Jayne and me, too, although I laughed hard since I'm a big fan of Don's.

Still, the comedy of insult is funny only when it occurs in the realm of make-believe. When a comedian in a nightclub says to a heckler, "Oh, you want to ad-lib? Good; I'll turn in my brain, and we'll start even," the audience laughs because they realize that the insult is first of all coming from a funny professional, and secondly that his purpose is to get a laugh. If one said the same thing to a stranger on a streetcar, the incident might, after a sufficient lapse of time, become amusing in the telling, but it would be supremely unfunny at the moment of its occurrence.

There are, nevertheless, certain areas wherein the humor of insult may be so delicately applied as to be genuinely laugh-provoking at the time, and if the application can take place in such a way as to puncture a vanity, the effect may be eminently satisfactory, even to the relative unfortunate who is the butt of the joke. I was the target one night when "Scatman" Carruthers, the late actor, singer, and songwriter, appeared on a program of mine originating from Hollywood.

The preceding week, if I may indulge in a necessary digression, had seen the entirely unmomentous premiere of what was my first motion picture. It was an undistinguished but pleasant hodgepodge of old Mack Sennett film footage featuring such greats as Ben Turpin, Gloria Swanson, W.C. Fields, Bing Crosby, the Keystone Kops, Franklyn Pangborn, and Mabel Normand, and my job had been to write and appear in several short scenes that would tie the potpourri together and give it some sort of storyline. For better or worse, the picture, called *Down Memory Lane,* was completed and released, and on the strength of this rather hesitant step in the direction of a film career, my agent had secured for me a booking on a popular radio dramatic program called "Hollywood Star Theater."

Lest the title seem presumptuous for a program that featured relative newcomers, let me explain that a real live Hollywood star was actually present at each broadcast. This luminary (it was Joan Bennett in the case of the program on which I appeared) functioned in a seemingly advisory capacity and appeared to sponsor the newcomer unleashed on each broadcast. In fact, the star's legitimate function was to add glamour and name appeal to a program that otherwise would not have enjoyed such a respectable rating. Be that as it may, I was rather proud of the way I had played a plain-talking cab driver who, after finding a dead blonde in the back of his taxi, had to work fast to avoid being arrested for the murder.

A year later, a half hour spent listening to the transcription of the broadcast convinced me that my confidence in my dramatic prowess had been somewhat misplaced. On the night of Scatman's appearance, however, I was still feeling a bit puffed up about my accomplishments. For the first few minutes of our interview, Carruthers and I discussed his recent recordings, debated musical viewpoints, and traded quips. In a momentary lull, he said, "Say, by the way, I heard you on that show the other night . . . that 'Hollywood Star Theater' thing. Man, you really surprised me."

"Oh?" I said, bracing myself for what I expected would be a compliment of my acting ability. "I surprised you?"

"Yeah," he said. "I didn't know you could drive a cab!"

But, to return to the reader's self-interest, suppose you are a young comedian trying to develop material. How would you go about writing a monologue that would be funny and acceptable to a wide range of people?

It's possible to start with some available slice of reality and create humor out of it. For instance, quite by chance, years ago on my old late-night radio show on the CBS station in Los Angeles, I discovered by reading items from small-town newspapers aloud that there was a strong vein of humor in them. I refer, of course, to accidental humor. If you've ever seen a newspaper from a really small community, you will be aware that they do not carry the same sorts of headlines one sees in the *New York Times* or the *Washington Post*. The smaller the town, the more likely that the news stories will be narrowly personal. I have actually read items such as: "Lucille and Mary Ellen Kneber Just Got Back from Cedar Rapids." That was the story in toto. Now, you string just five or six of those items together— all actually taken from a small town paper—read them aloud in front of an audience in a large city, and you can get screams.

The reason I mention this is that to this day, if I'm entertaining in a fairly small community, I make it a point to check the local papers to see if there's some event, some advertisement, some public announcement that I can use while on-stage. I remember one time when I was working in Greensboro, North Carolina. Glancing through the local paper a couple of hours before the show, I discovered that it included a special column consisting of brief reviews of the food and service at a dozen or so local restaurants. One of the restaurants referred to had an all-you-can-eat policy. As soon as I read the phrase, it reminded me that a few years earlier a musician friend had told me a funny story. A guy goes into an all-you-can-eat restaurant, pays his $5.95 and begins to pile all kinds of food on his plate—two steaks, several chicken legs, some appetizers, extra desserts. As soon as he does so, a big tough guy walks up to him and says, "Hey, you, that's all you can eat." That remembered joke naturally fit perfectly into the developing routine.

Although I was using the actual names of local restaurants in the monologue, I was aware that no one else present would have that particular news feature in front of him. Therefore I was free to use the name of a restaurant that I had actually seen in another city a couple years previously— the Saddle and Sirloin—which led me to say to my conductor, Terry Gibbs, "Terry, what was the name of that restaurant where we had dinner last night after the show? Oh, yes—the Saddle and Sirloin. But you were lucky. You had the sirloin."

In case any North Carolina historians want to research the matter, I found the restaurant review column in the Friday, April 11, 1986, edition of the *Greensboro News and Record*. The first restaurant mentioned was Madison's, at 616 Dolley Madison Road. The only thing that struck me of interest in that particular entry, however, was the peculiar spelling of *Dolley*.

The next restaurant recommended was the Cafe Pasta at 305 State Street. Since the foods mentioned were Italian, I simply recalled to mind a routine I had originally written about thirty-five years earlier based on my observation that the names of foods in Italian restaurants have always sounded to me like the names of gangsters. I visualize the first name of the dish as having quotation marks around it, as in "Meatballs" Marinara, "Chicken" Cacciatore, "Shrimps" Rigatoni.

Another restaurant the reviewer mentioned was the Equinox, located at the Friendly Shopping Center. Although the establishment specializes in "fish and other seafoods," nothing about that struck me funny at the moment, so I looked again at the name, at which time it occurred to me to say, "The Equinox is so named because you can select either the *equine* or the *ox*, both of which are very well prepared and served in a charmingly insouciant ambience." You know, that half-goofy jargon used in talking about wines or restaurants.

I also noticed that the local Greensboro restaurant where I'd had lunch, actually named Tijuana Fats, which of course served Mexican food, was not among those recommended, a fact I found perfectly understandable. But because of the relevance of the Spanish language, that led me into a standard routine in which I say that Spanish should really be the dominant international language because it is superior to all others—certainly to English, which is notoriously inconsistent as regards spelling and pronunciation. I then explain that, because literally anything said in the Spanish language sounds somehow lovely and romantic, this has been a helpful factor to those who write songs in that idiom. To prove the point, I sing the actual menu from a Mexican restaurant, but to the accompaniment of a lush, romantic and typically Latin ballad melody. Of course it's the contrast between the pretty melody and all the references to tortillas, tacos, and tostados that gets the laughs.

As I looked at the newspaper again, I saw that one of the recommended restaurants was a Japanese establishment named Asahi. At that point I was reminded of a very funny line that somebody, I can't remember who, had given me about three weeks earlier about a new Jewish-Japanese restaurant named Sosumi ("so-sue-me").

Next I noted that each mini-review referred to the credit cards that were accepted, so at this point I said, "And when eating there you can use various cards—Visa, American Express, Diners Club, a seven of spades— any damn card at all will be acceptable."

The last restaurant reviewed in that issue of the paper was Laredo's Neon *Cactus*. I italicized the word *cactus*, because it was that word that prompted me to say, "And you'll see they have actual cactus available at Laredo's. Consequently, there's no particular need for toothpicks."

Many of the most successful comedy monologues contain no actual jokes at all, but are funny because they touch on some experience familiar to everyone in the audience.

After once doing jokes about cliché social myths relating to storks, the sexual-physical structure of Chinese girls, and Coke-and-aspirin, I made the following observations:

> I've checked all this out with some bright people and have discovered that, no matter how intelligent you are, you believe certain things when you are very young that you later recognize as really dopey.
>
> One of *my* erroneous beliefs grew out of my ignorance of the word *round* in the phrase *a round of ammunition*. We've all heard that phrase hundreds of times: "We can't hold the Apaches off much longer, Captain! We've only got fourteen rounds of ammunition left!" I used to think that in that context the word *round* was somehow like the word *rasher* of bacon, or a *baker's dozen* of rolls. In other words, I thought it indicated a specific amount of ammunition. Come to think of it, it does. But I had no idea that the amount was *one*. I assumed that a round of ammunition meant about ten or fifteen bullets.
>
> Now, this is more than just a simple mathematical mistake, because what it means is that I totally misperceived the predicament of those poor doughboys and frontier cowboys—all those people who were about to be wiped out by the Germans, the Japanese, the Indians, or whoever. When Gary Cooper said that he only had six rounds of ammunition left, I was never really that worried about him because I figured that with sixty-seven bullets he could hold out till Thursday. Forgive me, Gary, wherever you are!

Another monologue I do that contains no joke lines touches on reality but borders on the outrageous. I call it "Women of the Street."

> You know, we live in a time of general collapse of standards, and I'm sure none of us need to be reminded of the dreadfully serious problems that trouble our society.
>
> Recently, public officials have been giving attention to one particular problem by cleaning out the red-light districts of certain major cities, trying to make the streets safe once again for just plain folks.
>
> Well, that's alright with me, but it doesn't answer one question: What do you do about all the, shall we say, women of the streets who will be

left unemployed? Since ours is a society in which pretty much *everything* is for sale, I propose a modest solution which would work something like this: (*walking over behind pitchman's counter*) A going-out-of-business sale at a house of ill repute. . . .

Yes, folks, *everything* must go—blondes, brunettes, redheads, baldies, wildies, hippies, junkies! Come on down, and if you mention my name before next Friday, you'll get a 15 percent reduction!

We've got *new* models, *old* models, models in all colors. I mean we've got whites, blacks, Orientals, half-breeds . . . you name it!

Why *rent* when you can *buy* at these once-in-a-lifetime low-low-low bargain prices?

Say, men, be the first guy on your block to own a strumpet! Imagine, a brazen hussy you can keep around the house for those days when the TV is on the blink and the ballgame's been rained out.

Help clean up your community! Get the women of the streets *off* the streets! Be a good neighbor. Take a hooker to lunch. Or—and this is for you real bargain-hunters—buy six and go into business for yourself!

Yes, men, no more wasting valuable money on overpriced magazines and crummy porno movies. Get the real thing, at these low, low, lost-our-lease sale prices!

The misuse of language in our society at present is so notorious that a number of books have been written about it. It sometimes seems that the coherent, grammatical English sentence should be added to the list of endangered species. Even our leaders are not immune from the virus of careless communication. The following monologue entertains the fantasy that if perhaps our greatest speaker among American presidents, Abraham Lincoln, were alive today and was going to deliver his immortal Gettysburg Address, it might come out sounding like this:

Four score and—uh—(you know) seven years ago—our fathers (like) brought forth on this continent, a new nation, conceived in liberty, and dedicated to the—uh—(you know) proposition that all men are, *like*, wow—created equal.

Now we are engaged in a—you know—great civil war, *all right?*—testing whether *that* nation, or (you know, like *any* nation) so conceived and so dedicated, can (like) long endure, you know what I'm saying?

We are met on a great battlefield of that war. We have come to dedicate a *portion* of that (you know) field, as a final resting place for those who here did the give-your-life thing that that *nation* might live. It is altogether fitting and (like, you know) proper that we should do this, okay?

But, *hey*, in a larger sense, we can not dedicate—we can not (like) consecrate—hallow—this ground. The brave men who struggled here, have (like) consecrated it, far above our *poor* power to add or (you know what I mean), detract.

The world will little note, nor long remember what we *say* here—but it can never forget what they *did* here, man.

Anyway, the bottom line is that it's for us the living, rather, to be dedicated to the unfinished work which they who (like) fought here have thus far so nobly advanced (you know—the whole nine yards). It is rather for us to be here dedicated to the great task remaining before us—that *from* these honored dead we take—you know, like—increased devotion that we here highly resolve that these dead shall *not* have died in *vain*—that this nation, under—you know—the man upstairs—shall have a new birth of freedom—and, *hey,* that government *of* the people, by the people, and, for the people, shall *not* perish from the earth!!

I'm outta here.

* * *

What can I explain to the reader about constructing a nonjoke monologue? First of all, there's no particular virtue in the trick itself. In other words, one would not start out with the deliberate intention of writing a monologue that had no jokes. If the thing makes sense, it will happen as a result of your having conceived certain comic ideas. In any event, what ends up as a monologue without jokes is closer to a humorous essay than a standard nightclub string of jokes connected only by a common theme.

And then, of course, there are successful comedians whose acts consist entirely of jokes that have no connective theme at all. The prime example would be Henny Youngman. As I once said, it would not matter if Henny did his act backwards. The individual jokes are invariably strong, and Henny has always gotten screams with them. Rodney Dangerfield jokes, too—with some exceptions—might be done in almost any order and still be as well received. There is of course, in Rodney's case, the fact that most of his jokes are self-demeaning and connected to the I-don't-get-no-respect idea.

A nonjoke monologue always starts with a funny thought. Voltaire, for example, imagined a scene in which a Catholic priest is explaining to a Native American the necessity for the Indian to confess his sins to the priest. Well, that sounds like a fair deal to the Indian, so he kneels down as instructed and tells the priest about every terrible thing he's ever done. And then, having completed that task, he forces the priest into a kneeling position and says, "Okay, now you tell me *your* sins."

Many of Bob Newhart's monologues don't have jokes in the Dangerfield or Youngman sense. They are little dramatic scenes in which Bob plays the various roles, if there are more than one. Consider, for example, his marvelous monologue in which he imagines that there are Madison Avenue-type public relations experts helping Abraham Lincoln write the Gettysburg address. Naturally, they give him a lot of stupid advice, like cutting the line about four score and seven years. "No, no, Abe," they say. "The people won't be able to figure out what that means. Just lay it right on the line. Say '87 years ago.' "

I haven't heard the routine in over thirty years, so I'm not even sure if that's one of the lines, but if it isn't, it ought to be, because it perfectly explains the point of the monologue. It's obvious that once the originator, and then later his or her audiences, buy the basic premise, all you need to do is give examples of what would follow, in some kind of imagined reality, and the ideas flow from the energy of the original conception.

An example of this is an open-ended monologue to which you can add or delete references to continually keep it fresh. I can cite from my own repertoire, for instance, a routine mentioned in volume 1 about silly-sounding product names. It occurred to me many years ago, that certain commercial products have what seem to be dumb names. Now, today, perhaps as long as thirty-five years after the original idea struck me, that routine can run to various lengths because it consists of a dozen or so examples of such products that have actually been distributed on the American marketplace. There's no specific, necessary beginning to the routine, nor does it have a formal end. In fact, I rarely recite the entire litany. I just keep running the specifics out until I sense that the audience has had enough of that subject. Then I move along to something else.

The first product I used in this connection was a popular soft drink called Dr. Swett's Root Beer. I've also used such brand names as Kelvinator, Hot Point, Smuckers, and Ben Gay. Here's part of the routine:

> And there's a kind of inexpensive candy which, in my opinion, has a stupid name—*Milk Duds*. I doubt that anybody ever actually got dressed during a snowstorm and said, "Honey, I'll be back in about an hour and a half. I'm going out to pick up some Milk Duds." No, you usually buy them at a movie theater while you're hanging around the lobby. But what a name for a product. The *milk* part of it I can understand, although I'd like to know what actual percentage of milk is in the candy. But *duds?* I can just see the guys inventing this stuff at the original candy factory. "I'm sorry to break the news to you, Chief, but that new milk chocolate you've invented has turned out to be a real dud."

And how about *Intensive Care* hand cream? "Yes, your husband is in the hospital, Mrs. Johnson. We picked up his body about an hour ago. No, he seems to be coming along just fine. Oh, there is one thing, his hands are in intensive care. We'll do our best, but you know what intensive care means."

But whatever products I refer to, I usually finish with a reference to *No Nonsense* panty hose, my monologue about which appears in *How to Be Funny*.

As you've seen, my monologues usually reflect my opinions. This point even extends to the world of fashion. The following are some monologues in which I hit on current trends. Apropos of the first is the fact that in 1957 I actually had the distinction of being named, by some organization, one of the ten best-dressed men in America, and—by another—one of the ten worst-dressed men.

Historians of the future are going to have quite an easy time telling what life was like in the present period because we are leaving behind such a massive accumulation of evidence—motion picture films, television tapes, recordings, newspapers, magazines, etc. But I don't think that people a thousand years from now will have an absolutely accurate picture of how we *dress*—what we actually wear on the streets and in our homes. The reason I say this is that I read what are called fashion magazines: *Vogue, Glamour, Bazaar, Gentlemen's Quarterly.*

These magazines do *not* show you how actual human beings dress. They do not even show you how professional models dress. All they show you is what professional models wear when they are working in fashion shows or in front of fashion photographers' cameras. I've known some models over the years, and I know some at present. On the street they dress the same as you and I. Men, particularly, do *not* dress like the male models in *Gentlemen's Quarterly.*

Then why, you might ask—if you are paying attention—has such a peculiar state of affairs come about? The answer is quite simple. If *Gentlemen's Quarterly* showed how men actually are attired, they would go out of business in six months because men's fashions change very slowly. I'm talking, of course, about actual typical American males—not punk rockers or other weird people.

Oh, lapels get a little wider or narrower every few years. Neckties get a little wider or narrower. But, for men, that's about it.

Occasionally young guys will wear stuff that's a little far out, but they don't get their ideas from *Gentlemen's Quarterly.* They get them from entertainers, or from the movies. Like, if Michael Jackson wears one white glove, suddenly three million young jerks have to wear one white glove.

A few years ago it became hip for about 1 percent of young guys to wear very cheap-looking sports jackets with the sleeves pushed up to the elbow. Now these jackets have to be cheap and skimpy because if you're wearing a good, classy Brooks Brothers or Ralph Lauren tweed jacket, you can't push the sleeves up. They'll fall right down again. But if you make a jacket out of polyester and unborn linoleum, then, when you push the sleeves up, they stay up. . . . At least until you take the jacket off.

Now, if your jacket sleeves are pushed up all day, they're gonna be wrinkled as hell when you take the thing off at night. What do you do? Run out to have them pressed and start the whole process all over?

That thought occurred to me a year or so ago when I was emceeing a Lenny Bruce comedy special on HBO. I pushed the sleeves of my jacket up and said to the audience, "What the hell is supposed to be so hip about this?"

A woman in the audience yelled out, "It's not hip anymore." And she was right. Sleeves pushed up were out, for about six months. Then they became slightly hip again, at least if you're a rock singer.

To use Michael Jackson for another example—he usually wears white socks with dark pants onstage. For the last fifty years, the only people in America who wore white socks with dark clothes were members of the Teamsters Union from Columbus, Ohio. The look was considered the squarest of the square. Now it's supposed to be hip, simply because Michael does it.

Don't you people have minds of your own?

I wrote another monologue about mode of dress for a television show on which I appeared some time back. Because of the good luck I'd had with the routine done at the Improv in Los Angeles, I rewrote it as follows. When I was announced, I walked on stage dressed in Levi's, a navy turtleneck under a blue work shirt (with the sleeves rolled up), and an open black vest—at the time typical garb for a twenty-five-year-old comic working in a comedy club.

Hi, good evening. I probably look a little *strange* to you, being dressed like this on a big, important television show. Ordinarily you'd expect to see me in a tuxedo, as befits my station. But this is the way most of the young comics work now, isn't it?

I saw one young comedian walk in here one night wearing a nice-looking, three-piece suit.

He was thrown out of the club.

They thought he was a *narc*.

The philosophical rationale of dressing like this when you do comedy is first of all—I guess—to inspire *sympathy*.

You identify with the proletariat.

You look like you can't *afford* a tuxedo.

You look like it's not even definite that you're in show business at all.

You were just walking by the club, on your way home from the car wash, and you heard people laughing, so you stuck your head in, and the next thing—WHAM!—you're on stage, getting screams, dressed like a guy on welfare.

But do you know why comedians dress like this? I checked into it and have actually discovered a reason.

It's because about twenty-five years ago a lot of the hippy folk and rock singers were always wearing overalls and Levi's and dumb country clothes because either they were poor or they had no taste.

But then they began to have hit records.

So they were booked to perform in the city, and on television, and all the young kids who wanted to be in show business saw these hicks walking around in these rube clothes. So the first thing that happens is that all the *big city* singers—all the Irish guys and Jewish guys and black guys, who wouldn't know a cow from a tree stump—they start dressing like hicks. And using phony hick *voices* when they sing. (*sing*) "Well-uh, mama, wanna getta sumpin' . . ."

And it works for them. They become millionaires.

So now the comedians think, "Hey, to heck with class and style and sharp threads. I'll start dressing like I just flunked out of junior college; maybe it'll work."

Another monologue I wrote not too long ago concerns the strange hairdos we began seeing on our young people about the time "punk" came in. The fad was picked up by a certain segment of the black male population.

I don't know about you, but I think we're seeing more weird hairdos— on men and women—than we ever have before.

Sometimes where the hairdressers go wrong is as regards the factor of exaggeration. They start with something creative, a cute little twist or curl or line. The first people who wear it look okay, but then other people say, "Hey, that's wild. I'm gonna do that and a little *more* of it," and at that point things go all to hell.

I saw a white guy at the airport the other day who had about nineteen pounds of hair sticking straight out the *back* of his head.

Now that would be a marvelous hairdo if you dig looking like a hydrocephalic.

And—listen carefully now because I don't want to hear any nonsense about racism—let's talk about the hairdos that *some* black folks wear.

I didn't mind when, about three or four years ago, some of the black athletes began wearing the flat top. Actually it looked like what the U.S. Marines used to wear back in World War II. It had the advantage of looking trim and neat. But then somebody got the idea of getting rid of the sideburns so that finally what some of the cats were wearing looked like they were totally bald, but had a hockey puck on top of their head.

My vote for the worst-looking hairdo in the country is the one Sinbad wears on one of my favorite programs, "It's Showtime at the Apollo." This man looks like his head was run over by a Goodyear tire.

And—to go back a few years—the corn-row was cute, particularly on pretty women, whether they were black or white. Well, come to think of it, almost everything looks good on pretty women.

That, of course, is why they never hire ugly people to work as models.

But as soon as the *dreadlocks* look came in, I checked off the bus. If that's authentic—in other words if you're from Jamaica, if you play in a reggae band, and if you have marijuana soup for breakfast—then it's a legitimate look for you.

But I'll tell you right now, if I go to see my dentist or my stockbroker, and he's got a dreadlocks haircut, he's not going to do a hell of a lot of business with me.

I happen to think that Whoopi Goldberg is a very funny woman. How she's managed to read cue cards all these years with her hair down in her eyes I have no idea, but I hope, just for her fans' sake, she'll eventually try some *variation* on the hairdo because—to speak frankly—it does not look too gorgeous.

Incidentally, there's no sense putting down punk rock hairdos because the whole *point* is to look weird, just as the whole point of punk music is to *play* weird.

Probably 90 percent of the American people put it down, but I'll say this for punk, it's given even a lot of ugly kids a chance to be popular.

So again—it's okay if you *want* to look rotten and sicko. Knock yourself out; it's a free country.

But the pathetic thing is when people want to look sensational and then they do dumb things to their hair. I'm sure nobody who knows Spike Lee could possibly accuse him of being anti-black. He's brilliant; our country should listen to what he's saying. But the funniest line in his movie *Do the Right Thing* is where those three middle-aged cats, who are sitting against the bright red brick wall commenting on life like a Greek chorus, have a conversation with the young loudmouth who is the chief trouble-maker in Spike Lee's story. You might recall the scene where this jerk tries to get the three older guys to take part in his boycott of the Italian pizza joint. One of the guys says, "Never mind that, man; what you *ought to be boycottin'* is the barber who did that to your hair."

As another example of a special-situation monologue, I'll close this chapter with a transcription of a routine I did in 1989, at the Las Vegas Comedy Convention, at which I was honored as a so-called legend of comedy. Combining a little prepared material with odds and ends of observations I had picked up while waiting to be introduced (see chapter 4), this is how the acceptance speech went:

BUDD FRIEDMAN: Please welcome . . . Mr. Steve Allen! (*applause, piano*)

STEVE: (*finding award plaque on the podium*) You never actually brought this up, Budd, but there's the implication that you're giving it to me, right? (*laughter*) Your implication . . . my inference. (*noticing plaque is Greek mask of comedy*) Ah, I hope I win one next year . . . then I'll have cufflinks! (*laughter*)

You know, really, I'm quite touched by this. As a matter of fact, I'm honored to be working in Las Vegas at all. If I didn't know where I was, if I'd been taken here blindfolded, I could tell that I'm in Vegas because of those slanted mirrors up there.

You can laugh, but there are people looking down through the one-way glass right now . . . to see if you're signing the right number on your room tab. (*laughter*)

Anyway, it's great to be working in a room with such a view of— (*looking outside*), a view of several construction cranes. (*laughter*)

That's all I ever see any more in Vegas when I look out the window. . . . Is it the *whooping* crane that is a vanishing species?

At three o'clock there'll be a seminar on how to take a thought of this sort and make an actual joke out of it. (*laughter*) I'm too busy at the moment . . . (*laughter/applause*) That can be your assignment for the afternoon. (*laughter*)

Our table was a little dragged because we were talking about the Lakers being wiped out in four. You know . . . the hometown comedy team. (*laughter*)

Also, draggy news just in from the world of sports. We all mourn the news of the passing of John Elway. He's still alive, but his passing sucks. (*laughter/applause*)

By the way—I have nothing but bad news—have you heard the sad news about the motion picture producer Cubby Broccoli? He's a vegetable. (*laughter*) *That* joke will also be discussed at three o'clock. (*laughter*)

Hey, wasn't Will Durst fantastic? (*laughter/applause*) That name— Durst. It sounds to me like the past perfect participle of some Elizabethan verb. Thou durst not be funnier than the guest of honor. (*laughter*)

I'm a little punchy today. This is not just one of those I'm-so-tired-I-have-to jokes about how tired I am. I really am punchy because I got very little sleep last night, and airplane flights always give me jet lag—even if it's only twenty minutes. (*laughter*)

I am so out of it, honestly, that I just almost did a line I originally ad-libbed about twenty years ago. As you know, if you have a good line that works, you keep throwing it in whenever it makes sense again; so I've used it probably every two years since then. In that first instance I was on a talk show, speaking spontaneously, and suddenly heard myself using a polysyllabic word—maybe it *was* the word *polysyllabic*, I don't know. (*laughter*) In any event, I suddenly stopped and said to the host, "By the way, how many other comedians can you think of who use words such as *polysyllabic?*" And the guy played accidental straight and said, "None at all." I said, "Right. That's why they're all in Las Vegas tonight making a million bucks and I'm stuck here!" (*laughter*) So that was the line I almost resurrected here: they're in Las Vegas and—oh, so am I! Forget the joke.

Anyway, while my observations this afternoon are, it seems to me (*to photographer*)—thank you, I work alone—anyway, it seems to me that my approaches to comedy are too diverse and complex to be subsumed under a single rubric—(*laughter*)

I feel, nevertheless, in all seriousness, that a few explanatory remarks might provide a certain amount of contextual enlightenment. (*laughter/applause*)

Hegel, close to Schopenhauer's chosen field in the philosophy of history, inveighed—as this audience is very well aware. . . . (*laughter*) But he made his famous distinction between the finite volitions of men and the astuteness of the idea, which, while working its way through men, obviously nevertheless often directs their wills to ends that they do not fully anticipate nor apprehend, even after they occur.

Nietzsche takes his clue from these, distinguishing between the finite empirical will of men and the apparent dichotomy—wait a minute—God, I'm sorry, this is the speech I'm giving *tomorrow* night! (*laughter*)

I told you I was out of it! (*laughter*) There's a philosopher's convention at the Silver Slipper (*laughter*) so I'll be delivering this. . . . (*laughter/applause*) Can't keep it straight. (*laughter*)

Anyway, I've never done the same show twice—Nobody's ever asked me to, come to think of— (*laughter*)

But really, it's nice to be called a legend, considering the fact that for forty years I've gotten away without having an actual act. There are some songs I do, and some jokes, but—(*laughter*) I've never had an act in the sense that Bill Cosby has an act, or Bob Newhart, or George Carlin.

I just talk about whatever is going on, and it usually works great—unless there's nothing much going on. (*laughter*) Then I kind of blend into the general nothing-going-on-ness. (*laughter*) But, working *with* what's going on here, I wonder if any of you actually had the foresight, or the saga, to look at this particular media release—the publicity release from—is it Levine Schneider or Levine *and* Schneider? You can't tell. Are either Levine *or* Schneider here? (*laughter*)

How do you like this? They publicize the thing, and they're not even here! Oh, Levine *is* here. Hi, Levine. Is it Levine and Schneider? (*Levine says: "Levine slash Schneider."*)

Ah, I hope I'm not there when that happens! (*laughter*)

Anyway, it's a remarkable document. And these things are historic. People are always asking me, "Did you ever realize, when you were thirty-six years old, and one night on the "Tonight" show . . . ?" No, you don't realize, when things are happening, that thirty years in the future they will be considered a big deal. But this today is a big deal. There are almost two hundred comedians here. Many of you will go on to major stardom, and here you're all treating each other like equals. It's not fair. (*laughter/applause*)

Anyway, get a copy of this. It'll be documentation, you know, when they write your life story. (*laughter*)

(*reading*) "Budd Friedman and Eddie Kritzer have announced plans—this is before the fact—for the Second Annual Comedy Convention at the Riviera Hotel in Las Vegas . . . blah, blah . . . Friedman, founder and co-owner of the Improvisation Comedy Clubs, and Kritzer, a radio, television and feature film producer, stressed that while the focus of the convention will be for carefully screened comics . . ." (*laughter*)

Good, okay. If it hasn't happened to you, and you'd *like* to get screened in the next few minutes, (*laughter*) I'll be available in the lobby. (*laughter*)

(*continues reading*) "to showcase . . ." *Showcase*. That means low bread! (*laughter/applause*)

(*continues reading*) "It will also include extensive seminars hosted by casting agents, talent bookers, managers, TV directors, publicists, comedy writers, and the like." There *is* nothing else like all those categories! (*laughter*) People of that *ilk*, they might have said. (*laughter*)

Anyway (*reading*) "they will probe in depth . . ."—(*Steve laughs*) And if you're going to probe, why the hell not do it in depth? (*laughter*) ". . . every aspect of what Friedman and Kritzer refer to as the remarkable comedy explosion."

Now the fact that there are already some four million people who have referred to it as the comedy explosion isn't terribly significant. (*laughter*) Comedy explosion could mean we're all bombing . . . but that's another matter. (*laughter*) (*reading*) "All participants will be welcomed to the convention at a gala cocktail party on Monday, June 2 . . ." I missed that. Was it gala? (*laughter/applause*)

Okay. (*reading*) "The keynote breakfast will be held the following morning, which will feature Budd Friedman, along with a special superstar guest of honor." Who *was* that, Budd? (*Budd says "you"*) Oh, that was you, too? You played both parts. (*laughter*)

(*pretending to read*) Together Friedman and Kritzer are currently producing a thrilling action disaster motion picture titled *The Day Irwin Allen Stood Still.* . . . (*laughter*) And they are also executive consultants to the American Comedy Awards. (*Steve laughs*) God help us. (*laughter/applause*)

Actually, Budd—while he is in a sense the godfather of stand-up comedy, and—no jokes about that—he *does* deserve a great hand for that. . . . (*applause*) Yeah. Be that as it may, it always occurred to me that there was something a little questionable about the *name* of the club, the Improv. Because I'm an amateur historian of comedy—I love to laugh at comedians and write about them, do books about them—I investigated this, and I discovered that the last comic to actually *improvise* anything at the Improv— it occurred one night in 1972 . . . (*laughter*) . . . when a young comic who is no longer with us, named Lenny Jackie . . . Lenny got drunk and forgot his act and *had* to improvise. (*laughter*) There's been no improvisation since then. A lot of great people, but no improvisation. (*laughter*) Another matter altogether.

Anyway, it's a fun-filled laugh-fest. (*laughter*) The world will little note nor long remember whatever it was I've said for the last few minutes, but a lot of the guys thought it might make a little sense if I did one actual routine, which thank God only takes about two minutes. So I'll do it.

It has to do with the fact that—(*to pianist*) Can I have a little noodling, Sam? You all remember Noodling Sam . . . (*laughter*)

Real soft. . . . Thank you.

Anyway—he was working at . . . somewhere, I guess. (*laughter*) What the hell am I talking about? Oh, yes. You all remember rock music that's been so popular, up to this morning. A lot of people of my generation make a mistake. They put down rock music in toto. (*Steve laughs*) Who was Judy Garland's dog, I think. . . . (*laughter*) We must keep these things straight. (*laughter*)

Anyway, that's wrong. There is good and bad in all categories. In the old days of Gershwin and Berlin and Porter, not all the music then was great; we just remember the better songs. But people, even professional critics, often put down particularly the lyrics of rock songs. Sure, most of them are pretty lightweight, some you can't understand, but if you look into a particular number and make a wise selection, you can sometimes find philosophical profundity, emotional sensitivity and spiritual depth. So, if I may . . . Sam, that's lovely. Keep playing something like that. I'm going to recite the lyric of one of the rock classics of the last twenty-five years and *not* do the melody, so you can concentrate on the words. I make no comment about them, I simply say they are worthy of your careful attention.

(*reciting*) "I can't get no satisfaction. I *can't* get no satisfaction. (*laughter*) I can't get no satisfaction. I can't get no . . . I can't get *no* . . . I can't get no satisfaction.

"No, no, no, no. (*laughter*) Hey, hey, hey. (*laughter*) That's what I say. (*laughter/applause*) I can't get no satisfaction. (*laughter*) I can't get *no* satisfaction. (*laughter*)

"When I'm watching my TV, and the man comes on and he tells me . . . how white my shirts can be. . . . Well, he can't be a man, 'cause he don't smoke the same cigarettes as me, and *I* . . . can't get no satisfaction. (*laughter*) I can't get no . . . girl with *action*."—Schmuck finally thought of a rhyme!—(*laughter/applause*)

" 'Cause I try, and I try, and I try, and I try, but I can't get no satisfaction. I can't get no—no, no, no, no no. Yeah, yeah, yeah. No, no, no. I can't get no satisfaction."

Now don't tell me they don't write great rock lyrics once in awhile. (*laughter/applause*) Thank you. I feel like I'm working a lounge! (*laughter*) And why not? (*laughter*)

By way of contrast, and I'll finish right here if I may—and I'm capable of it—that's the kind of lyric they write lately. There's another way they used to do it, in the old days. The old days, as *old*, don't mean a damn, but *quality* is important.

And I'll take about forty-three more seconds of your time to just quickly tiptoe through a lyric by a man named Lorenz Hart. I select it not because it's the best, but because it's typical of the way it used to be.

(*Steve sings "My Romance"*)

6

Playing Straight

The "straightman" typically is given little credit by audiences, yet he or she may be critical to the success of a comic sketch or routine. What *is* the significance of a straightman's role?

In a routine, the straightplayer represents the point of contact between all the verbal or physical craziness that's happening on the one hand, and the audience, on the other. That's why straightmen often refer to the audience when putting questions to the comedian, as in: "Do you expect these fine ladies and gentlemen . . ." The public usually doesn't appreciate the abilities of people who play straight, except when there's something else they do—comedy, playing a musical instrument, tap dancing, or whatever. In the comedy business, of course, the ability to play good straight is much appreciated, although this appreciation has diminished somewhat in recent years since new people getting into it seem to have no interest in being straightmen or women.

Think about it. Why would anyone *want* to play straight? Most people would prefer to be the one doing the jokes. As a result, there is hardly anyone in show business under forty who even knows *how* to play straight, except in the case of such obvious exceptions as two-person comedy teams where either one plays straight for the other all the time or they take turns, as did my former partner, Wendell Noble, and I when we worked in radio in the 1940s. He did a funny character with a Mexican accent by the name of Manuel Labor and I would play straightman, setting up the jokes for Manuel. But if I did Claude Horribly, my goofy Mortimer Snerd–type character, then Wendell played straight for me. Here's one exchange from our "Smile Time" show (1947):

CLAUDE: (*goofy voice*) Gosh, Wendell, I've got a date tonight, but I don't really know how to act with a girl. You know about hugging and kissing and all that.

WENDELL: Do you mean, Claude, that your father never took you aside and explained to you about the birds and the bees?

CLAUDE: Oh, sure he did. But I checked that out, and I think it's a lot of nonsense.

WENDELL: What do you mean, you checked it out?

CLAUDE: Well, I got a bird and a bee one time and put 'em in a cage together, and they dang near killed each other.

In the old days, forty or fifty years ago, there were a good many people in vaudeville and burlesque who were gifted at playing straight because there was a certain amount of changing of personnel in various acts. And, of course, those who were good at the task—say George Burns or Bud Abbott—could perform that service for almost any comedian. George is also a great comedian, but some of the best straightmen in the business have been comics. Jackie Gleason and Art Carney played straight for each other. Bob Hope had the knack. Jack Benny was so good at it he made people seem funny who really weren't. On the radio shows Jack and Bob did back in the forties, many of the jokes were given to announcers, wives, singers, or bandleaders—people not noted for their humor. Nevertheless, the stars could help these supporting players get big laughs by reacting to them.

Is there any basic requirement for playing straight? Only what is, I suppose, obvious—that the straightman's job is to help the comic get laughs. Is there any one right way to do that? Well, there are vague parameters, I suppose, but different performers have their own approaches to playing straight. Some of the old-timers—Bud Abbott was a good example—dominated and browbeat the comic, treating him as if he were stupid. They were forever trying to straighten the poor schlub out.

A slight variation on that involves what I call the smart-guy/dumb-guy relationship, which many of the old comedy teams had. The smart one, usually the straightman, was a bit of a con man, forever trying to talk his dumber friend into something, trying to manipulate him.

In slightly later relationships, in vaudeville, the straightman would also function as master of ceremonies. The comic would seem to be interrupting some more sensible sort of performance, such as a dance number, vocal, or an instrumental turn. My mother, in fact, used to work in exactly that way with whomever did straight for her. My father did it, but after he died (when I was about a year and a half old), she had to use other partners, some of whom were women. The two of these that I remember, Lonnie Nace and Flossie Everett, were rather like what used to be called, in burlesque, the Talking Woman. The Talking Woman was one who was not necessarily funny herself, but who was onstage chiefly to accommodate the comics she worked with. Usually she was attractive, so that she could be used in the context of sexual innuendos. The comedians flirted with her. The Talking Woman was a bit like a master of ceremonies.

I've had a number of people play straight for me over the years and have been asked often who, of all of them and all I've seen, would I consider to be the best. The answer may surprise you—my wife Jayne. She has performed the same service for Milton Berle and Red Skelton, both of whom thought of her as a Talking Woman. There is, of course, a great deal more to Jayne's abilities than playing straight, but she, nevertheless, is the best I've ever seen at it, partly because she approaches the assignment as if she were doing Shakespeare or Shaw. And though it may sound odd, that's exactly the approach a straightman ought to take. It's up to the comic in a sketch to horse around, take a pie in the face, say wild, zany things. The straightman must be more realistic.

Jayne has often played straight for me when I do my wackier characters, such as Sen. Philip Buster or Dr. Mal Practice. She never breaks up, never gets out of character, and always treats the subject matter, however preposterous, as if she were a serious inquiring reporter on a newscast or documentary.

In the sketch that follows, Jayne talks to another of my characters— Homer Hayseed, the Country Philosopher. The character speaks in poetic rural exaggeration of which *nervous as a long-tailed cat in a roomful of rockin' chairs* is a classic example. Homer can communicate in no other way.

JAYNE: Good morning. It's time once again for "Unusual People Who Do Unusual Things." Our unusual visitor this morning is that beloved country philosopher, the sage of Arkansas, the paprika of Oklahoma, the rosemary of Texas—*Homer Hayseed*. Good morning, Homer. Are you glad to be with us this morning?

HOMER: Just as happy as a plowhorse when the crops are all in, ma'am.

JAYNE: That's nice. Are you pleased by what you've found here in Los Angeles?

HOMER: I'm as pleased as a dumplin' simmerin' in a mess of hog fat.

JAYNE: That's lovely. How do you feel about being on television?

HOMER: I'm just as happy as a ticklish snake crawlin' through a blackberry bush.

JAYNE: You don't say.

HOMER: Oh? I thought I did. You know, Miss Meadows, your skin's just as white as the inside of a toadstool in Tuscaloosa.

JAYNE: It is?

HOMER: Yep. You're just as pretty as a new-laid egg. I'll bet you're as proud as a peacock with two tails.

JAYNE: Well, really, I—Let's get back to you, Mr. Hayseed. How are you enjoying this tour you're on?

HOMER: I'm just as happy as a dead pig in the sunshine.

JAYNE: I see. Well, when you visited the larger cities of the East, did you ever feel that you were in any danger on the streets?

HOMER: Nope. I was just as safe as a possum in a pie. Just as calm as a hog on ice.

JAYNE: But some of the criminal types who—

HOMER: I know what you mean. There are some people who're as crooked as a dog's hind leg.

JAYNE: Is that right?

HOMER: Yes, ma'am. Just as sure as a goose goes barefoot.

JAYNE: What have you been doing in town, Mr. Hayseed?

HOMER: I've been steppin' out like a chicken in high oats.

JAYNE: Well, have your fans been glad to meet you in person?

HOMER: Glad? Listen, the women've been chasin' after me like pigs after a pumpkin.

JAYNE: Yes, that's very interesting. Well, Mr. Hayseed, it's been awfully nice of you to appear on our program, particularly since you're not being paid.

HOMER: I'm not?

JAYNE: No, I don't believe so.

HOMER: (*rather curtly*) Well, then, I'd just as soon shinny up a palm tree with an armload of goose grease.

JAYNE: Well, thank you very much, sir.

HOMER: Did I ever tell you about my brother? Why he's so lazy he stops plowin' to spit.

JAYNE: Thank you very much for these bits of rural wisdom and homespun philosophy, Mr. Hayseed.

HOMER: My sister was so ugly she had to blindfold the baby before she could feed him.

(*During fade out, Homer is still shouting metaphors, similes, etc.*) There ain't room enough around here to cuss a cat without gettin' hair in your mouth. . . . It's so quiet around here you could hear a cricket clear its throat. . . . I'm just as sassy as a . . .

In another example, in one of a series of takeoffs from my syndicated show of the early sixties, Jayne plays a straight-faced television host interviewing a hit songwriting team of the Irving Berlin era. The songwriters are well along in years, and their minds are still set in the 1920s and 1930s. Louis Nye paired with me in the original routine. Later sketches had me as Charlie Rise and Gabe Dell playing Danny Shine, the team of Rise and Shine.

JAYNE: Today I would like to present two of Tin Pan Alley's most distinguished members, Mr. Danny Shine and Mr. Charles Rise.

Their last appearance met with such favorable response that we phoned them to see if they were available to appear again tonight. Unfortunately they were. So here they are once again—Rise and Shine.

VOICE: (*singing*) "The Whole World Is Stealing My Song."

(*Steve and Gabe enter, wearing straw hats and 1930s attire. Gabe is carrying a violin case and bow, which he places on piano but never uses.*)

JAYNE: Hello, fellows.

STEVE: Hello, baby, sugar!

GABE: How are ya, sweetheart, honey, sugarplum?

JAYNE: Fine. Say, how did you gentlemen get started in the songwriting business?

STEVE: Well, Miss Meadows, I started out as a musician. I played the organ, but after a few years I had to give it up.

JAYNE: How come?

STEVE: My monkey died.

GABE: Yeah. And I took the place of the monkey.

JAYNE: I'm not surprised. It must have been rough for you in those early days.

STEVE: Rough? Why, we couldn't even afford a piano. And to write the words to our songs we used a secondhand typewriter with a broken *W*.

JAYNE: A broken *W*?

STEVE: Yes.

GABE: That's when we wrote our first song entitled "I Vant A Vonderful Varm Voman." . . . But we didn't allow ourselves to get carried away by success, because lots of composers, ya know, have written just one hit and you never hear of them again.

STEVE: Yeah, like Francis Scott Key. . . . But we knew we was on our way later that year when we wrote our first Broadway show, *Funky Follies of 1942*. Do you remember this song?

(*They go to piano. Gabe sits down. Steve, standing, leans over Gabe and starts to play.*)

GABE: (*singing*) When your little ole lips—

JAYNE: (*interrupting*) Pardon me for interrupting, gentlemen, but, er, *you* play the piano and he does the *singing*?

STEVE: Yeah. Why?

JAYNE: Well, why don't *you* sit down and let *him* stand up?

STEVE: (*looking at Jayne, then Gabe*) Nineteen years! How come *we* never thought of that? (*They switch places.*)

JAYNE: Tell me, what was the first song you actually had recorded?

STEVE: That was in 1942, and the nation was hearing the first Rise and Shine song, "My Son, the Soldier." It goes like this (*singing*):

> *If you have a boy in the service*
> *And you want to do something nice,*
> *Just send a salami*
> *To your boy in the Army*
> *And let him cut off a slice.*

Believe it or not, Jayne, that song never sold. It's hard to figure the public. As a matter of fact, things were so rough for us back in those days, that there were times we went a week without eating.

GABE: Yeah. We were starving! Our minds were constantly on food. That's how come we wrote our first novelty song—"Knockwurst and Beans."

JAYNE: Who published it?

STEVE: Nobody. As soon as we finished it, we ate it.

JAYNE: When did you fellows get your first taste of real success?

STEVE: We got lucky the following year. That's when we had our first big hit.

GABE: That's right. I was hit by a bus on Broadway and 49th Street. We collected $2,700.

JAYNE: And that was enough money to take you to California, where your luck finally changed. You went to work in motion pictures.

STEVE: That's right. And we wrote this haunting torch song for a Lyle Talbot musical (*singing*):
> *There's a million kinds of cigarette filters*
> *But here's one that's really hip*
> *Put a sardine in your filter*
> *And have a gefilte tip.*

JAYNE: Please get off the stage, would you?

*   *   *

Who are other good straightpeople? Strangely, there are almost no women who do this sort of thing, so Jayne's been an exception in that regard, too. Dean Martin was a fine straightman in working with Jerry Lewis, although he always had his own sort of funniness going. Dan Rowan was originally the comic of the Dan Rowan–Dick Martin team, but they eventually reversed roles. Dan was very skilled at playing straight. So is Dick Smothers.

I have acted as straightman quite a bit over the years, in addition to doing my own nonsense. I often happily played straight for Louis Nye, Tom Poston, Don Knotts, Bill Dana, Dayton Allen, Pat Harrington, Tim Conway, or the rest of the old gang. Unlike Jayne, however, I would sometimes get so amused at what the fellows were doing that I would break up.

In a two-person comedy act, the one playing straight provides an important service of introducing joke topics, and it's essential that he or she really tack them to the bulletin board, so to speak, so the audience knows precisely what is being discussed.

There are jokes heard only within the comedy business that relate to playing straight. For example, a straightman is walking along the beach at a popular resort one sunny day when, suddenly, a man out in the water starts thrashing about and shouting "Help!" The straightman looks at the guy, then gestures at the hundreds of bystanders and shouts, "Are you asking these nice ladies and gentlemen to believe you need *help?*"

To digress for a moment from the subject of playing straight, it's interesting that every trade, every profession, has its own inside jokes that are rarely shared with the public. Show business has a good many of them. Some of them are minor classics. One goes back to at least the 1940s. Since it could have come out of a European circus background it might be even older than that. It concerns two young fellows who are very close friends. Each is bright, ambitious, and seems destined for success. But they become separated in following their divergent paths and don't see each other for a very long time. Then one day one of the men, now middle-aged, happens to attend the circus in a distant city. It's a typical circus, with a couple of dozen elephants. Suddenly, to his shock, the visitor sees that the raggedy-looking attendant sweeping up after the elephants is his old school chum. After the circus is over, he waits around to see his former friend. "Harry," he says, "it's wonderful to see you again, but let me speak very frankly. I must say I'm shocked to see you in this condition—poor, wearing ragged clothing, and suffering the daily indignity of cleaning the filth from elephants. Please take my advice. You've got to quit this job."

"What," the friend replies, "and get out of show business?"

Another classic story, of more recent vintage, concerns a comedian who has just finished his night's work in a Las Vegas nightclub and is upstairs in his hotel room cooling off. Suddenly the telephone rings. When the comic picks it up, he hears a woman's voice. "Hello, is this Jackie Slater?"

"Yes, it is," the comic says.

"Oh, good," the woman says. "I'm so glad I caught you. I saw you perform tonight, Mr. Slater, and I just had to tell you that I've never been so impressed in my life. I've been a fan of yours for years, but tonight you were absolutely magnificent out there on stage. You were witty, quick, charming, irresistible."

"Well," the comedian says, "you're very kind, but I—"

"As a matter of fact," the woman says, "I'd really appreciate it if I could just run up to your room and tell you, in person, how absolutely marvelous I thought you were. Your warmth, your charm—"

"Well, that's very nice," the comic says, "but you don't have to do that."

"No," the woman says. "I absolutely must. Believe me, I'm not ordinarily affected by this sort of thing, but I thought you were so magnificent that I've just got to do something to thank you for thrilling me this deeply. As a matter of fact, Mr. Slater—insane as this may sound—if I could just come up to your room, I would be happy to return this wonderful favor you've done for me by placing my body at your disposal. I hope you're not shocked. I'm not a cheap woman; but I just want you to know that if you permit me to come upstairs I will pour out to you all the tenderness, the affection, the erotic excitement that you've made me feel."

At that point there is a slight pause, after which the comedian says, "Tell me, did you see the first or the second show?"

What both of these stories have in common is a reference to the tendency of those in show business to concentrate on the trade to the exclusion of other, and frequently more important, considerations.

7

Plagiarism

In this chapter we'll be considering the problem of plagiarism. The best advice I can give to would-be humorists about the subject would be to resolve never to be personally guilty of it. One way to help lower the statistics on any crime is not to commit it oneself.

Another piece of advice is that if you encounter instances in which other performers are taking important jokes or perhaps whole routines from you, you should at once register a protest, or have an agent, manager, or attorney do so on your behalf. It would be nice to be able to report that a formal protest is always followed by a concession of guilt and an abject apology. This is rarely the case, although sometimes the guilty performer can be shamed into stopping his or her use of your material. The letter of warning ought not to be angry or accusative in tone because there are instances where the comedian in question has purchased a joke or routine, in all innocence, from a writer who stole it but passed it off as original work.

Can one copyright or legally protect pieces of comedy material? Certainly. A letter to either Writer's Guild-East (New York) or Writer's Guild-West (Los Angeles) will bring specific information about how to go about this. The Los Angeles office address is 8955 Beverly Blvd., Los Angeles, CA 90048. People may still steal your brainchild, but if they discover that it is legally protected, your position will be stronger.

It has often been said that, for whatever mysterious reasons, I am the most borrowed-from comedian of modern times. If this is true, there must be a number of components to the explanation. One is that I've been doing comedy, on radio and television, as well as in concert and club appearances, for fifty years. But that can't be the only explanation, because people like Milton Berle, George Burns, and Bob Hope have been performing longer

121

than that, and nobody ever seems to take their material.

More important, then, may be the fact that there are many ingredients to my comedy. To say that is by no means to praise myself, since it's theoretically possible that, as regards all such factors, my actual performances could be lousy. The point is that by setting so many different sorts of comedy on the counter, so to speak, I have apparently become easy prey for the shoplifters in the business.

Another part of the explanation is that some of the comic forms that were developed on my shows over the years, particularly on the comedy-and-talk shows, were so casual, so easy in approach, that they may have seemed to less original practitioners of the comic arts somehow automatically in the public domain from the very moment of their conception. Wandering through a studio audience with a hand microphone would be one example. I was certainly not the first human being to carry a microphone up a theater aisle. Quizmasters, game show hosts, and radio announcers have been doing that since the early days of radio. I was simply the first comedian to do it, the first one to get laughs by doing it. So that fact didn't give me much protection against plagiarism. Some others probably reasoned, "I could do that as well as Steve Allen does," and so they simply appropriated the idea, probably without a twinge of guilt.

As we've already discussed, the main ingredient of my nightclub and concert act involves giving funny answers to questions written by people in the audience. A number of entertainers—most notably Johnny Carson—have borrowed the routine. But again, I was obviously not the first public speaker to answer written questions. That sort of thing has been going on for centuries. Here too, however, I was the first *comedian* to do so. In this instance, also, I suppose, the plagiarists justified their theft by referring to the noncomic precedent.

The primary thing, however, that other entertainers have borrowed from me seems to be essentially an attitude, a style. To their credit, scores of young entertainers have told me as much. Quite a few people in radio over the years have mentioned that they listened to me so often during their high school and college days that they just naturally picked up that casual style of comedy. Sometimes when you make something look easy—or if, in fact, it *is* easy for you—the very ease of your work can make a strong impression on others. Consider, for example, Bing Crosby's singing style. In the 1920s, 1930s, and 1940s, Crosby was not only a fine and successful singer but also enormously influential. Perry Como, for example, has acknowledged that what he does for a living is basically just sing like Bing. I think if Crosby had worked in a hard-sell, frenetic style, very few other singers, if any, would have imitated him. But he always made it seem so off the cuff, so what's-the-big-deal, that other vocalists just came to think that that was how one was *supposed* to sing.

The same thing was true of Frank Sinatra, who influenced dozens of younger male vocalists. In Frank's case, too, the dominant element was the ease, the naturalness.

But in my case, there have been more than enough thefts of actual jokes, routines, and sketches. Every time you read an article about David Letterman, two things stand out. First, the writer mentions the extent to which I have influenced David's style, and secondly, David himself brings up the point. And as far as I'm concerned that takes the curse off it. I truly appreciate the compliments David has paid me, for the public record.

Of course, when we say that one entertainer has influenced another, we're usually talking about a situation in which the copier just naturally has something in common, so far as his overall personality is concerned, with the original. Had I never been born, David Letterman would no doubt work pretty much as he does. Most of the imitativeness of his show comes, perhaps, from his staff people who are using ideas originated on my programs—things like taking cameras out into the street or down the halls outside the studio.

For whatever reasons, from my earliest days in radio, I felt uncomfortable limiting myself to standard show-business hoke, a geniality I knew was often false anyway or that showed exaggerated respect for things that were not necessarily worthy of it. In my case, it was not a matter of a conscious decision to be irreverent or disrespectful. As I saw it, I was simply being realistic about references to networks, sponsors, advertising agencies, commercial products, and political figures. David, among others, has picked that up from me.

Jack Paar was the host of the "Tonight" show for a full five years and was deservedly successful at it. Why don't people borrow from him? Probably because Jack had a narrower, more uniquely quirky personality than I do. It sounds odd to say, but I've met hundreds of people rather like myself. In fact, they often come up to me in airports or restaurants and say that their friends have told them they're like me. Some of them even look like me, and a good many more speak more or less as I do. But Jack, as I say, had a more unusual style of delivery. He would often become emotional on the air. He would stutter, get angry, become involved in feuds, say sarcastic things, some of which were quite funny. For whatever reasons, other young entertainers apparently didn't sense anything in Jack that they wanted to emulate, although to say as much is certainly not to be critical of him. It's interesting that over the years, although he started out as a comedian, his image was finally just that of talk-show host. He was witty, but I have never heard his name come up in public or private discussion of the history of television *comedy*. That's odd.

The same thing happened to Garry Moore. When Garry was young, he worked purely as a comedian, and he was quite a funny one. But over the years he gradually just became lovable, cute Garry Moore. He was finally referred to strictly as a "TV personality," whatever that is. Today he is hardly recalled as a comedian at all, even though, as I say, he did a lot of funny things during his early radio days on a delightful network radio show, broadcast from Chicago, called "Club Matinee," on which he shared hosting duties with another funny gentleman, Ransom Sherman.

As I mentioned in *Hi-Ho, Steverino!* (published by Barricade Books) Johnny Carson, a superb talk-show host, has the worst reputation in the field of comedy when it comes to doing other people's material. Although there's been only occasional reference to this in the media, it's a matter of common knowledge in the business. Part of the reason for overlooking the problem is that the "Tonight" show—regardless of who the host is—is a tremendously important promotional outlet. All the publicity people and agencies are constantly trying to place actors, entertainers, writers, and other notables on the various talk shows. Since the "Tonight" show is the most important of them, it's naturally their number one target. Johnny had a fairly long list of people he would not permit to be booked on the show, but even those who were on that list didn't want to speak for the record in saying anything critical. I guess they figured, why become involved in controversy?

Dick Cavett was quite courageous about Johnny's habit of borrowing other people's material without permission. In his autobiography he wrote:

I'm sure that Johnny is as riddled with doubts about his identity as any of us who have gravitated toward comedy for a living, and I think it shows in his work. His style is an accretion of Bennyisms, Grouchoisms, Hopeisms, and, to drop the ism-ism, later additions of Don Rickles, Don Adams, Dean Martin, and a large dose of Jonathan Winters. Here and there are touches of both Allens, Fred and Steve. Fred Allen had a department called The Mighty Allen Art Players, a witty adaptation of Stanislavsky's name for his company, and Steve Allen's Question Man went into swami drag and became Johnny's Carnac. Also, Johnny's appropriation of Oliver Hardy's look of dismay into the lens was a shrewd choice for television.

Dick was absolutely right, but at that time his own late-night program was opposite the "Tonight" show so there was no reason why he should withhold comment on what he knew was the case. Jonathan Winters has also been outspoken about Carson's stealing his Aunt Blabby character.

One odd aspect of the Question Man matter is that I didn't do the routine on the original "Tonight" show, but on my prime-time NBC Sunday night comedy series. The show had twenty-five or thirty million people watching it every week. In other words, there were scores of millions of witnesses to the eventual plagiarism. The fellow who originally created the routine—a Los Angeles radio comic by the name of Bob Arbogast—tried to stop Carson from doing the Question Man. I refer to him in the foreword of my book *The Question Man:*

> On the title page of this book it says "by Steve Allen."
> That's a dirty lie.
> I wrote only part of the book. No sooner had we introduced the Question Man on our TV show last year than we began to receive Question Man jokes from all over, even from my writers.
> Leonard Stern, Bill Dana and Don Hinkley from our staff threw a batch into the hat, a high-school girl in Philadelphia sent me a couple, and a funny man by the name of Bob Arbogast not only contributed a number of jokes but also provided us with the somewhat unnerving information that he had thought of the Question Man idea itself several years before we did.
> As the reader presumably knows, the Question Man joke is a new gag form in that the punchline comes *before* the straight line. It is the Question Man's feeling, in other words, that there are millions of questions that have been answered, but that nobody has ever bothered about the millions of *answers* for which there are no questions.

It's obvious that Arbogast had no luck in complaining since Johnny went right on doing that routine for years. As soon as I first heard from Arbogast, I wrote to him saying that I would leave to him the decision as to whether I should just stop doing it altogether—which I would have been glad to do—or send him payment for the idea every time we performed the sketch. Bob decided the latter course made more sense. Perhaps Johnny will leave Arbogast something in his will, in a last-minute paroxysm of guilt.

Another routine I did years before Johnny was "The Late Show Pitchman," the monologue in which I did commercials for crazy products and gave funny names to the movies presumably being shown. The two characters—mine and Johnny's—even looked alike, down to the crazy wig and mustache. And the physical structure of the routine is precisely the same, involving the use of brief old black-and-white clips from actual movies, mostly from the 1920s and 1930s, and then doing commercials for slicers, dicers, handy-dandy rotobroilers, spot removers, or whatever.

Sometimes we deliberately ran the same movie clip of fourteen guys fighting and rolling over tables again and again in one sketch. Other times we would use several clips, and I'd give the films titles like *The Bowery Boys Meet the Pope.* We also used the film bits in other sketches, including "Report to the Nation," "The Allen Crime Report," and "Big Bill Allen's Sports Round-up." There was no other show in the early 1950s that made comic use of old film clips in that precise way.

Eventually, though, it became a common TV comic device, and Johnny took the whole pitchman routine, even calling his character Art Fern—*fern* being a double-talk word I popularized. The basic draft of the routine, on our old "Tonight" show, was written by Stan Burns and Herb Sargent. I never did understand why the Writer's Guild did not come to their defense.

And then there were the funny sketches where we would show tight close-up shots of actual people in our studio audience and weave a soap opera-type storyline around them. That was one of our regular routines on the old "Tonight" show, starting in 1954. The sketches were basically written by Stan and Herb, and I would add a good deal of ad-lib comedy by keeping my eye on the TV monitor and, if one of the visitors scratched his nose, removed his glasses, frowned, or something of that sort, incorporate reference to that into the text. Johnny apparently made no switch at all when he appropriated the routine years later, except that he deleted the ad-libbing.

Another thing many have mentioned over the years is that the tight, little "pip-squeak" voice Johnny sometimes did was stolen from Jackie Gleason's Reginald Van Gleason character. As the years pass, however, such truths tend to become obscured. Gleason was never too thrilled about Johnny doing the characterization, but I heard a young emcee recently doing the voice in such a way as to lead the audience to think he was imitating Johnny Carson, when actually Gleason was the originator.

To sum up: If you become the victim of plagiarism, raise hell. It doesn't make a great deal of sense to make a fuss about an individual joke, unless, that is, it is of truly key importance in your act. Some years ago I used to do a character called Dr. Mal Practice. There was nothing original in the characterization itself—half the comedians in the business, over the last century, have occasionally portrayed goofy doctors.

But in this case I personally wrote a joke that always got an enormous laugh. The exchange went as follows:

MS. MEADOWS: Doctor, you are also a brain surgeon, is that right?

DOCTOR: Well, yes, I am a brain surgeon. Whether it's right is a separate question, but I remember one time when I was performing a pre-frontal lobotomy and I—no, wait a minute. Was it a pre-frontal lobotomy—or a free bottle in front o' me?

In time I began to hear reports that other comics were doing the joke. I finally identified one of them, and my attorney wrote to his manager, after which the line was deleted from the fellow's act.

But, as I say, unless the joke is truly one of your own origination and important to the success of a particular routine, it's time-wasting to make an issue of thefts of individual lines.

8

How to Play Hoaxes
and Practical Jokeses

Since my youth I have enjoyed playing occasional practical jokes and have
even staged some outrageous hoaxes. Two of the wildest involved albums
of jazz piano music I recorded under fictitious names: *Buck Hammer* was
supposedly a shy, black boogie-woogie pioneer whose album was released
posthumously, and *Mary Anne Jackson* was, according to the liner notes,
a black pianist and composer who performed with "bold authority," mainly
in Europe. The picture of Buck Hammer shown on the record cover was
an artist's sketch, and the photo of Mary Anne Jackson was actually a
photograph of one of our former housekeepers, named Mary Sears. I not
only did the piano playing on both albums but wrote the liner notes, in
the deliberately stuffy, overly analytical style of some critics.

I fooled some real critics with those, who gave Hammer and Jackson
splendid reviews. *Downbeat* magazine awarded Hammer three-and-a-half
stars, and the *New York Herald Tribune* said the pianist's death was a terrible
loss to the world of jazz.

Another of my more ambitious put-ons was a multiple hoax, a book
of poetry called *A Flash of Swallows*. It was published under the name
William Christopher Stevens, who was billed as "one of Australia's best-
known poets." Besides writing the entirely serious poems, I made up jacket
blurbs from imaginary critics and sculpted a statue of Stevens (actually of
bandleader Skitch Henderson) that was pictured on the book's back cover
and attributed to the purely fictional sculptor Luigi Goldoni. Of course I
took the photograph of the sculpture, crediting it to yet another nonexistent
personage I chose to call, appropriately, Janus, after the two-faced god.

129

But although the Buck Hammer and Mary Ann Jackson hoaxes fooled a few disc jockeys and jazz critics, the hoax that attracted the widest audience was one we played on Louis Nye on my Sunday night NBC show. That was actually a high-risk proposition all around because in those days our show was on the air live, with perhaps thirty million people watching every Sunday.

Once in a great while, in the days of live sketch-comedy programs, something would go wrong. An actor would forget his lines, a piece of scenery would fall down, somebody would hold up the wrong cue card—somehow a show would momentarily get loused up. Since you couldn't yell "Stop the tape," the performers had to do some nimble ad-libbing around the problem.

In any event, the plot line of this particular stunt involved setting Louis up as the patsy. From the first day of rehearsal that week, Tom Poston pretended to be having a drinking problem. So far as I know, in reality, Tom wasn't drinking at all. But when the guys would take their lunch break, he would go to a neighborhood bar, order a shot of bourbon, and, when Louis wasn't looking, rub a little of the liquid on his lapel. Now Tom does a great drunk. Every comedian in the world, of course, knows how to act drunk, although many of us are no better at it than your neighborhood class clown, but some—Foster Brooks is probably the best example—are masterful at it. Tom is one of them.

Anyway, by Wednesday Tom had not only totally convinced Louis that he was a semi-alcoholic, but, with the help of Don Knotts, had added the twist that, "No matter what happens, we have to be sure Steve doesn't find out about this because you know how he feels about people who drink." Everyone familiar with the gifted Don Knotts, of course, knows that his specialty is acting nervous, so it was not surprising that by Saturday, poor Louis was convinced that Don's jitters were for real and consequently actually thought Tom's job might be in jeopardy.

In reality, everyone on the show was in on the gag except Louis.

All week, in addition to their participation in other segments of the show, Louis and Don had been rehearsing a sketch that was supposed to take place in a seedy waterfront saloon. Louis played the part of a Mafia gangster, and Don played one of his flunkies.

I should mention another important ingredient of the hoax: the audience had to be in on it. To accomplish this, just before the sketch started, I signaled for the boom microphone to be lowered right into the picture so that I could speak just an inch or two away from it, in a semi-whisper that could not be heard backstage. As extra insurance, Bill Harbach, our producer, engaged Louis in conversation at the same moment, so Louis' concentration would be on what Bill was saying.

As the sketch began, Don and Louis, in character, walk into a dive, and stand at the bar. While they're waiting for service, Don says, "Big Al, I gotta go make a phone call. I'll be right back." At that he walks a few feet to a phone booth, sits down, drops a coin in the slot, and pretends to forget his lines—totally—in such a way that everyone in the studio audience, and the millions watching around the country, had not the slightest doubt that his memory had failed him completely. And at this point there was no way Louis could help him by ad-libbing, because he was still about twelve feet away, at the bar.

Naturally Dwight Hemion, the camera director, was taking close-up reaction shots of Louis as he listened, with growing consternation, to Don talking gibberish in the phone booth.

The script next called for Louis to say to the bartender, "Give me a double." All week long he had been served ginger ale, which has the color of liquor. But now—need I say it?—he got the real thing, a double scotch. Naturally, we had set it up in the script that "he downs the drink in one gulp." When Louis did that with the actual booze, his eyes practically crossed.

The audience, knowing what was going on, howled. Louis, of course, began to be puzzled by the laughter, because ostensibly nothing funny had yet happened in the sketch, as Louis perceived it.

At this point, Don continued to deliberately garble his lines. Now, if you're in a scene and another actor doesn't give you the right cue, you can hardly just go ahead as if nothing had happened because your next line may not make sense. Consequently, Louis had to keep revising the text, which he did quite well, although he was still puzzled by all the hysterical laughter.

Then Tom came in. The scene, as rehearsed, called for him to confront Louis, call him a squealer and a fink, and finally pull a gun and shoot him. But from the moment of Tom's entrance he appeared to be high as a kite. His speeches were partly unintelligible and when he reached inside his pocket to pull out a gun, there was no gun. So he pulled out what he did find, a pack of cigarettes, which he pointed, with a goofy smile, at Louis. Louis was then supposed to pull his own gun and fire first. But when Louis pulled the trigger, the gun would not fire. He thereupon proceeded to pantomime that he had a knife, with which he "stabbed" Tom. It was great fun.

A hoax has something in common with magic—show business magic, that is—it's a simple matter of fooling the observer. You're putting something over on someone, and as long as a third party serves as the audience and no one is really hurt or badly frightened, the situation can be very funny. But the connection with magic has long interested me. I dabbled in magic at the age of about twenty-five and the idea of combining it with humor occurred to me almost at once.

Suppose you learn a bit about magic and want to add funniness to it. How do you do that? To answer, let me give you an example I recall when I walked into a dime store with a friend who had to make a few small purchases. As often happens when two people go shopping, they separate once they're in the store, and each attends to his or her own interests and makes his or her own purchases. In this instance, once I saw that the young lady was otherwise involved, I made certain preparations and then a few minutes later, flipping a quarter to attract her attention, said, "Would you like to see me make this quarter disappear?"

"All right," she said, just to be cooperative. So I did a simple bit of hand-shtick and the quarter did seem to vanish.

"Would you like to know where it went?" I said.

"Okay," she said.

"Then look in that cooking pot behind you." Just to humor me she opened the pot and, sure enough, there was a quarter inside. During the next couple of minutes she found the same newly vanished quarter in three other locations in the store.

How did I do it? Magicians are not supposed to reveal how their tricks are done, for the obvious reason that if they do eventually few people would bother to see magic shows since they would already know how the effects are achieved. But because this is not the kind of stunt that anyone is ever likely to do on stage, no harm can come of my revealing the behind-the-scenes machinations: All I did was wait until my friend's attention was concentrated elsewhere and then hide four separate quarters in or under items of merchandise in different parts of the store. After that, all I had to do was the disappearing-coin pass and then, seemingly while wandering idly about the store, ask the young lady to find the missing quarter for herself. Of course it was necessary for her to return the quarter to me in each case. I would then make it disappear again so that each time she seemed to be finding the same coin. I assumed—correctly as it turned out—that she would not bother to check the dates on the quarters, but if this had been a serious concern, the trick could have been set up anyway by just selecting four quarters all minted in the same year.

My friend was kind enough to laugh at the trick, as it escalated, but of course audiences have been laughing at the combination of magic and comedy for centuries. There are some comedians who deliberately pretend to be terrible at their craft so that the audience laughs at the combination of their ineptitude and the cleverness with which the stunts are staged. In other cases, even when the bumbling approach is not employed, audiences often respond to certain tricks with laughter as well as gasps of astonishment and applause.

That reminds me of a line I did when traveling in China a few years ago. Our travel bureau hosts had taken our touring party, the evening before, to see a sensational variety show featuring acrobats, people who did remarkable feats of balancing on bicycles, animal trainers, and—the star of the show—a marvelous magician. Every one of his tricks had to do with producing fish, some of them actually alive and swimming, from here, there, and God knows where. He would wave a fishing pole through the air and suddenly there, wriggling on the hook, would be a fish. No matter where his hands moved, they seemed to be able to find fish. Finally he had large bowls of them swimming on-stage and assistants carried off a good many others.

The next day, with another group of hosts, we were discussing China's economic problems, and in particular the special difficulties posed by having to feed that country's enormous population. "Well," I said, "if there's ever a food shortage again, you don't have to turn to Marx or your economists. You need only call in that magician we saw last night; he could provide fish for a good part of your population," at which even the most serious Maoist present laughed heartily.

I doubt that anyone actually requires how-to type instructions as regards perpetrating hoaxes and practical jokes, and specific examples are probably better than abstract reasoning.

I remember one hoax broadcast on television that worked out wonderfully well. The story started late one afternoon when I got a phone call from Washington, from the secretary of then-Sen. Barry Goldwater. "Mr. Allen," she said, "the senator was supposed to fly out to Los Angeles yesterday to serve as master of ceremonies at a dinner held by the Fighter Pilots Association tonight, but a very important Senate vote came up, which means he hasn't been able to get to California. We hate to be calling you about this at the last minute, but the senator wonders if there would be any chance that you might be able to replace him at the dinner."

As it happened I had no appointments for that evening, so I said, "Give the senator my best regards and tell him that I happen to be free this evening and will be happy to attend the dinner."

The event was staged at the Hollywood Palladium, which was not far from the production offices I then occupied. One of the guest speakers, as it turns out, was a man I had at that time never heard of—the wonderful Foster Brooks. I noticed during the dinner that he was a distinguished-looking, bearded gentleman who looked as if he might be a scholar. He came over to me, introduced himself, and said, "When you introduce me, please don't say anything about the fact that I'm going to tell some funny stories. Just refer to me as if I were a serious speaker."

When the time came for his introduction, I followed his instructions and then sat back attentively to see what he would say. Inasmuch as Foster has since that time become a nationally popular entertainer the reader will know what sort of presentation he did at the Fighter Pilots' dinner. His imitation of a bumbling speaker who has had too much to drink is a true classic of its kind; his every remark was greeted with uproarious laughter. At the end of the evening I said to him, "Foster, have you ever appeared on television?"

"No," he said. "But I'd like to."

"Well," I said, "you've got a deal. In fact, I'd like you to be a guest on my show sometime within the next few days."

Chapter two of our hoax story involved the booking of Ralph Edwards, of "This Is Your Life" fame, as a guest. My wife Jayne and singer Steve Lawrence also appeared that day.

After Steve and Jayne had done their turns, I introduced Edwards. Before indicating that he should sit with the other guests, I met Ralph at center-stage and engaged him in a moment or two of talk-show chitchat. Then, fixing him with a level and seemingly serious look, I said, "Ralph, I suppose that over the years there have been many times when you might have expected what we have scheduled for our show today," by which, of course, I meant turning the tables on Edwards and doing a surprise television production recalling the significant details of *his* life.

"Oh, no," he said, in seemingly genuine terror, sensing my drift.

"Oh, *yes*," I responded. "Ralph Edwards, this is *your* life!" at which point I turned to receive a large green leatherette book which looked much like the one Ralph held on his own program when he would suddenly announce to a startled guest that the reason he had been asked to appear at a studio was a ruse and that, in fact, his own past was about to be laid bare.

"We have one of your old friends backstage at this very moment, Ralph," I said. "I'm sure you'll recall this voice."

In reality there was no possible way Ralph could recall the speaker because the man backstage was no old friend of Edwards' but simply Foster

Brooks, whom I had instructed to speak as if he were only slightly rather than heavily intoxicated. "Hello, Ralph," Foster said, still not visible to those of us onstage. "Yes, I remember you very well because I gave you your first job at the radio station in Denver where you got your start. I remember predicting that you would enjoy great success because I could see that you were a bright, energetic, and personable young fellow. I'm very pleased at all the wonderful things that have happened to you over the years."

In saying this, Foster gave a very faint verbal hint that he might have had a drink or two, but in such a way that no one could be sure.

Ralph, being an experienced showman and wanting to be cooperative with what he thought was a sincere tribute to himself, pretended that he recognized the voice, and when I said, "You know who that is, don't you, Ralph?" he responded by saying, "Yes, I *think* I do."

"That's right," I said. "It's Brooks Fosterson, who was the general manager at the station in Denver where you indeed did your first radio work. And here he is to greet you again after all these years."

Naturally, when Foster walked onstage, Ralph didn't recognize him at all; I assume that he thought, since Brooks wore a heavy beard, that that feature alone might have made him hard to recognize. In any event, the two men embraced and greeted each other warmly, after which I invited them both over to the sofa to make themselves comfortable. At this point, Foster pretended to become very garrulous and answered my first question about Ralph at extended length. Little by little, too, he made it seem that he was heavily intoxicated.

At this point Jayne, who like everyone else fell for the hoax, assumed that Brooks was indeed a stuffy old inebriate who was (1) lousing up a sincere tribute to Ralph Edwards, and (2) ruining her husband's program. Consequently, she began giving Brooks contemptuous glances that revealed the angry emotions she was feeling. Since our camera director, naturally, was in on the whole thing, he took close-ups of Jayne without her realizing it.

For the next several minutes the audience's laughter was uncontrolled. They, too, believed that Brooks was actually drunk, but the things he was saying were so funny that they nevertheless enjoyed the embarrassment that all of us on the stage appeared to feel. In another few minutes, it had become apparent, even to the benumbed Edwards, that the whole thing was a put-on, but I shall never forget the richness of the first part of the interview with Foster in which he so perfectly acted the part of a drunk that I'm sure he fooled not only everyone in the studio but the millions watching us in various parts of the country as well.

* * *

Why do we so enjoy participating in, or at least reading about, stories of this sort? It's probably a combination of simple playfulness and another, less-attractive element of human nature.

Perhaps the heartiest laughter in the history of television was that evoked by certain features on the old "Candid Camera" show, and on the "Candid Mike" radio version that preceded it. What you're dealing with in the case of hoaxes is reality, not just comedians telling jokes or doing sketches. And, of course, comedians aren't the only show business people who have perpetrated stunts of this sort. Musicians, too, have gotten into that particular act. Why musicians should be more given to playing practical jokes than watchmakers or milkmen is not clear. Perhaps it is because music itself is an adult form of play, a making-believe with sounds, and the people who indulge in its practice are therefore by their very natures more constituted to engage in other forms of folderol. Or maybe it's just that, because of the higher profile of their profession, more people become *aware* of their foolery.

One of the more notorious cases in point, as regards musicians, involves Richard Himber, a composer-conductor best known for his long association with the old Studebaker Champions radio show. For several years Himber and his orchestra performed happily on the program; and although he was respected by his men for his musicianship there were nonetheless evidences of an insurrectionist spirit on the part of a few of the orchestra members: they objected to his taskmaster approach. The result was that one afternoon some of his musicians put into action a scheme so classic that it has since been imitated by production groups assigned to other radio programs.

The clock is the yardstick of radio. The medium deals in sound, but its basic commodity is time. So thoroughly ingrained in the radio mind is this concept that occasionally more thought is given to making sure that a particular program gets off the air on time than is devoted to seeing that it is good. And so the men who temporarily shook Himber's hold on his sanity used time as their weapon.

The stocky, red-haired leader had rehearsed his men until shortly before airtime and then left the studio for a few minutes of relaxation before the broadcast. While he was out of the building, every clock and watch in sight was turned exactly seven minutes fast, including Himber's own stopwatch, which he had left on the conductor's stand. Thus it was that at approximately seven minutes before airtime he tapped commandingly for attention and lifted his baton, ready to lead the orchestra through the opening theme.

When the producer (who was in on the gag) pointed an index finger in Himber's direction, he confidently lowered his baton and smiled encouragingly at his string section. Two of the violinists responded thinly, but Himber blanched when he saw that the other members of the section were not even attempting to play. One man was tying a shoelace.

At this point the brass swept in with a blood-chilling discord, there was an uncalled-for crash of tympani, and a saxophone player was observed to be tuning up. Frantic, Himber rapped his stand for order and hissed a venomous command for attention.

"What are you doing?" he whispered. "We're on the air! Take it again, from the top!" To that the trombone player delivered a raucous raspberry, and the drummer took out a cigarette.

Stupefied, Himber looked on helpless as another of his players strode casually to a water cooler and two more announced, in audible and vulgar terms, that they were heading for the men's room.

Visions of angry sponsors and puzzled listeners from coast to coast must have filled Himber's sweat-beaded brow. Fortunately, just before he reached the point of collapse, an announcer walked over and explained that it was a joke, that there were still five minutes to go before airtime.

It was a full two years before Himber was able to laugh about the incident.

I would say my most grandiose practical joke was the one I played on the people of Arizona during the 1944 Democratic national convention in Chicago.

It was a period of unutterable boredom in radio stations across the land, because almost all regular daytime programming was canceled. For hours at a time the stations would simply broadcast whatever fare came in over the national network line from convention headquarters. There was nothing whatever for the local announcers to do but identify their stations every thirty minutes.

During moments when nothing was evident but the slow, soft mumble of the giant convention crowd, I noticed that the public-address system in the auditorium in Chicago could occasionally be heard in the background, amplifying announcements that frequently had no direct connection with the activities of the convention. "Will delegate Charles Samuels of St. Louis, Missouri, please call his home," a distant voice would cry.

An idea formed in my mind.

Knowing that Ray Busey, a Phoenix paint dealer who would later be elected mayor, was in Chicago, I instructed an engineer to open a microphone in our largest studio, walked into the room, stood as far away from the mike as possible, and imitated the distant, nasal sound of the voice that came over the air from the public-address system in Chicago. "Attention, please," I called. "Will Mr. Ray Busey of Phoenix, Arizona, please go to the parking lot behind the auditorium. Someone has just covered his car with whipped cream."

The engineer then cut off the mike, and we both sat down to await developments. Believe it or not there were none. Emboldened by this lack of censure, my friend and I took another crack at the thing a few minutes later. He opened the mike again, and, muffling my voice, I said, "Mr. Ray Busey of the Arizona delegation, will you please call home at once? They have just discovered that green paint is leaking under the door of your shop."

Evidently my imitation of the Chicago stadium announcer was exact enough to still all suspicions that might have been aroused by the content of my remarks. The other announcers and I had another two days of laughs of this sort before the joke wore thin.

Besides these and a few other hoaxes I've actually played out, I've thought of some that I never got around to springing. Years ago I read that a group of quadruplets—women—were in town. It occurred to me that it would be a wild idea to involve them in what I'm sure would be one of the great practical jokes of all time. I would take them to any busy downtown office building, and position them on, say, the fourth, fifth, sixth and seventh floors, standing just a few feet from one of the elevator shafts. Five minutes later I would bring a friend into the building and, blocking his view of the elevator button panel, press each of those floors' buttons. Now remember, on each of these floors we have a young woman, looking exactly like her three sisters and wearing precisely the same clothing.

As the elevator stopped on the fourth floor, I would look at the first young lady and say, "Are you coming in?" To which she would reply, "No. Thank you."

Five seconds later the elevator would stop at the next floor. So far as my friend could tell, the very same young woman would be standing there, and I would again say, "Are you coming in?" She would, as planned, give precisely the same answer I had received at the earlier floor. Can you imagine the mental state of the fellow I'm with when exactly the same thing happens four times and he knows it's a physical impossibility for that woman to have appeared on four separate floors within just a few seconds?!

Then there is one of the best pranks I've ever dreamed up, but which was, unfortunately, also never acted out. It relates to eating—anything and everything. Back in 1948, when I was living in Los Angeles and television was new, there was a program that used to book guests who did unusual things for a living. Some of these were more or less standard freak-type carnival or circus attractions; others were people with unusual hobbies. Today, David Letterman would interview them.

In any event, I planned to go on the show as "the man with the cast-iron stomach." In those days, if something was said to be made of cast-iron it was assumed it could withstand almost anything. Since I was already recognizable in Los Angeles, I planned to disguise myself by wearing dark glasses, adding a mustache and a wig, and speaking in a Texas or New York dialect.

The first demonstration I planned to perform involved emptying a bottle of Parker's fountain pen ink, washing the bottle carefully and then refilling it with grape juice. On the program I naturally planned to allege that I was drinking a bottle of ink.

I was also going to announce that my stomach was so strong I was able to eat steel wool kitchen scouring pads. To pull this off, I intended to remove the actual pads from the box and replace them with similarly shaped Shredded Wheat, to which a little food coloring might be added and a slight sprinkling of powdered sugar, so they would seem to be impregnated with soap.

I also planned to have a tailor remove the two buttons on the front of one of my sports jackets and replace them with slices of carrot, vegetable-colored in brown. At the appropriate moment, I would, of course, rip them off my jacket, pop them into my mouth, and chew away.

My intentions about all of this were quite serious, if the word itself doesn't seem ridiculous in such a context. Unfortunately, at that point I got so busy doing a nightly radio show that I never found time to act out the fantasy.

9

Writing TV Satires and Other Sketches

I have been asked many times if I think there will ever be a second golden age of TV comedy. Although my answer may seem biased, I have to say that I don't think so. The reason has nothing to do with a shortage of funny people. Exactly the reverse is the case, in fact. There are twenty times as many professionally funny performers in the business now as there were in the 1950s. But there is a logjam on the desk of television programming executives who are convinced, perhaps quite rightly, that putting sketch comedy on in prime time will not produce big ratings.

There is not a great deal of evidence to support their belief, but there is some. Several years ago, when Steve Martin, Lily Tomlin, and Richard Pryor were all new in the business, red hot in terms of media attention and even greater popular favorites than they are today, they were presented on network television starring in their own comedy specials. The ratings were surprisingly low.

It does not automatically follow that the same thing would happen today. My own view is that if one of the networks had the good sense to bring back something like the old "Colgate Comedy Hour"—that is, a program scheduled at the same time, on the same night, week after week, with a different comedy star hosting each time—a viewing habit would quickly develop. The trouble with specials, even those that get strong ratings and good word-of-mouth, is that the most common comment is "I heard you had a very funny show last Thursday. I didn't know it was on so I missed it."

How much of what is wrong generally with TV can be blamed on the network executives? I'll say a word in defense of them here. They are not to blame for the system. Like the performers, they are only cogs in the machine. They, too, are kept on only so long as the shows they commission deliver high ratings; their jobs are no more secure than those of the comedians. One day they are running a network, the next day they can be looking for work.

It *is* true that they may give you a good deal of advice on how to run your show, but you get that anyway. If you're in a common line of work, you rarely run into people who, though not of your profession, nevertheless consider themselves qualified as an authority on it. Neither brain surgeons, plumbers, TV repairmen, nor insurance salesmen receive any appreciable amount of helpful suggestions from outsiders. We may complain about the prices they charge us, perhaps, but we don't consider ourselves qualified to take issue with them.

In contrast, we all apparently regard ourselves as experts on the subject of comedy. Each of us is convinced that our individual sense of humor is absolutely top-notch, and we also know that others' are often deficient.

As regards satire, some writers feel it is more difficult to bring off than more conventional sketches. I do not agree. In fact, having a specific target to make fun of immediately provides a focus and direction that may not be present in other contexts. The object of a satire is always specific, although it may also be generic in the sense that it refers to a particular category or class.

There is no getting away from the fact that there is an element of cruelty in all satire, although the spectrum ranges from the harshly critical to genial spoofing. There is generally, in the minds of the creators and perpetrators of satirical sketches, the background sense that the selected target has it coming, that there is something inherently criticizable that deserves more than the adulatory attention that seems to be lavished upon almost every public presentation, particularly in our celebrity-addicted society.

The components of any specific satire obviously must be related to the original that is being made fun of. The foibles, idiosyncrasies, nervous mannerisms, or other aspects of the original will be recognized as such by audiences and therefore should be incorporated into the parody. But note that not everything related to a specific original is automatically a satire. For example, one of my most dependable routines since the early 1950s is an exercise in extroversion called Letters-to-the-Editor, which is explained in fuller detail in chapter 14.

Another instance of something that's related to reality but is not satire is the Man-on-the-Street sketch, a staple of my comedy and/or talk shows. As every newspaper reader knows, journals the world over have long published the comments of citizens about a specific question of the day.

The question itself may be entirely serious—"Do you believe the Russians will ever return to communism?" "Should the British people do away with the monarchy?" "Can we balance the budget without raising taxes?" Or it may have an element of the ridiculous—"Do you believe Elvis Presley is still alive?" "Have you, personally, ever been abducted by a space alien?" "If Madonna were not so famous, would you consider her a common slut?" But my purpose was never to satirize this journalistic staple, merely to present a sampling of "average citizens" doing big jokes about the issue at hand.

Parenthetically, do you know the names of the three performers who were the original "men on the street"? If you say Louis Nye, Don Knotts, and Tom Poston, you're wrong. It was indeed these three funny gentlemen who are best remembered in the context of the man-on-the-street sketches, but the original three were Louis Nye, bandleader Skitch Henderson, and Marilyn Jacobs, who was actually a secretary on the staff of my show at the time and had no particular interest in a performing career.

All right, so much for instances that were funny but not satirical. Here's an example of the real article.

❖   ❖   ❖

In 1967 I created a satire called "The Prickly Heat Telethon," which years later was included by the Showtime cable channel in a salute they did to comedy and "TV, The Way It Was." The basic idea for the sketch had originally occurred to me in the early 1950s, when Dean Martin, Jerry Lewis, and other popular comedians began doing fundraising telethons to help in the campaigns against various diseases. It would naturally be in the poorest possible taste to make fun of such diseases or their unfortunate victims, and nothing of the sort ever crossed my mind. But it did strike me, after seeing three or four such telethons, that they had quickly become ritualized.

First of all, there was The Star. At the beginning of a program he would be bright-eyed and oozing charm, full of ginger. A day or two later, however, he was a frazzled wreck of a man, irritable and short-tempered, hollow-eyed, and either listlessly dragging himself across the stage or crackling with the strangely intense energy induced by pep pills.

There also always seemed to be some delicatessen owner trying to get free plugs for the sandwiches and coffee he had provided "at no cost," a medical director or two somewhat befuddled about being on television, children who had canvassed their own neighborhoods to raise a few pennies or dollars, and, perhaps most notably, a peculiar mixture of big stars and theatrical nonentities who could not possibly get on television except on telethons.

All of this began to seem funny to me. Eventually I made a few rough notes for a sketch. During the 1950s and early 1960s, however, I considered the subject matter too touchy. I was afraid that if we did such a sketch some would erroneously assume that I was heartlessly insensitive to the plight of disease victims themselves. By 1967, however, American humor had become more frank; it finally became possible for us to present "The Prickly Heat Telethon" satire. To this day I sometimes show a tape of it when I've been invited to lecture on the subject of television comedy. It makes audiences laugh even more heartily now than it originally did. Here's the script:

THE PRICKLY HEAT TELETHON

STEVE: You know, television is quite remarkable. Besides being a source of entertainment, some of the time anyway, it also serves us in another important area. For example, each year large sums of money are raised for worthwhile charities by means of that venerable institution, The Telethon. Thanks to these telethons the day may come when we've conquered all the serious diseases. But when that day finally arrives, what will happen to all the people who now make a living working on telethons? They'll probably identify another problem and do a telethon about that. We'd like to show you what might happen when that day finally arrives.

SCENE: *Typical telethon setup. Double-level panel with pretty girls and second-rate actors answering phones. Small band area stage left. Master of ceremonies at center stage. Large backdrop sign says: "National Association for Prickly Heat. 14th Annual Telethon." On stage left is a tote board that will give money totals throughout the evening.*

MUSIC: *"We're Having a Heat Wave"—very corny, show-opening style. Up and fade for announcer's voice.*

ANNOUNCER: From the heart of Manhattan into *your* hearts, ladies and gentlemen, it's the Fourteenth Annual Prickly Heat Telethon, bringing you the greatest names in show business in a special fundraising program that kicks off this year's campaign against Prickly Heat. And here is your master of ceremonies, Steve Maudlin.

STEVE: (*enters*) Thank you, Bob, and hello, America. Well, sir, here we are with the big annual Prickly Heat Telethon, and once again we're depending on you good people out there to stay up all night . . . miss work in the morning . . . call us on the telephone . . . make your pledges . . .

send in that money, tote that barge, lift that bale, and help stamp out this terrible scourge, Prickly Heat.

We've got a lot of the biggest names in show business over here on the phones tonight, waiting for your calls. I mean people like Conrad Nagel, Helen Twelvetrees, Guinn "Big Boy" Williams, and Barton MacLaine, God rest their souls.

Camera does a loose pan of double-layered panel as Steve mentions names.

STEVE: We've got Farciot Eduardo, Lionel Atwill, Slim Summerville, and Honeychild Wilder! Imagine that, these wonderful people, some of whom came out of retirement this evening to spend a few hours here with you, mooching drinks and sandwiches all night long, great troupers that they are. Yes, we cleaned out the Lambs Club, ladies and gentlemen, to bring you this star-studded line-up.

Now remember, our goal this year is two million dollars! At the moment let's see how much we've raised in pledges and contributions. The first total is . . .

MUSIC: *Trumpet fanfare.*

Camera on tote board as numbers spin. A weird-looking girl in tights— Ruth Buzzi—smiles inanely. 76 CENTS comes up.

STEVE: Seventy-six cents! Seventy-six, that's the spirit, folks! Remember, Prickly Heat can strike anywhere. On the nape of your neck. Behind your knees. In the small of your back. In the still of the night. It can strike without regard to faith, creed, or religion. So give until it hurts. Remember, the itch you save . . . could be your own.

Do you realize, my friends, that a man gets Prickly Heat in the city of New York every twenty-nine seconds? And we have that man here tonight!

Camera pans to Kenny Solms, who sits scratching like mad.

STEVE: He's dead game, ladies and gentlemen, and I know you're greatly impressed with his courage. So keep that phone call coming in. In New Jersey the number to call is Epidermis four, nine six seven eight. (*super number in white*) And on Long Island the number is Soothingsalve five, seven thousand. (*super number*) And . . . if you're watching in Massachusetts, I want to congratulate you on your great TV reception—and I don't understand it at all.

And now let's get to a little entertainment here, folks, and I do mean little. I give you a very clever young comic who has just come over here . . . between shows . . . from the Copacabana in downtown Boise, Idaho—that very witty, snappy young funster! Let's welcome the King of Mirth—Lenny Jackie!

MUSIC: *"Fine and Dandy" up and fade.*

COMIC (*John Byner*): Thank you, Steve Maudlin, and good evening, ladies and germs. I wanna tell you, it's terrific to be here for this great cause, whatever it is. (*Drummer does rim shot.*)

Zowie! Ha-ha! What is this, an audience or an oil painting? Ha-ha-ha! Yes, sir! I just want to tell ya . . . a funny thing happened to me on the way to the studio tonight. A bum came up to me and said, "Hey, buddy, I haven't had a bite in three days!"

Then there was the time when these two Armenians got off a streetcar in downtown Boston—I know you're out there, folks, I can hear you breathing!

And now I'd like to give you my impression of Lionel Barrymore. (*turns away, then back*) Listen, Jocko—you're the guy who gave it to my brothah—in the back! . . . Don't applaud, folks, just throw money.

But seriously, folks . . . I don't have to do this for a living. I can always sell tennis shoes to Howard Hughes. These are the jokes, folks. (*to Steve*) Too hip for the room, Steve. Going right over their heads. . . . Come on, folks, laugh it up. I laughed at *you!*

People are crazy today. Take my wife . . . please. And that's why I say:

MUSIC: *Slow two-beat Dixie tag phrase.*

COMIC: Just keep laughin' . . . keep smiling . . . Right in your mouth!

MUSIC: *"Fine and Dandy" again—very fast.*

Comic runs back for four million bows. Steve can't get him off.

STEVE: How about that, folks? Isn't that a great talent? Oh, it isn't? Okay. By the way, we'd like to thank Sam Krelman of Sam's Delicatessen for all the sandwiches and coffee served here tonight. Sam, come over here and take a bow. He's a sweetheart! Sam, gosh darn ya.

SAM (*Louis Nye*): Thank you, folks. Thank you, Steve. I just want to say that I'm behind this thing one hundred percent. I know what a terrible scrooge Prickly Heat is, and—

STEVE: Not scrooge, Sam. Scourge!

SAM: It's that too! Because I feel this thing so strongly . . . in my heart . . . that I am personally *giving* you all these sandwiches and coffee and other leftovers this evening. At cost! I got a pastrami, a liverwurst, cole slaw, pickles, and our special Southern Fried Tzichken. Steve Maudlin, you're doing a wonderful job. America loves you.

STEVE: How about that Sam? Beautiful! Thank you so much. . . . Okay, get off. . . . So what's that new total now, gang? The total *is* . . .

MUSIC: *Fanfare.*

STEVE: A dollar and a quarter! Well, we're not getting off to the fastest start in the world with our telethon this evening, but I know you're not going to let us down, are you folks? Remember, one person in twenty will get Prickly Heat this year. And he'll give it to the other nineteen, if I know these people! So there's no getting away from this thing. It's reached epidermic proportions. So we're not going to give up. We're gonna stay on your TV for seventy-two straight hours.

And now let's get back to some more wonderful entertainment. During the next few minutes you're going to see Sabu Weintraub and his All-Girl Elephants. You're going to see that great rock group, the Four Garbage Cans. You're going to see the world figure skating champ, lovely Patricia Zelman, who, trouper that she is, has agreed to come out here tonight and skate her heart out, right here on our stage, even though we have no ice. Now that's courage.

That's what made America what it is! And some people say there's no God!

You're also going to see a powerful dramatic reading by Modus Vivendi, star of the Broadway hit, *A Hat Full of Pencils.* Modus, you know, just two weeks ago, right here on this stage, won the Clarence Derwent Award for being the only actor on Broadway who knows who Clarence Derwent was.

So, alright—we'll start some of that great entertainment right now, while you folks keep those calls coming in. And now, in response to a special request from the National Rifle Association, here is the very lovely Jennie-boo Gigliani doing her exciting specialty musical number, "The Hills Are Alive, With the Sound of Gunshots."

MUSIC: *"Sabre Dance" dissolving to a brief Ragtime phrase and then a Dixieland passage.*

During this we take a close-up of the hands of the clock moving from 11:05 to 2:45.

STEVE: How 'bout that? Let's hear it for a guy who—in my humble opinion—pound for pound was the greatest boxing champ of all time . . . "Hershey-Bar" Harrison. And thanks so much to a wonderful woman from our studio audience who permitted the champ to give her a real good pasting for this wonderful cause tonight.

Well, we're now in our fourteenth hour and that means it's time to meet and greet the Prickly Heat Foundation's medical advisor, the eminent authority on malpractice, Dr. Seymour Clyde.

The doctor (Dayton Allen) enters, dressed like a nut, and walks right off the other side of the stage. Eventually he is located.

DOCTOR: Good evening, Mr. Maudlin, and hello to all of you Prickly Heaters out there.

STEVE: Dr. Clyde, you are the head of the National Prickly Heat Home for the Itchy, aren't you?

DOCTOR: Yes, Mr. Maudlin, and I just want to tell your audience that the fight against Prickly Heat can be won. The secret is in research. Some doctors don't understand it. I know one surgeon who treated a patient for two years for kidney trouble . . . and two years later that patient died of *heart* trouble.

STEVE: Really?

DOCTOR: Yes! But not with me. If I treat you for kidney trouble, you *die* of kidney trouble!

STEVE: I see.

DOCTOR: And you don't have to wait two years to do it either.

STEVE: Doctor, that's a very old joke.

DOCTOR: Listen, you're no spring chicken yourself.

STEVE: At the present time, doctor, you are the *head* of the National Prickly Heat Institute, are you not?

DOCTOR: Who says I'm not? Of course I am. I *discovered* Prickly Heat many years ago. I got a *patent* on it. Anybody wants this thing, they got to come to me. I got a corner on it. Anytime anybody itches I get a nickel.

STEVE: How did you get started in the field?

DOCTOR: Well, I didn't start in the field. I started in a hospital.

STEVE: But when you started working on Prickly Heat . . .

DOCTOR: I started from scratch, believe me.

STEVE: But can we now beat this thing?

DOCTOR: I wouldn't recommend that. Maybe you could rub it a little. But no beating. At the first sign of an attack, take two aspirins and get in bed. With anybody. If pain persists or is unusually severe, well, that's the breaks of the game. But just to show you my heart's in the right place, I am going to make a donation to this cause myself tonight.

STEVE: How's that?

DOCTOR: I am not going to charge you for this call.

STEVE: Thank you, doctor, and good night. (*doctor leaves*) Well now, let's go over to the telephone panel here. They say a lot of calls are coming in. (*crosses to people at panel*) Right here we've got that great motion picture star, Mr. Chuck Roast. Evening, Chuck.

CHUCK: Evening, Steve. (*he's on the phone*) I'm handling a call here. (*into phone*) What is your name, sir? (*makes notes*) Lyle Socks? And you're giving ten dollars? Wonderful. Where are you calling from, Lyle? Oh, the other end of the panel.

Camera pulls back to show another actor down the line, waving at Chuck.

LYLE: Yes, I'm down here, Chuck. How are you?

CHUCK: Fine, Lyle. How's yourself?

STEVE: Well, let's move along. . . . Right here we have that lovely lady of the silver screen, Lila Lipstick.

LILA (*Jayne Meadows*): Hello, Mr. Maudlin, darling. It's so wonderful to be here for this great disease.

STEVE: Well, it's great to have you, Miss Lipstick. You're a wonderful person.

LILA: How true. Thank you. I'm glad to take part in this campaign because, you see, this is my favorite disease. And I know what I'm talking about, too, because we had Prickly Heat in my own family.

STEVE: Oh, that's too bad. On your mother's side or your father's side?

LILA: No, on my side! Right over here. (*she scratches her side*) Could I mention my latest picture?

STEVE: Certainly. What is it?

LILA: I forget.

STEVE: Good. Will you do a song for us a little later?

LILA: I'm determined. It's part of the deal.

STEVE: Right. Thank you, dear. How about that, folks? A great humanitarian and a credit to her race. And speaking of race, folks, look who's taking phone calls. The wonderful black actor, George Token. Hi, George. Listen, next time do me a favor—don't sit on the back of the panel, okay? . . . . That's right, ladies and gentlemen, television can educate you about these things!

   And now for some more entertainment for all you prickly heaters out there. Who's backstage right now? Oh, great! . . . Folks, let's welcome the

King of the Tap Dancers, tapping and traipsing, tripping his way back into your hearts. Here is . . . "Mr. Taps" himself—Tappy Tapperson!

CUE APPLAUSE

MUSIC: *Fast, peppy tap dance number*

SOUND EFFECT: *Lightning-quick taps on a hard floor*

A tap dancer runs out on stage and starts to do a wild number. We move in to his feet, then dissolve to the clock again, which this time moves from 2:50 to 6:45.

ANNOUNCER: We'll rejoin the fourteenth annual Prickly Heat Telethon right after this message.

FADE OUT to actual commercial break

FADE IN after commercial, still on the tap dance music and sound effects of taps. We see a close up of the tap dancer's feet, then dissolve to clocks as the hands turn. Dissolve to calendar with the pages starting to fall: June 28, 29, 30, etc. Tap dance sound effects continue.

CUE APPLAUSE

STEVE: How about that, ladies and gentlemen? Let's hear it for Tappy Tapperson! Great little trouper he is. Thank you, Sappy—er, Tappy, for two-and-one-half days of great dancing! Talk about time-steps.

Dancer collapses from exhaustion. Camera moves into a closeup of his shoe soles, which are frayed, tattered, falling off.

STEVE: Oh, by the way—(*turns to black man on panel, George Token*) How about that, George? Not bad . . . considering, I mean, eh? (*to camera*) These people know about such things, folks.

Stagehands and production assistants rush on-stage and drag the tap dancer's dead body off into the wings.

STEVE: Well, sir, we're going into our third day on the air. Remember, folks, we're trying to raise two million dollars for this wonderful disease— Prickly Heat. Now let's go once again . . . to the tote board! The total is now . . .

MUSIC: *Fanfare*

Ruth Buzzi at tote board points to the numbers as they roll into position. The figure is now $127.15.

STEVE: One twenty-seven, fifteen. Folks, I don't think you're trying! I'll tell you what I'm going to do. I'm going to give you a chance to make some more pledges right now. My voice is beginning to give out. I've lost seven pounds since we came on the air. Now, folks, I'm doing my part . . . What's the *matter* with you people out there?

Steve is suddenly distracted as a little boy in a Boy Scout uniform approaches him. The child is carrying a tin can with some coins in it.

STEVE: Well, what have we here?

SMALL BOY: Mr. Maudlin, I've been watching your show, sir, and I wanted to do something to help the fund-raising drive.

STEVE: That's wonderful, sonny. Well, bless your heart! You're a little scout of some kind. Have you raised some money?

SMALL BOY: Yes I have, sir. I went all over the neighborhood and asked people for money. And I broke open my piggy bank.

STEVE: Isn't that wonderful, folks? Imagine that!

SMALL BOY: You see, my mother and father had Prickly Heat.

STEVE: Aww, you poor little son-of-a-gun.

SMALL BOY: Yes, and they were so busy scratching they didn't have much time for me. So anyway, I raised this money and here it is. (*hands Steve a few coins*)

STEVE: How much is it?

SMALL BOY: Twenty-seven cents.

STEVE: (*shoves boy as drummer does rim shot*) Get off the stage, you little crum! Get this punk out of here! Stop that kid, he's stealing a cookie back there!

   And now, I'd like to introduce once again, that lovely lady of the silver screen, Lila Lipstick.

LILA: (*enters*) Good evening again, Steve. It's simply marvelous of me to be here with you for this worthy cause. Now I'd like to sing for all you wonderful people a song from my latest album. (*sings*)

FORGETTING

> I can't forget that you've forgotten me.
> Please don't forget that I forgot to forget you.
> You forgot that I forget
> To forget the night we met
> I forgot you were so pettable;
> It was all so—unforgettable.

We can't forget what we forgot before,
And when forgetting is forgotten once more,
If your heart forgets, well, let it,
If you've forgotten me—

STEVE: (*walks in, gives her disgusted look*) Forget it.

LILA: But I'm not finished.

STEVE: That's what you think, sister. While you were singing seventy-nine dollars in pledges were withdrawn! And now, folks, let's get back over here to the panel and meet some of these other wonderful celebrities. Why, look who's there! It's one of your favorite Hollywood leading men, ladies and gentlemen, Mr. Gear Shift. Good evening, Gear.

GEAR: Good evening, Steve. It's wonderful to be here with you tonight.

STEVE: Let's see, Gear, you wanted to tell the folks what your latest picture is?

GEAR: Well, actually, Steve, I haven't made a picture in quite some time. But I'm working quite steadily.

STEVE: Oh, really? On Broadway?

GEAR: No.

STEVE: In a TV series?

GEAR: No. I work mostly on these telethons. Tonight I'm here with you to help stamp out Prickly Heat, and I just came back from Portland, Oregon, where I appeared on their annual Flat Feet Telethon. That goes over very big up there, you know. There are a lot of people who suffer from flat feet, and they're trying to stamp out flat feet! . . . That joke got nothing in Portland either, by the way.

But all seriousness aside—I stole that from you, Steve—two weeks ago I emceed another wonderful telethon in Cedar Rapids, Iowa. It was the big annual Halitosis Telethon. We're trying to wipe out bad breath, you know. It can strike anywhere . . . and I wish you'd move back a little bit, Steve, now that I think of it.

We did get a few complaints from the garlic people, but in general the folks back in Cedar Rapids were really behind us. And I'm glad a lot of them weren't in *front* of us, I'll tell you that.

STEVE: Where will you be working next, Gear? If at all?

GEAR: Well, next Tuesday I fly to Boise, Idaho, for their big annual Hoof-and-Mouth Disease Telethon. It's the second greatest killer of cattle, you know.

STEVE: Oh really? What is the *first* killer?

GEAR: *We* are, Steve. *People.* Yes, it's terrible, but people kill more cattle by far than hoof-and-mouth disease ever could. I'm thinking of organizing an Anti-People

Telethon next year. I think eventually we've got to stamp out people, even at the risk of putting myself out of work in the long run. But there *are* some things more important than a man's career.

STEVE: Well, thanks very much, Gear Shift. I know you're going to stay right here on the telephones all night! We'll be looking for you on local TV channels around the country during the next few weeks.

Now, let's see what our grand total is. As we go to the tote board (*camera on tote board*), the total is . . .

MUSIC: *Fanfare*

STEVE: Twenty-seven dollars and fourteen cents! May I remind you, ladies and gentlemen, that our objective is two million dollars! Now, please! Keep those calls and pledges coming in! (*beginning to get nasty*) Wait a minute! I've just been given a note that tells me we have a large donation coming in. And here to make that donation in person is one of the leaders in the business community, Mr. Phil—or "Filthy" as his friends call him—Rich! Filthy Rich, come on out here, Phil!

Filthy Rich enters.

RICH: Good evening, Steve.

STEVE: Good evening, Mr. Rich.

RICH: You can call me Filthy.

STEVE: Tell me, Filthy, how much is it you're prepared to donate this evening?

RICH: Well, Steve, I know what a serious problem Prickly Heat is. It's kind of gotten under my collar, you might say. Now I want nothing in return for this marvelous gesture I'm making. But I want you to know my firm stands behind me as I present this check to you tonight. By my firm I mean, of course, the Rich Manufacturing Company, located at 1769 Longbranch Avenue in Teaneck, New Jersey, where the New Jersey turnpike meets Highway 29 and we're open twenty-four hours a day to welcome you to our lovely showrooms.

STEVE: Well, thank you, Mr. Rich. Actually, we are not permitted to broadcast commercial messages, but I was just wondering if—

RICH: Oh, I have no selfish motive in coming here tonight, Steve. My company, which has branches in thirty-eight states, wants to make this donation to this wonderful cause. Remember folks, we're open from eight in the morning till three o'clock the next morning, working around the clock for your dining and dancing pleasure.

Come in and place a downpayment. Ask about our layaway plan. Some of our salesmen speak Spanish. Some of 'em don't. Two of them don't speak at all. Special courtesies extended to prickly heaters. We are an equal opportunity employer. Vets, no money down. Member FDIC.

If you have suffered from Prickly Heat, we'll put you on our training program so that you can work on our assembly line with one hand while you're doing a little scratching with the other.

STEVE: Thank you very much, Mr. Rich, but I was wondering exactly how much your donation—

RICH: I personally am making my donation anonymously, Steve. We've all got to get behind this thing and put it over big. Everybody over at our main showrooms out in Teaneck is looking in tonight. Hi, Harry! (*waves*) Hello, Mabel! I'm on TV.

STEVE: Mr. Rich, we're running a little short of time. May I see your check? What is the size of it?

RICH: The size of it? (*hands check to Steve*) It's about five-and-a-half by seven inches. And now I'll say good night, folks. We look to see you all soon at our main showrooms in Teaneck. Drop in and tell them Phil Rich himself sent you. (*exits*)

STEVE: (*looking at check*) Twelve dollars and fifty cents. (*crumples check and throws it on the floor*) And now on with our show. Let's check the clock and see what time it is. (*looks at clock*) Well, sir, it's four in the morning. We've been on for two days—I think—and we're still going strong. And now again, it's time for a little entertainment. A lot of wonderful people are donating their services to keep you folks entertained, and our next guest is seen regularly on his very own early morning television show on Station W-OY-VEY. Here is Goofo the Clown. Come on out here, Goofo.

Goofo enters. He speaks like Mortimer Snerd, as do all television clowns.

GOOFO: Hello, boys and girls. I know that a lot of you are still up at four in the morning, and it's wonderful to look out there and see your sleepy, stupid-looking little faces. This is your old friend, Goofo the Clown, here to tell you exactly what to do. Tiptoe into daddy's and mommy's room right now, kids. That's it. Be sure to take the TV set with you. Be very quiet.

Now, you'll see daddy's watch and mommy's jewelry somewhere. Take them and put them in a large envelope and address it personally to Goofo the Clown, in care of Box 27, Grand Central Station, New York.

That's it for now, boys and girls. And remember . . . get that envelope in the mail . . . or I'll getcha! Good night, ya little suckers.

STEVE: Good night, Goofo, and thanks so much for being here tonight. Isn't he a great trouper, folks? And I know that all you little punk—er—kids, are going to do exactly what he said. Whatever it was . . . I wasn't listening.

Well, that brings us up to the last few minutes of our big annual telethon, ladies and gentlemen. Let's get back to the tote board and see how much money has been raised up to this moment. The new total is . . .

MUSIC: *Fanfare*

STEVE: One hundred and seven dollars! Okay, no more Mr. Nice Guy! You don't give money? Okay, go ahead, sister. Talk your brains out!

LILA: My friends, my own dear mother and father—bless them, they've gone now —(*looks at watch*) They'll be back in about twenty minutes. But they taught me, out of their own heroic suffering, that this disease strikes without regard for *nationality, tribe, or ethnic background*. All wonderful causes in themselves. . . . And so I say to you, dig down into your hearts . . . (*begins to cry*) Oh, I can't go on!

STEVE: You're telling me! Thank you, and goodnight.

CUE APPLAUSE

COMIC (*John Byner*): Oh, Steve, I've been over here on the phones . . .

STEVE: Oh, yes, Lenny.

COMIC: I have to catch a plane to my next telethon now, but first how about a special thanks to the wonderful boys in the band, who have agreed to work for *scale* tonight . . . which is twice as much as they usually get.

STEVE: Right. Thank you, Lenny. We needed that. And that reminds me. How about a word of thanks, folks, for our wonderful stagehands, who have agreed to work this entire show at standard double-time for overtime rates.

SOUND EFFECT: *Splat of sandbag as it falls next to Steve*

STEVE: Just kidding, fellas. Wonderful bunch of guys. But folks, I've been here for three-and-a-half days and all you people are able to come up with is a lousy $107! You expect to see big stars for that kind of money? Forget it! I'm sending the rest of the stars home! Frank, Dino, Sammy, go home. That's it. Liz and Richard, out! And take Eddie with you!
    That shows how long *they've* been backstage!
    Now, folks, I'm getting really steamed. I came here to bring you entertainment and fun. But you don't *want* entertainment and fun. Folks, I'm burning up now. I'm not going to stand for this. I'm losing my voice. I tell you what I'm going to do. Hold my breath—yes, hold my breath! . . . until that tote board goes up! (*takes deep breath and holds it*)

MUSIC: *Suspenseful theme*

Clock moves from 7:00 to 11:00, stops, then moves four more hours.

SOUND EFFECTS: *Clock ticking*

MUSIC: "*Sting*"

STEVE: (*He is on the floor, almost passed out.*) Very funny, folks! Okay, you win this time! Oh, incidentally, doctor, you saved my life.

DOCTOR: That's right. You owe me a penny.

STEVE: Listen, I'll tell you something. As soon as I go off the air this morning I'm catching a plane to Chicago where I'm emceeing another telethon altogether. One aimed at stamping out the greatest killer of them all . . . *Natural Causes*. Tell you what. Hold all those Prickly Heat checks and make them out to Natural Causes. Believe me, a much better cause than this one. This whole thing stinks here. Well, that's our telethon for this year. . . . You people are disgusting! (*exits, babbling and throwing a tantrum*)

Camera shows everyone on panel and in audience is asleep.

MUSIC: *Play off with "Playing the Field"*

* * *

One of my oldest and most reliable comedy satires is one of the first I ever wrote, "From High Atop—." The basic idea of it occurred to me when I was in high school, although I didn't put it on paper until I was in college. In those days, which were part of a marvelous, truly golden era of American popular music, every night you could lie in bed, perhaps with the lights out, listening to one or another of the great orchestras of the 1930s or 1940s— Benny Goodman, Count Basie, Tommy Dorsey, Jimmy Dorsey, Glenn Miller, Duke Ellington, Harry James. The broadcasts seemed rarely to come from radio studios but rather from ballrooms and dance halls across the country.

I don't know who the first radio announcers were who did the introductions of the bands and the individual songs on these shows, but they were a bit like the local newscasters of the present day in that they all seemed to talk alike, in the same artificially sophisticated, sing-song style. Anyway, I used to amuse my high school friends by rattling on like one of these announcers:

Good evening, ladies and gentlemen, out there along the radio airwaves. From the Solitary Confinement Room on the delightful Devil's Island, my friends, high atop the Sherman Hotel in downtown Lackawanna, Pennsylvania, it's the music of Joe Banana and His Bunch, featuring music with appeal.

As sidewalk humor, the routine had its limitations. It could only be done properly later, after I had gotten into radio and had orchestras available to me. That meant that I could prepare satirical songs and parodies that the bands and singers would perform so that the satire was full-fledged rather than only in the form of a monologue.

One odd thing about this routine is that there aren't a lot of Americans still alive who ever heard those original dance band "remotes," as they were called. Some of the people laughing at the routine today are twenty-five years old. They cannot possibly have been exposed to the original form being satirized, but I suppose they laugh at the crazy references to imaginary hotels and dance halls, the wild song lyrics, and the individual performers.

Strangely enough, even though the routine has been presented perhaps thirty-five times over the years, I've never had to write thirty-five completely separate versions of it. What I do is freshen the references each time, using names recently in the news. And, of course, I have so many comedy songs in my repertoire that any three or four of them will suffice for a given performance of the sketch. Here's one version:

FROM HIGH ATOP—

MUSIC: *"Last Night I Saw You" in 1930s Sammy Kaye–style. Up and fade.*

Ballroom with revolving mirror-ball. Boy and girl singers, seated, snapping fingers in unison. Old-fashioned floor mike downstage. Steve in dumb-looking tux and slick hair. Pianist noodles under the following.

STEVE: Good evening, Latvians and Germans out there along the radio airwaves. From the beautiful Lucille *Ball* Room, high atop the fabulous Del Mafia Hotel, in the heart of downtown Gallup, New Mexico, just a short forty-five-minute drive from the ball-bearing center of the world—Leavenworth, Kansas—the National Broadjumping Company is sending your way the Rancid Rhythms of Fletcher Castoria and his makes-you-want-to-call-the-cops music.

Yes, direct from the stunning new Laundry Room of the glamorous Iran-Contra Hotel, a refreshing two-and-a-half-mile swim across Lake Michigan, just underneath the heart of downtown Birmingham, Alabama, where the Ohio River meets the Panama Canal to form the St. Lawrence Seaway, it's another seventeen solid hours of danceable, pranceable, horrible melodies on your radio.

And now, little Spacey Sissek asks the musical question: "Smarty Pants?"

MUSIC: *Spacey Sissek sings "Smarty Pants?"*

GIRL: *Smarty Pants,*
You're such a rotten little smarty pants.
There's nothin' you don't know
About romance,
Smarty pants.

You think you know it all;
Be careful or you'll blow it all.

You're such a brain
You give me such a pain
With that old song and dance.
Girls don't like you;
That big I.Q.
Won't get you romance.
Hey, big thinkah,
You're a fink, ya
Rotten Smarty Pants.

STEVE: Thank you, Spacey, that was sickening. Friends, in case you're just joining our Jerky Jamboree, the Mutual Bumrushing Company is heaving your way the hair-curling selections of Peter Principle and his Twelve Angry Men, coming to you direct from the brand-new Locker Room of the beautiful Ayatollah Khomeini Hotel, a short haul from the mouth-watering fig fields of the 1934 Mississippi State Fair Grounds, on the banks of the old Amazon River, just across from the pearl of the Orient, Zimbabwe, Rhodesia.

Yes, the Crumbling Block-Busting System is unloading its musical trash basket right into your living rooms, representing the brain-numbing selections of John Birch and his Society Orchestra, direct from the breathtaking new Men's Room on the seventy-sixth floor of the William Ruckles' house on the outskirts of Los Alamos, New Mexico, just a thrilling ten-second rocket flight from the cotton-pickin' and chicken-pluckin' center of the Great Northwest, Capetown, South Africa . . . yowsah!

And now, turn up your radios, roll up the rugs, and plug up your ears, as we listen to handsome Neal Down, singing the romantic ballad, "Mouth-to-Mouth Resuscitation."

MUSIC: *"Mouth-to-Mouth Resuscitation"*

SINGER: *I was in swimming*
When quick as a wink
I was caught in the undertow
And I started to sink.
But you, wonderful you
Were there to save me,
And I'll never forget, my dear,
How you gave me—

Mouth-to-mouth resuscitation
That's what pulled me through.
Mouth-to-mouth resuscitation
Brought me close to you.
I opened my eyes

And there you were, up above me,
Upside down, it is true,
But somehow I knew
You'd love me.

Mouth-to-mouth resuscitation,
That's what did the trick.
It was such a strange sensation,
Did it make you sick?
There were people standing around,
Looking down at us on the ground.
Now, it's sweeping the nation,
Mouth-to-mouth resuscitation.

STEVE: Ah, yes, isn't he lovely? . . . Friends, if you're tuning in late, the American Back-Breaking System is shoving down your throats the sweetest music this side of Sodom and Gomorrah, played by the king of Latin rhythms, Judeo Christian and his Illegal Immigrants.

And it's all coming your way direct from the freshly repainted Broom Closet of Frank Daily's Meadowbrook, high atop the New Flophouse Hilton, built with a $47 million loan from the Teamsters' Central States Pension Fund, under *very* questionable circumstances, ladies and gentlemen.

And now, Sammy and his Goyim Gorillas challenge their chops as our romantic lovebirds—Linda Lipstick and Modus Vivendi—return to offer this enchanting invitation—"Let's Go To Lake Louise and Banff."

LET'S GO TO LAKE LOUISE AND BANFF

Let's go to Lake Louise and Banff.
Where we can hug and squeeze—and banff.
There's nothing to it
Let's just do it,
Baby:

Let's go to Lake Louise and Banff.
We'll shoot the breeze and banff.
It's a snap dear.
Shut your trap, dear.
Let's just hit the road.

> *Others*
> *May go to Rio or Rome.*
> *Let those mothers*
> *Know anywhere I hang my hat*
> *Is home.*

Let's go to Lake Louise and Banff.
By twos and threes, let's banff.
Last time we did it,
We really did it right.
I don't know about you
But I could have banffed all night!

Song ends.

CUE APPLAUSE

STEVE: Ah, yes, aren't they wonderful? And folks, they're available because they've just been fired! Yes, you're listening to another musical massacre by the old King Kong of the keyboard, Karl Klutz and His Misguided Missiles, coming to you from the lovely International Head Shop Festival, in the heart of the nation's Quicksand Center, Three Mile Island, Pennsylvania.

MUSIC: *"Last Night I Saw You"*

Establish and fade to background.

STEVE: Well, friends, the old clock on the wall says our Saturday Night Dancing Party is on its last legs. So, until next time, this is your announcer, Mike Side, mike-side saying toodle-oo, a bit of a tweet-tweet, a fond adieu, a yock-she-mosh, a bit of a pip-pip, a punch in the mouth, pleasant dreams, an *au revoir,* and *auf wiedersehen,* good night, goodbye, lots of health, lots of fun, lotsa luck. . . .   This is NBK, the National Brainwashing Kompany.

MUSIC: *Up to playoff*

Close-up of mirror-ball.

*   *   *

Sometimes a satire can be combined with a "what if—" idea. For example, several years ago I was asked, by Bob Thiele of Coral Records, to write some special material for Ricky Vera, an appealing little Mexican-American boy who had become popular from appearances on Hoagy Carmichael's TV show. "Dragnet" was in the top ten then, so the question occurred to me—what if there were a "Dragnet" show on the level of a young child? The result was called:

DRAGNET GOES TO KINDERGARTEN

BOY: I'm five years old. My name's Friday. Friday Morning. I'm a kid!

MUSIC: *First four notes of "Dragnet" theme*

BOY: It happened at 3:25 last Monday. I was on my way home from kindergarten when I noticed it was missing—my *lollipop!*

MUSIC: *Second five notes of "Dragnet" theme.*

BOY: My teacher, Miss Brown, had given me the lollipop for good behavior. It was a good lollipop. Strawberry. I made up my mind to get it back. At 3:29 I checked back at the playground. Two strange kids were playing in the sandpile. I checked their pockets. It was just as I thought—they were full of sand!

MUSIC: *Brief phrase*

BOY: Three forty-five. There was a man selling ice cream bars at the school gate.

SOUND EFFECT: *Good humor jingle-bells, but they play "Dragnet" theme*

BOY: I decided to question him. . . . Hello, mister.

MAN: What can I do for ya, son?

BOY: I'm looking for a strawberry, sucker.

MAN: What?

BOY: I mean, I'm looking for a strawberry *sucker.*

MAN: Get lost.

MUSIC: *Brief phrase*

BOY: I marked him in my book as a possible five-eighteen and went across the street to the candy store. It was 3:59. There were some tough kids playing Tap the Ice-Box. It looked suspicious. They had one kid locked in an ice-box, and the others were playing taps. I broke up the game and booked them all on a four-twelve. The kid who'd been in the ice-box demanded protection. I walked him around the corner, and we watched the gang. They started to play hopscotch. It looked phony. Then I knew—someone was throwing the game!

MUSIC: *Brief phrase*

BOY: The kid I was with said he had to leave. Said he had to go finish beating the erasers for Miss Brown. I checked under his fingernails. Chalk dust! He was telling the truth.

MUSIC: *Chord. Sustain under briefly*

BOY: Four-oh-six. It was getting late. Still no lollipop. I had to move fast. My friend, Donovan, came by. He's in the first grade. He had a kiddie car with a wagon in the back. I jumped into the wagon. "All right, Donovan! Go to the corner of Fourteenth and Caterpillar, and step on it!"

MUSIC: *Brief phrase*

BOY: Fourteenth Street. The neighborhood of the rival school—P.S. 87. It was a rough section. The school was so tough even the *teachers* played hooky. It was so tough they printed the report cards on sandpaper. The schoolyard looked peaceful enough, but I was in over my head. I knew it. I saw the janitor feeding the pigeons. Then I noticed. He was feeding them to his family.

MUSIC: *"Dragnet" phrase*

BOY: I told Donovan to pick me up in ten minutes. It was 4:19. Then I saw him—the toughest kid in the neighborhood. Fatso!

MUSIC: *Stinger chord*

BOY: He was big. At least three feet six. He was a man-mountain! He must have weighed eighty pounds! I could tell he was in second grade. He had that look. Tired. Cynical. Sophisticated. There was something odd about his face. Something strange about his mouth. Then I saw it—sticking out of his mouth . . . my sucker!

MUSIC: *"Dragnet" phrase*

BOY: Alright, Fatso. This is it.

FATSO: (*sounding older, tough*) Listen, bud. You're asking for a licking!

BOY: That's right. I'd like to lick my sucker again, if you don't mind.

FATSO: Scram, punk!

BOY: Listen, Fatso . . . you tough?

FATSO: Yeah!!

BOY: (*pause, then meekly*) I knew it the minute I looked at ya. (*pause*) Would you mind giving me my sucker? I've gotta be home in exactly ten minutes.

FATSO: Why?

BOY: Gotta take my nap.

Fatso laughs.

BOY: When he started laughing, he took the sucker out of his mouth. I saw my chance. I grabbed the sucker, started to run. Donovan came by just in time. I jumped in the wagon. It was downhill now. It was easy. We got away. I felt good inside. I had it again. My lollipop!

MUSIC: *"Dragnet" closing music. Hold under.*

BOY: The story you have just heard was true. Only the flavor was changed to protect the sucker.

MUSIC: *Up to finish*

Notice how, in the above speeches, the phrases are the short, declarative sentences that characterized the "Dragnet" show dialogue. Observe, also, how the time of day is tracked, Sgt. Joe Friday–style, to build suspense. In satirizing the narrative from "Dragnet," I also applied quick little shockers following mild statements. For example: "I saw the janitor feeding the pigeons. Then I noticed. He was feeding them to his family."

The piece ends with a takeoff on what was "Dragnet"'s signature line: "The story you have just heard was true. Only the names have been changed to protect the innocent."

*   *   *

One of every comedy writer's favorite targets to parody has been the television commercial. Here is a routine I wrote for Sid Caesar, though it was eventually performed by Steve Landesburg on a CBS "Comedy Zone" show. The monologue is a satire not on a specific television commercial but on the entire genre in which a headache sufferer, apparently not knowing he is visible to a television camera, describes his headache in excruciating detail.

This is a "consumer testimonial" type of ad, wherein people talk about how a particular remedy came to their rescue. I added the "what if" factor —what if the announcer couldn't shut the guy up, and he just went on and on, theoretically for all eternity, trying to tell the world about his headache? This is funny for the added reason that none of us really care about the poor guy's headache in the first place.

Notice how I use the technique of exaggeration interlaced with crazy word/sentence switches in describing the pain.

THE HEADACHE

HOST: We all have had headaches. Some of us are no doubt suffering through one at the moment. Perhaps for a few of you out there this program might even be responsible for that. But that possibility notwithstanding, I've never been sure why we keep seeing television commercials in which Just Plain Folks—who evidently do not know they are being filmed by a hidden camera—describe their headaches to us. Do you really need anyone to describe a headache to you?

I thought not. . . . But it happens on television all the time.

Cut to grainy, 16mm shot of Sid Caesar-type comedian in a medium-close shot. He is looking slightly off camera.

VOICE: Could you describe your headache?

MAN: Sure. It will give me great pleasure. Well, at first it seemed to start at the base of my neck. (*touches various parts of his head, massages them, squeezes them, etc. as he mentions them*) And then it swirled around here, hiding just behind the rim of my collar, until it began to creep—insidiously—up the left side of my neck. . . and then suddenly—wham!—it struck my left ear.

VOICE: Without warning?

MAN: Certainly without warning! A headache doesn't put an ad in the paper, you know. Anyway, it went from my left ear, right through my *medulla oblongata*, and out the right ear. Then it worked its way through my sinuses here, and then right over the top of my left eyebrow, across the bridge of my nose, down around my upper lip. Then it struck, like a knife, into the left side of my face. I was dazed with pain.

Then it ran, like a nervous titter, along the top of my gums and down through my throat. And then suddenly—headaches are like this, you know—they do things when you least expect them, like in "Candid Camera." Anyway, it suddenly shot back up along the right side of my face, tiptoed across the wrinkles in my forehead, then surreptitiously smashed a blitzkrieg, a sneak attack, right up under the edge of my hairpiece. Right here. See where I mean? And then, just when I was ready to cry havoc, it zoomed down the other side of my face, went right up my left nostril—

VOICE: Sir, I think we've heard quite enough about your headache for the time being.

MAN: Are you kidding? I'm just getting started. This is the *easy* part. (*like Jolson*) You ain't heard nothin' yet!

HOST: And now, ladies and gentlemen, we're—(*he's interrupted*) What?! I've just been told that the guy with the headache is *still* telling us about it.

MAN: You wanna talk headaches you came to the right man. And I say that without fear of Contra Costa County. You know what an *ache* is? You know what a *head* is? Well, you put them together, Jack, and you've got a headache *par excellence*, if you'll pardon my French. I'm talking about a headache that sometimes strikes in the middle of the night, when I'm sound asleep. Suddenly I find it doin'-the-Huckle-buck across my chin, and right through my moustache. Then, with the pounding beat of its mighty hooves, it runs roughshod across the base of my spine, up through my decolletage—

VOICE: A headache . . . in the base of your spine?

MAN: You looking for an argument? You did *ask* me about my headache, you know! I repeat—it zooms up, like the space shuttle, right from the base of my spine into my cranium, to every pore, every hair follicle, every skin eruption that made my life hideous through my teenage years. Every fiber of my being is crying for mercy! The pain is excruciating. It's phenomenal. It's salacious. (*sings*) It's delightful. It's de-lovely. It's a pain that doesn't just move, doesn't just creep, it marches—boots, boots marching up and down again. Boots, boots, pounding on my crown again.

VOICE: Sir, please.

MAN: Pain to the right of them, pain to the left of them, into the valley of death marched the six hundred. For it was crawlin' and it stunk, but of all the drinks I've drunk, you're a better man than I am, *Gunga Din!* Ya see, that's the monstrous thing about headaches like mine. You never know when they're gonna strike. Why, you're walking along the street, or you're at a party . . . (*singing*)

> *Or else you're alone and then you suddenly dig.*
> *You're lookin' in someone's eyes.*
> *You suddenly realize*
> *That this could be a pain that's something big.*

The last time I suffered from a headache, I sat me down by the waters of Babylon—

VOICE: Yes, you certainly do.

MAN: Do what?

VOICE: Babble on. Sir, we have no more interest in your headache!

HOST: Ladies and gentlemen, I've just been handed this news bulletin. It seems that the man with the headache has refused to be silenced. S.W.A.T.

teams, however, have the building surrounded, and we expect to open negotiations with the gentleman shortly.

MAN: Don't try to stop me, buster. You asked about my headache, and I'm going to tell you about it! How can you say you have no further interest in my headache? Where's your basic human decency? Your sympathy? Your empathy? Where's your sister? Bring her down here, and I'll tell *her* about my headache. Are there millions of people watching me right now? Good! All you people out there, your headaches are nothing, nothing—ya got that?—compared to mine. I have the King Kong of headaches. The hydrogen bomb of headaches. *Hitler* should have had such a headache!

VOICE: Sir, if you'll just stop for a moment—control yourself. . . . That's it. What I've been trying to tell you is that we have something that will *help* your headache. Look there on the table in front of you.

Camera shot widens out somewhat to show an Excedrin- or Tylenol-type bottle with "PAINAWAY" printed on it in large letters.

MAN: What's this?

VOICE: That's *Painaway*, sir, the fastest headache remedy available without a prescription or a handgun.

MAN: Painaway? How many should I take?

VOICE: Painaway is very powerful, sir. I would think that one tablet a month should suffice.

MAN: That's what *you* think. You don't have my headache. Here, gimme some of that stuff!

He pours out six or seven Painaway tablets, puts them into his mouth, and begins to crunch them up.

MAN: Ahhh, I think I'm beginning to feel a little better already. At least my mouth has gone totally numb. Can you still understand what I'm saying?

VOICE: Yes, I'm afraid we can.

MAN: Good, that means my tongue is still working—which is more than I can say for my sister's husband. . . . Yes, I'm beginning to get the clear impression that at some point in the future, perhaps along about mid-November, these tablets might possibly begin to take away the pain, the turmoil, the heartbreak of psoriasis of my headache. The Gargantua of headaches. The Pretty Boy Floyd of headaches. The Al Capone of headaches.

A disembodied hand, holding a large, easily recognizable blackjack, comes in and zaps the man on the head with it. His eyes close, and he sinks slowly out of the picture.

HOST: That's *one* way to end a headache! . . . And now, ladies and gentlemen—What? Oh, no! Folks, we've just received word that the man who insisted on describing his headache is still at it. Let's check back and see if—

MAN: Forget the checking. I'm still here because my head is *killing* me. Now, you asked me where my headache *starts*. Well, sometimes it starts at the base of my skull, and sometimes it starts way down around Forty-second Street, zooms up Seventh Avenue, takes a cab over to Madison, and when I come out of the building where I work—whammo!—it hits me right in the mouth. Then it works its way through my upper palate, up past the post-nasal dripworks, up the Monongahela Valley, through the Cumberland Gap and along the Old Chisholm Trail to the temples, where I feel the excruciating beat, beat, beat of the tom-toms . . . when the evening shadows fall.

Sometimes I try to fight it. My left brain says to my right brain, "Listen, mate, how about sending down a few endorphins to clear out the endorphinage here?" And my right brain says to my left brain that a headache like this can strike at any time of day. Why, when the sun goes down and the tide goes out and the people gather around and they all begin to shout, "Hey, hey, that's a pain, it's a treat to beat your feet on your Mississippi brain."

You want to talk *pain?* I got such a headache even my *dandruff* hurts. I've got such a headache that when I use Head and Shoulders, even my *shoulders* hurt. If somebody tries to give me a head *start,* I always say, "Don't start with the kind of head *I* got!" You know, the doctor tries to tell me that my headaches are all psychological. But forget him. He's psycho, and I'm logical. Sometimes the pain starts in that great mysterious area between the small of the back and the nape of the neck. Somewhere between the top-o'-the-mark and the back-o'-me-hand. Suddenly the eagle has landed, and it sinks its merciless talons into my skull, through skin and bone, through muck and mire, through Mork and Mindy, and tiptoes through my two lips, and at *that* point, all *hell* breaks loose.

VOICE: Sir, watch your language because we're—

MAN: Why? What's wrong? Can't you stand the *truth?* That's the kind of *headache* I got. Moreover, and I say this with my mouth, my headache is hell bent for leather, whatever that means. At this point, I will take *anything* for my headache. I don't care what I use—Anacin, aspirin, cleaning fluid, chicken fat, punk music—I'll take it and kiss your hand for giving it to me.

But, you know, it's a funny thing. At other times, it starts right here at the temples. See? Right here where Ronald Reagan applies his Grecian Formula. And then it suddenly swoops down until it reaches my chinny-chin-chin.

VOICE: Sir, would you like to see *real* pain?

MAN: I was—Why, yes, that would be interesting.

VOICE: Okay.

A fist comes in frame and smacks the man apparently right on the kisser. The punch is actually pulled, of course, but a sound effect makes it sound like a right to the chops in a Clint Eastwood movie. The man's head snaps back. His eyes cross, and he sinks out of the picture. But suddenly, with a goofy smile, he rises back up into it.

MAN: You know, that was very interesting. When I first felt the full force of the blow, the pain started right here—right in the *kisser*, as we say. Then it gradually spread, traveling over the intricate network of nature's delicate tracery, beneath the epidermis. And then the pain continued to spread, like an enormous mushroom cloud, until I—

At this point, two hands come into the picture, from just below camera, grab the man by the throat and start to strangle him. Despite gagging and choking, he manages to sputter out a few more words.

MAN: And then suddenly, in the still of the night . . . as I gaze from my window . . . at the moon in its flight . . . my thoughts all turn to pain. . . and the agony goes from—

*   *   *

Very well, so much for examples of satire. The great majority of sketches over the years—going back to vaudeville and Broadway—have not been satirical. In my own experience, I find that ideas for sketches come at any time, any place. For example, one afternoon while listening to the radio, I heard the phrase, *star-spangled celebration*. I immediately focused on the word *spangled*. It's hard to explain why, but ever since childhood certain words simply sound different to me than to others. In a way, they call for attention. And in this case I considered *spangle*, used as a verb.

In about half an hour, I had written this interview-sketch.

REPORTER: And what do you do for a living, sir?

GUEST: I'm a spangler by trade.

REPORTER: A spangler? And exactly what does a spangler do?

GUEST: Well, I think you could have figured that out for yourself. What a spangler does is spangle. At least I spangle. My brother-in-law spangles, too. We're members of the Spanglers' Union, Local 106.

REPORTER: Well, sir, I did grasp that a spangler would spangle. But the problem is, I'm not quite sure what the verb *to spangle* means.

GUEST: Boy, you don't get around much, do you? Ever hear of the little ditty called "The Star-Spangled Banner"?

REPORTER: Yes. Of course.

GUEST: Well, who do you think spangles all them stars on them there banners? You want a nice, neat spangling job, you'd better call a union man every time. That's why all the stars are so neat on all them flags. 'Cuz one of us spanglers worked with them stars. Now, if Francis Scott Key had written about a star-*splattered* banner, then, hell, you could just dump 'em out of a bucket. Wouldn't matter where they fell. But he didn't say star-splattered banner, did he? He said star-*spangled* banner. Spangling is much neater than splattering.

REPORTER: So then if a flagmaker was a stickler for accuracy, he'd have to—

GUEST: Oh, no. For that you'd have to call a stickler. The Sticklers' Union can give you the names of lots of sticklers. You call one of them guys in, and they will stickle for you real good.

REPORTER: Well, sir, I can't help noticing, with your lovely wife and children over there, that you're a good family man. In fact, just before we came on the air, I noticed you dandling your little daughter on your knee.

GUEST: Yes, that's right. I can do that all I want now because I was formerly a member of Dandlers' Local 86. You don't see much knee-dandling any more. It used to be very big in Europe.

REPORTER: But don't people usually do their own dandling?

GUEST: Oh, sure they do. But man is not born with the knowledge of how to dandle. So you either have to go to dandling school, or just take a little casual instruction from your friendly neighborhood dandler. At least, that's how it used to be in the old country.

REPORTER: What old country?

GUEST: Any old country. . . . Who cares?

REPORTER: Is that right? Well, I'll be horn-swoggled!

GUEST: Then you'll have to call a professional swoggler. If you're in the market, I can put you in touch with a very good horn-swoggler. And I know quite a few swashbucklers, too, if you'd ever like to have your swash buckled.

REPORTER: Sir—

GUEST: Yes?

REPORTER: Please go away.

*　*　*

Another piece I wrote, "Having a Good Time," can actually be classified as either a sketch or a brief one-act play. It makes a somewhat unusual sketch because, although there are laughs in it, it's essentially serious. I got the idea for it while sitting on a park bench in New York, watching a prostitute working the area. It occurred to me that since our worlds were so far apart it would be difficult to carry on a conversation that would make sense to us both. That's all there was to the genesis of the idea. After that I just started to dictate dialogue, without having any idea where it would lead.

THE SCENE: *A secluded area of a public park, at night. Two lampposts are visible, greenery, a park bench, etc.*

After a moment, Roger Stileger, a scholar in his mid-fifties, attractive, moderately urbane but bookish, enters. He sighs deeply, looks at his watch, places his old-fashioned briefcase on the bench, seats himself, and rubs his eyes tiredly.

A few moments later, sounds of an argument between a man and a woman are heard off stage. The woman appears, speaking to someone off stage. She is young, quite pretty, and dark-skinned—perhaps part black, part Latino.

BETTY: Yeah? Well, you know where you can stick it, Jack! (*to herself*) Dirty bastard.

She seats herself at the other end of the park bench, takes off one shoe and begins to massage her foot. After a moment she realizes she is not alone.

BETTY: How you doin'?

ROGER: What?

BETTY: I said, how you doin'?

ROGER: Oh. Why, fine, thank you.

BETTY: You wanna have a good time?

ROGER: (*considers the question briefly, then nods*) More than anything in the world.

BETTY: You got it.

ROGER: I beg your pardon.

BETTY: I asked you if you wanna have a good time.

ROGER: Yes. Everyone wants to have a good time. The American people, in fact, expend an inordinate amount of their energies in the attempt.

BETTY: What the hell you talkin' about?

ROGER: I was about to ask you the same thing.

BETTY: Let's get down to business. Twenty-five bucks.

ROGER: I have the impression I'm listening to a badly-edited tape recording. What *about* twenty-five bucks?

BETTY: That's how much it'll cost ya.

ROGER: How much *what* will cost me?

BETTY: How much a good time will cost you.

ROGER: How can you possibly know that? A good time could conceivably cost nothing at all, in financial terms, or it might rob me of my life's savings.

BETTY: You crazy?

ROGER: There were times when my late wife thought so—but, no, I'm not. How about yourself?

BETTY: Hey, Jack, do you know what I am?

ROGER: You would appear to be a young, pretty woman of Latino extraction, and perhaps black ancestry as well.

BETTY: Hey, what the hell are *you*—Ted Koppel? Listen, I asked you if you wanted to have a little action. If you do, just get up the scratch and we can get to it.

ROGER: (*truth suddenly dawns on him*) Ahh, I see. You're a prostitute.

BETTY: (*sarcastically*) Hey, man, don't ever go on "Let's Make A Deal."

You wouldn't win doodley-squat.

ROGER: I do not know what doodley-squat is, although I have never liked the sound of the term. Nor have I ever watched "Let's Make A Deal," which I take it is a television program. Nor, I'm sorry to say, am I interested in your sexual favors.

BETTY: Who said anything about doin' you any favors?

ROGER: Young lady—if I may use the term—I sat on this bench a moment ago because I was seized by a feeling of utter exhaustion.

BETTY: Then you ain't cruisin'?

ROGER: That is correct.

BETTY: Then you don't want to make it with me, no way at all?

ROGER: I'm afraid not.

BETTY: You gay?

ROGER: I have moments of gaiety. But I am not, as it happens, homosexual.

BETTY: Well, you certainly are a wise-ass.

ROGER: It's not my intention to be.

BETTY: Ain't you got the scratch?

ROGER: The what?

BETTY: The money, the twenty-five.

ROGER: If you'll forgive me for saying so, I don't think it's any of your business how much money I have.

BETTY: What I meant was—if you ain't holdin' right now, we could go someplace where you could *get* the bread, you know?

ROGER: Why are you so persistent?

BETTY: Why are you so goddamn nosey? You sound like the law.

ROGER: (*chuckling*) No, I'm not a policeman.

BETTY: What *do* you do?

ROGER: I teach. But I find myself curious—why do you keep bringing up the subject of your, er, availability?

BETTY: Why the fuck do ya think? I happen to need twenty-five dollars right now.

ROGER: Why didn't you say so? If your need is that desperate, I'll be happy to *give* you twenty-five dollars.

BETTY: What do you want for it?

ROGER: Nothing.

BETTY: You puttin' me on?

ROGER: No.

BETTY: No schoolteacher I ever knew could afford to go around handin' out money. You teach at one of the schools around the neighborhood?

ROGER: No, I teach at the university.

BETTY: Lookin' at your shoes I'd say you do pretty good.

ROGER: What do you mean?

BETTY: I size up guys by their shoes. Guy's got a sharp pair of shoes, he usually does pretty well.

ROGER: To judge by *your* shoes, you're not doing very well. Why, may I ask, do you work as a prostitute?

BETTY: Because I'm too nervous to steal. (*laughs*) That's an old joke.

ROGER: Then there's honesty in you.

BETTY: What makes you say that?

ROGER: Because you told an old joke and then confessed. That shows your case isn't hopeless. But you still haven't answered my question. Why are you a prostitute?

BETTY: Because I have these funny habits I have to support—like eatin', drinkin', wearin' clothing, sleepin' with a roof over my head. All that stuff costs money, you know.

ROGER: Indeed it does. The whole human race has to worry about such things. But other people have regular jobs. Why did you choose this?

BETTY: I never did. It chose me. I got on junk, I needed money. I still need it.

ROGER: There are other ways of making it. Did you ever stop to think that there isn't much future in your present profession?

BETTY: Oh, yeah. I think of it all the time.

ROGER: I don't run into too many fifty-year-old prostitutes. Do you?

BETTY: I don't think you run into too many prostitutes of any age.

ROGER: You're right about that.

BETTY: Don't I turn you on at all?

ROGER: Appeal to me sexually, you mean?

BETTY: Yeah.

ROGER: It's an interesting question. I've already described you as pretty. There's part of my consciousness that's quite prepared to concentrate on that prettiness. I might even entertain a momentary fantasy or two—about you, I mean. But I choose *not* to have sexual contact with you.

BETTY: Why not?

ROGER: Well, you might be carrying a venereal disease, for one thing.

BETTY: Yeah, I might. But I ain't. I'm clean.

ROGER: It's a relative term.

BETTY: So what you're saying is—you're chicken. If you *knew* I didn't have VD, you'd jump on my bones, right?

ROGER: No, I would not. I guess it's that I think you're wasting your life, and I see no reason why I should help you to do it.

BETTY: Give me the twenty-five bucks.

ROGER: Very well.

He takes out his wallet, withdraws two tens and a five, and hands them to her.

BETTY: Thanks.

ROGER: My pleasure.

BETTY: (*laughs*) Well, I'm glad you're into *some* kinda pleasure. . . . You sure you don't want somethin' for this?

ROGER: What would I want for it?

BETTY: I don't know, a hand job?

ROGER: (*solemnly*) A hand . . . job. That's sad.

BETTY: If you ain't tried it, don't knock it. You don't look to me like no guy who's got ten chicks hanging all over him.

ROGER: I'm not. One doesn't need ten, you know. One will do. In fact, one is much preferable.

BETTY: Unless you tried ten all at once you'll never know.

ROGER: (*chuckles*) Scientifically speaking, I suppose you're right.

BETTY: (*stands up and tucks the money safely away*) Well, hey, thanks for the bread. You sure I can't give you nothin' for it?

ROGER: You already have.

BETTY: I didn't give you a damned thing.

ROGER: You gave me my life.

BETTY: (*considers this peculiar observation briefly*) I guess there can be well-dressed crazy people, too.

ROGER: (*laughs*) What I meant was, something about this peculiar conversation has made me change my mind.

BETTY: About what?

ROGER: (*quite calmly*) About killing myself.

BETTY: (*stares at him, truly perplexed*) Killin' yourself?

ROGER: Yes.

BETTY: Why'd you do a stupid thing like that?

ROGER: I'm afraid it would take me quite a few hours to properly answer that question.

BETTY: Well, I ain't got no few hours.

ROGER: I, by way of contrast, now probably have another forty years or so, thanks to you.

BETTY: (*with a shrewd look*) Hey, Jack, if I gave you that much, how about layin' another twenty-five on me?

ROGER: (*laughs*) That would come to about fifty dollars an hour—not far below the professional rate for this sort of service. Oddly enough, I have only seven dollars left at the moment.

BETTY: Then why the fuck did you give me twenty-five bucks?

ROGER: For the soundest of reasons. I thought I wasn't going to be needing it anymore.

BETTY: Then why didn't you give me the other seven?

ROGER: Because you only asked for twenty-five.

BETTY: Shoot, if I knew you was gonna buy the farm I coulda asked for everything you got in the world. . . . How were you gonna do it?

ROGER: (*takes revolver out of briefcase*) With this.

BETTY: But now you ain't gonna do it, right?

ROGER: That's right.

BETTY: Then you ain't gonna be needin' that piece.

ROGER: Right again.

BETTY: Then give it to me.

ROGER: Very well. (*he rises with gun in hand*)

MAN'S VOICE (*offstage*): All right, you son of a bitch, drop that gun!

Roger whirls, startled, and faces offstage, still holding the revolver.

MAN'S VOICE: Get back, lady.

Betty jumps back a few feet, panicked.

MAN'S VOICE: Drop it!

ROGER: But I was just—

He gestures with the gun toward Betty. Two shots ring out. Roger groans and crumples to the bench, then to the ground.

MAN'S VOICE: You okay, lady?

Betty, stricken, staggers to the bench, sits and begins to weep as the curtain slowly falls.

❋   ❋   ❋

We've already talked about nonjoke comic monologues, but what about the creation of nonjoke humorous sketches? Are they feasible? Of course. For example, not long ago, I wrote a nonjoke sketch based on an easily recognizable subject, but one that would be appropriate only for certain audiences. You would not present material of this sort—or the preceding sketch—to an audience consisting largely of children, or, for that matter, to a television audience. The material requires the context of a sophisticated theatrical revue.

In introducing it here, I'll first note that, by the late 1970s, it had become common to see, in a corner of the television screen, the tiny figure of an interpreter using sign language to communicate to hearing-impaired viewers the general gist of newscasts, dramas, documentaries, and other forms of entertainment.

While watching a newscast one evening in which there was reference to the crime of rape, it occurred to me that one of these television signing specialists might find himself in an embarrassing situation if the signal for some common word were so pictorial that he seemed to be making an indecent gesture—when, in reality, the translator simply was rendering a perfectly respectable word, such as *rape, intercourse, breast,* or whatever.

You will see that, with a single exception, there are no jokes or inherently funny lines in the panel discussion that comprises the spoken text of the following scene. Not only are the words precisely what we would expect of a serious and responsible discussion by a panel of academic authorities, but in the performance of the sketch the players are specifically warned against "playing it for laughs." Doing so would, in fact, have the paradoxical effect of diminishing the laughter, whereas if the sketch is performed perfectly straight-faced, the laughter will be heartier because of the incongruity between what the panelists are saying and what the unfortunate young man —a last-minute replacement signing specialist—is forced to do as a result of their repeated references to matters sexual.

To go over the last point from another angle, such a sketch would be highly objectionable if a broad-comedian—say, Jerry Lewis or Milton Berle—played the part of the translator. Jerry and Milton, as consummate practitioners of their craft, would get laughs, but appropriately so only at a men's smoker or bawdy revue. Better casting for the role of the interpreter would be someone like Christopher Guest, Bill Murray, or Martin Short. The realistic, non-show-biz quality of such performers would increase the atmosphere of reality and hence make the scene funnier.

HELP FOR THE HEARING-IMPAIRED

A living room–type set in a television studio. All that is required is a table or two to accommodate four guest panelists and the host, a couple of potted palms, and some sort of simple backdrop, perhaps with bookshelves and a window. At the start of our scene, the panelists are already in position. The host enters and speaks to the camera.

HOST: Good evening, and welcome again to "Dialogues in Democracy." Tonight our panel discussion brings together once again four distinguished experts well-qualified to comment on one of the pressing problems facing our society. This evening's discussion will deal, specifically, with the crisis of sexual identity in the modern world. And now our panel. . . .

First of all we have the Rev. Dr. Thomas Whitman, of Union Theological Seminary. Next is Prof. Gertrude Albertson of the Population Control Council, Dr. Mortimer Klein of the psychiatric department of Mt. Sinai Hospital, and Prof. Stephen Marquette of the Institute of Forensic Psychiatry at Yale University.

Incidentally, our hearing-impaired viewers will be glad to hear—(*in square manner, as if making a joke*) or should I say will be glad to *see*—that this evening's discussion will be rendered in *sign language* by Mr. Ralph Forman, of the National Council for the Deaf.

A serious-faced young man steps quickly into an oval frame, which gives the audience a view of him more or less from the waist up. A square of black velvet can hang below the frame so that we see only that portion of him surrounded by the oval.

REPLACEMENT: No, no, I'm not Mr. Forman.

HOST: You're not?

REPLACEMENT: No, Mr. Forman was unavoidably detained, so he sent me over to fill in for him. I don't even know what's going to be discussed.

HOST: Oh, I see. Well, thank you very much for being with us.

REPLACEMENT: You're welcome.

From this point on he gives a straightforward sign language rendering of everything said. At least a few of the gestures should be easily understood by the audience. This can be done as regards words such as big, small, smile, etc. In general, however, unless the comic playing this part wishes to do a bit of authentic research, the bulk of the hand gestures will be innocuous and faked, rather than legitimate. The laughs will come from certain familiar all-too-explicit sexual gestures.

HOST: Now, then—Dr. Klein, you are, quite properly, recognized as one of our society's leading authorities in the area of sex research.

At hearing the words sex research, the replacement signer does a very slight take, looking to the group at center stage, then, with a quick eyebrow shrug, gets back to work.

HOST: Which was the first of your books, by the way, to achieve international recognition?

KLEIN: That was one titled *Repressed Sexuality and Patterns of Masturbation.*

A fraction of a second after hearing the key words, the signer pantomimes the words, finishing with the classic male street gesture for masturbation.

NOTE: *It is important that the comic maintain his dignified, genteel demeanor throughout and not break up or "camp" his approach.*

ALBERTSON: Yes, that was the first work of yours, doctor, that attracted the attention of those of us at the Sex Behavior Institute. I clearly recall perceiving at once the underlying importance of your findings to my own studies on homosexuality.

At this the replacement does another slight take, then the classic vaude-ville or nightclub-comic gestures to indicate gayness, the little finger across one eyebrow, a pursing of the lips, etc.

KLEIN: Thank you very much.

HOST: Dr. Whitman, what recent changes, if any, do you detect as regards society's sexual standards?

WHITMAN: Well, the question is a bit too general, if I may say so. Some things change, others do not. It's quite clear, for example, that the once rigid Victorian attitudes towards masturbation (*replacement again makes the gesture*) are no longer dominant. Today people are much more tolerant about masturbation, whereas concerning *other* forms of sexual function society's attitudes today, even in this period of so-called sexual freedom, are actually *stricter* than ever.

MARQUETTE: What specifics are you referring to?

WHITMAN: Well, consider *rape.*

Replacement makes the classic Italian gesture of thrusting the right fist into the air while slapping the right upper arm with the left hand and making a fierce face.

HOST: Rape?

WHITMAN: Yes, rape. (*Replacement makes the same gesture each time.*)

HOST: Very well. So far we've mentioned *homosexuality, masturbation,* and *rape.* To what other aspects of sexual behavior do you feel we ought to direct our attention this evening?

ALBERTSON: My own feeling is that we should explore the fascination of the American male with the female's secondary sexual organs.

HOST: Which are?

ALBERTSON: The breasts, of course.

Replacement makes the appropriate two-handed gesture. By this point he is doing more exaggerated but still serious-faced takes to the panel, conveying the idea that he is personally quite shocked by the entire discussion. He conveys an "I can't believe this is happening" attitude, while still making his gestures as explicit as possible.

HOST: The breasts.

ALBERTSON: Yes. Now you see, in certain Latin American cultures, by way of contrast, the primary object of sexual fascination on the part of the male is the buttocks. While most American men prefer a woman to be slim-hipped, youthful, and trim, the average Cuban, Mexican, or South American is more stimulated by women with large, fully rounded hips. There is far less concentration, as my research has borne out, on the part of Latins generally, with the female mammalia.

HOST: What other cultural differences do you note between the Anglo and the Latin communities, very generally speaking?

KLEIN: The South American culture, specifically, is on the one hand old-fashioned and respectful, perhaps more so than the American, but then once the male's sexual intentions have been clarified, he moves directly to his task, we might say. For example, he is less concerned than North American culture in placing emphasis on foreplay.

From this point on, it is not necessary to indicate in the script all the various places where sign language gestures relate to the key words. The gestures themselves, for the most part, seem—if judged in isolation—vulgar, shocking. The conversation continues on its level of dignity and intelligence, with not a trace of joking, simpering, or aren't-we-devils? attitude.

KLEIN: It's also significant, in my view, that the Latin attitude toward *rape* is markedly different from our own. Both cultures approach the subject seriously, needless to say, but definitions of what constitutes rape would be different in the two cultures.

    For example, if an adult American male were, let us say, to rip open a woman's blouse and fondle her against her will, this might be legally construed, in certain states, as incidental to, or contributing to, a case of rape. Whereas in a South American state, it might be considered one of the prerogatives of machismo to not only rip open a blouse, fondle the mammalia, or forcibly discard other garments—(*replacement rips open his own shirt, pulls out a pair of shorts that have been positioned in front of his body but inside his trousers*)—even to the accompaniment of hortatory inducements to oral sex. The courts would deal very severely with such behavior here, although even within the United States there are, of course, regional differences, some of which involve race. In the case of the white man, for example, if the victimized female is black—

Replacement makes a sort of old-fashioned carrying-the-tray comedy shuffling step.

HOST: Rev. Whitman, I wonder what you might perceive as one of the obvious aspects of male sexual immaturity in contemporary society?

WHITMAN: I would say that it's primarily a matter of lack of social control. The mature adult male has no difficulty whatever in discussing the most intimate or important aspects of sexuality in a disinterested and responsible fashion. The immature male, on the other hand, perhaps because in our culture he is almost daily bombarded by sexually stimulating input— we're talking now about the advertisements for pantyhose, the full-color girdle ads in the Sunday *New York Times*, the so-called "jiggle" factor on such television series as "Harry's Girls," "Charlie's Angels," and "Irving's Prostitutes"—all of this, as I say, keeps the immature American male in a state of semi-arousal so that any additional stimuli, which may be relatively innocuous—may serve to set off a spasm of uncontrolled behavior.

ALBERTSON: I quite agree, doctor. It is refreshing indeed to be able to discuss these matters with such responsible gentlemen as yourselves. I would certainly not be able, in the average social context, to discuss male or female masturbation, foreplay, oral-genital patterns—

As the replacement signer listens to the woman saying these words, he begins to fall victim to the very behavior she is criticizing. He now breathes rather heavily as he continues with his sign language; he stares intently at the woman as she continues.

ALBERTSON: Some young men, it is quite clear, could not listen to a responsible discussion about *rape, orgasm,* multiple *female* orgasm, *group* sex, the employment of extra verbal or pictorial forms of sexual stimulation; mutual masturbation short of orgasm or leading to orgasm, either individually, sequentially, or simultaneously; the importance of the articulated verbal component in intercourse, the use of whispered, or for that matter, shouted terms of endearment or arousal—"Oh, baby, yes, yes, do it!"— and that sort of thing. Many immature American males, as I say, are simply incapable of accommodating—

The replacement at this point is driven crazy by the words, his own gestures, etc. He flips out, runs to the table, and flings himself on Dr. Albertson. The others try to restrain him.

*   *   *

A few of years ago, I wrote a nonjoke sketch dealing with the subject of genetic engineering, a subject then much in the news. Notice, though, how in the piece reality is stretched to absurd limits.

HOST: Naturally we couldn't operate successfully here in the "Comedy Zone" unless we had some very important connections. Some of these— though you may find it hard to believe—are with the *future*. We are able to take you at this moment, in fact, to the year 3047.

Now, it's interesting that very often, when people conjecture about the future, they predict a totalitarian state of the sort envisioned by George Orwell or Aldous Huxley. But our own connections to the future indicate that just the opposite will be the case. Freedom will have been greatly enhanced. So greatly, in fact, that the Creator will, at that point, put us on earth with nothing more than *brains*.

Cut to the corner of a laboratory. Greenish and purplish lights around the edges, plus low-key, ominous "Star Wars" background music clue us to the realization that there are weird vibes here. A "Donovan's Brain" setup is visible. What appears to be an actual brain is in a clear tank, perhaps under a plastic shell, floating in some pale greenish bubbling liquid, illuminated by dramatic side lights. A strange-looking individual—perhaps totally bald and wearing a futuristic jacket—stands at the side of the platform, communicating in the manner of a friendly automobile dealer, circa 1984.

HOST: (*voiceover*) In fact, freedom will be so complete that you'll actually get to choose what systems you want to add to your own body.

SALESMAN: (*He makes notes on a clipboard.*) All right, sir, now you probably won't want to stay in one place, so may I assume you'll want a body with *legs* attached to it? Okay. (*a light glows*) Fine. That'll be eight hundred dollars.

And I assume you'll want a *vision* system? Okay, that means eyes. The hookup to the brain will be made at no extra charge for installation.

You'll be wanting to hear and *smell* things, I assume? Okay, that's auditory and olfactory systems. Twelve hundred dollars each, with the usual ears and nose wiring thrown in.

Next, one of the more interesting options. Will you want to be able to reproduce at least approximations of yourself? Reproductive systems are available. But I warn you, they're far from trouble-free. In fact, the history of the race to the present shows that there are still a lot of bugs in this particular mechanism, largely because, once installed, the systems tend to get out of control. Just as the fuel-ingestion system—eating, drinking, and all that—tends to have pretty omnivorous interests, so the reproductive systems frequently show remarkably poor powers of discrimination. People are constantly making wrong choices. And sometimes, even after they've made reasonably wise choices, the systems themselves, apparently operating almost independently, continue to send out signals and to be prepared to function far beyond the race's need, in terms of the primary functional purpose. If you'll take my advice, you'll just skip this one. It's true that it's importantly connected to the pleasure system, but the pleasure receptors can be operated by other means. The decision, of course, is yours. Wadda'ya say? (*brain turns from side to side*) No? All right, sir, but don't say I didn't warn you.

MUSIC: *Brief play-off*

10

Creating Comic Essays

The first thing we need to establish about comic essays is that there is no one right tone. There are different approaches, different styles. As a matter of fact, each humorist, especially the better ones, has an identifiable voice. Art Buchwald and Russell Baker both amuse us, but no one would have the slightest difficulty telling which of these funny gentlemen wrote a given piece. Erma Bombeck, Andy Rooney, and Dave Barry have their own styles.

The best advice for young humorists who want to explore this particular avenue of expression is the point made in *How to Be Funny:* Read the masters. Track down everything of Robert Benchley's that was ever published. Read all the James Thurber you can get your hands on. S. J. Perelman, too. And, of course, Woody Allen. Saturate yourself with this kind of fare. Read it morning, noon, and night for weeks. The point is not that you should borrow so much as a syllable from any of these outstanding humorists but rather that you should prepare your mind to think in a strange, loose, even silly way, which is what all great literary humorists do.

Benchley and Woody Allen often write essays that are satirical, pieces that make fun of a particular style of serious writing. Woody sometimes uses a sort of *New York Review of Books* intellectual discourse as the framework on which to hang his marvelous jokes and non sequiturs. Benchley would sometimes take on a particular target—a treasurer's report to a social organization, or an action story by Hemingway, for example. Obviously, to write a satire of that sort you must first familiarize yourself with the original. I do not suggest that you, too, must satirize Hemingway or Kiwanis lectures. Select your own targets. Actually, strangely, these almost have a way of selecting you. By that I mean that something about the serious form just strikes you funny. That's usually how it starts, with that moment of something, as I say, suddenly presenting its absurd side, though it was intended to be totally serious.

There is no reason to limit yourself to this one form of comic essay, however. Russell Baker doesn't satirize the form of anything. He just shares with us his own witty or insightful ideas about whatever is going on in the contemporary world. Erma Bombeck, too, does not deal in satires on serious models. Andy Rooney writes, and usually delivers on "60 Minutes," low-key but always funny commentaries on aspects of modern life that most of us take for granted, or at least don't pay particular attention to.

Do I have a favorite humorist? Something in me doesn't like to specify favorites because in citing one you're ruling out a great many other gifted practitioners of the same art, but I've always been a pushover for Benchley. Another of my favorites is a man who sometimes isn't appreciated as a humorist at all: Jim Murray, the gifted sportswriter for the *Los Angeles Times*. He crams more funny lines into one of his daily columns than the average comedian's writers give him on Oscar night. But Jim's jokes are more than just laugh-provoking. They often have an insightful or poetic element to them. I strongly recommend that any student of the art of literary humor get a published collection of Murray's work, or simply subscribe to the *Los Angeles Times* and give Jim's columns careful study. They'll make you laugh your head off, though sometimes they can make you cry.

Twice in my life I've tried to read aloud a column Murray wrote some years ago about the Special Olympics, in which, as most everyone knows, the participants are mentally or otherwise handicapped children. In both cases I could not retain enough emotional control to complete the reading. Murray's artistry is that powerful. In fact, he may be the only humorist who makes you laugh and cry with the same ease. If any of the readers of this book are interested in athletics, they will already know that Murray is a giant in the field of sports journalism as well. I also direct your attention to Al Martinez, of the *Los Angeles Times*. His essays are often serious and touching, but when he's in a funny mood, he certainly exhibits the comic gift.

Another form of humorous essay is exemplified by Thurber's "The Night the Bed Fell Down," which every student of humor ought to know almost by heart. It's interesting that the style of writing is quite straightforward— no Benchley, Woody Allen, or Perelman jokes or crazy twists. The tone is very matter of fact. The reason the story is a classic, nevertheless, is that the events described are hilariously funny.

I employed this same plain-speaking style in recounting an actual experience, the text of which follows, that my aunt, my mother and I had when I was sixteen and Orson Welles sprang his famous *War of the Worlds* broadcast on an unsuspecting nation.

THE END OF THE WORLD

It was in the year of our Lord 1938—the last year, I briefly thought, that the Lord was to vouchsafe—that my mother, my Aunt Margaret, and I (along with several million other Americans) went through an experience that not many people will ever be privileged to share. We were on hand when the world came to an end.

The occasion was the famous Orson Welles *War of the Worlds* broadcast. I have never before told the story of my own response to that broadcast, because I have seen the reaction of those not victimized by Welles to those who were. It is the standard reaction of the level-headed citizen to the crackpot. In my own defense, and in that of all the other crackpots who went squawking off into that unforgettable night like startled chickens, I offer a word of explanation. Admittedly anybody who heard the entire Welles broadcast from beginning to end and believed a word of it should be under observation. Unfortunately, millions did not have the opportunity. For various reasons a great many people did not hear the first few minutes of the show. If some of these were in the mood for dance music they accepted what a randomly discovered orchestra was playing, lit cigarettes, or picked up magazines and settled back to listen.

In a room on the eighth floor of the Hotel Raleigh, an ancient and rundown hostelry on Chicago's Near North Side that was our home that year, I was lying on the floor reading a book. Feeling in the mood for background music, I turned on our radio, fiddled with the dial until I heard dance music, and returned to my book. In the adjoining room, Aunt Margaret and my mother were sitting side-saddle on the bed playing cards.

After a moment, the music was interrupted by a special "flash" from the CBS news department—the authenticity of which there was not the slightest reason to doubt—to the effect that, from his observatory, a scientist had just detected a series of mysterious explosions of a gaseous nature on the planet Mars. After this fascinating bit of intelligence, the announcer said, "And now we return you to the program in progress," and music was heard once more. I ask the reader: Would you doubt anything Walter Cronkite or John Chancellor told you on their evening newscast? Of course not.

There soon followed a series of news items, each more exciting than its predecessor, revealing that the strange explosions on Mars had caused a downpour of meteors in the general area of Princeton, New Jersey. By this time the music had been entirely forgotten, I had cast aside my book, and, sitting cross-legged by the radio, listened with mounting horror while the network news department went into action to bring America's radio listeners up-to-the-minute coverage on what was transpiring in New Jersey.

More meteors had landed, it seemed, and one of them, in crashing to earth, had caused the death of several hundred people. CBS at once dispatched a crew to the scene, and it was not long before firsthand reports began coming in. Up to now there was not the slightest reason for those who had tuned in the dance music—assuming their general ignorance of science—to question the truth of a word that had been broadcast. This granted, there was no particular reason for being suspicious of what immediately followed.

With disbelief rising in his throat, a special-events man on the scene near Princeton reported that one of the Martian meteors appeared to be no meteor at all, but some sort of spaceship. It actually appeared, he said, although one could scarcely believe one's ears, that this giant blob of metal, half-buried in the New Jersey mud, was not a blind, inert fragment shrugged off by some burly planet hurtling through infinity. Rather, it appeared to have been "fashioned" somehow. Bolts and hinges were in evidence.

The National Guard had roped off the area, allowing no one near the gargantuan hulk. This, as far as one could determine, was simply a formal precaution, for it seemed clear that even if some strange form of life had made the flight from Mars inside the meteor, it could certainly not have survived the crushing impact when the weird craft plunged into the earth.

By this time my mother and Aunt Mag were also huddled around the speaker, wide-eyed. The contents of the news broadcast were inherently unbelievable, and yet we had it on the authority of the Columbia Broadcasting System that such things were actually happening.

But if our credulity had been strained up to now, it had yet to face the acid test. The network next presented an army officer who made a dignified plea for calm, stating that the National Guard and the New Jersey police had the situation completely in hand. He requested that motorists give the area a wide berth and concluded with a few words conveying his complete assurance that it would be only a matter of hours until order had been restored.

But it at once developed that his confidence had been badly misplaced. The network interrupted his sermon with another report from the scene, frankly emotional in nature, which confirmed the suspicions that there might be life of some kind inside one of the rockets. Fearful listeners were now treated to the benumbing description, by a patently frightened newsman, of the emergence of strange, leathery creatures from the spaceship.

I suppose if one has been convinced that there is life on Mars it matters little whether Martians be leathery, rubbery, or made of Philadelphia cream cheese. The description of grotesque monsters by this time seemed in no detail too fantastic; what *was* fantastic was that there were any creatures in the rocket at all. Their slavering mouths, jellylike eyes, and the devastating fire they directed toward the soldiers who dared stand and face them were all minor almost unimportant details and even now they are not clear in my mind.

The National Guard troops dispatched to the scene were massacred almost at once by the huge interplanetary invaders (there were several of them now, for other ships were landing), and in the confusion of the battle the network's facilities were impaired and its "man on the spot" was cut off in mid-sentence.

CBS, however, was equal to the occasion. Civic and government spokesmen were rushed to microphones; dutifully—and ineffectively, as it turned out—they instructed the populace not to panic. An airplane was sent up over the trouble area and the network continued its blow-by-blow description from the clouds. My mother, my aunt and I didn't wait to hear more. We looked at each other, hardly knowing what to say.

"Good God," Aunt Mag gasped, her face pale, "what's going on?"

"I don't know," I said. "What do you think we ought to do?"

"There's only one thing *to* do," my mother responded. "We can all go over to church and wait there to see what happens." She referred to the Holy Name Cathedral not many blocks from our hotel.

"I don't know if that's such a good idea," I said. "There might be crowds."

Just then we heard the word *Chicago* on the radio. "More spaceships have been reported," a voice intoned. "Observers have seen them over Cleveland, Detroit and Chicago."

"Jesus, Mary and Joseph!" Aunt Mag shouted. "We'll be killed right here in this hotel!" She ran back into the other room and grabbed her coat.

"What are you doing, Maggie?" my mother asked.

"What do you think?" Mag said. "We can't stay here and be killed. Let's get out of here."

"You're right," Mother said. "We'll go over to the church. Who has the key to the room?"

"Who the hell cares about locking the door?" Mag said. "It doesn't matter now."

I was putting on my coat, still too shocked to say much. Oddly enough, and this I recall quite clearly, my predominant emotion was not fear but blank stupefaction. I remember saying "Gosh," idiotically, over and over, and frowning and shaking my head from side to side. I couldn't believe it, and yet I had to, on the basis of years of conditioning. CBS News had never lied to me before.

Aunt Mag was still fluttering around the room. The door was now ajar, but she was like a bird that, with its cage opened, doesn't know just where to fly.

"What are you looking for?" Mother asked.

"My glasses," Mag said, in a mixture of anger and panic.

"You're not going to have time to read anything, Maggie," Mother told her. "Just get your hat and let's get the hell out of here!"

"If I don't need my glasses, what good is my hat?" said my aunt.

"Never mind," said my mother. "Let's go."

They both stopped to look at me. Perhaps I was a bit pale.

"Are you all right?" my mother asked.

"Gosh," I said, resourcefully, and we headed for the door. By this time people all over the nation were reacting similarly. Many stayed glued to their radios and heard the reassuring conclusion to the program, but millions, like us, rushed off wildly. They had not heard the introduction to the broadcast, and they did not stay to be reassured by its finale.

Police stations, newspapers, and churches were badly shaken by the first wave of frightened, fleeing citizens. In one New Jersey town, a terrified man rushed into the First Baptist Church during evening services and announced that the end was at hand. The pastor made a futile attempt to quiet his flock by leading them in a prayer for deliverance.

Switchboards at CBS stations from coast to coast were clogged for hours by callers, some angry, some panicky.

In New York's Harlem more than one police station was besieged by terror-stricken men and women seeking refuge.

Conscience-plagued sinners all over the country began making efforts to return stolen money, confess undisclosed sins and right old wrongs. People in houses rushed into the streets, and people on the streets rushed into houses.

About this time Welles and the members of his cast, glancing toward the control room of their studio, perceived that it was crowded with policemen. They must have finished the program in a state almost as disturbed as that of many of their listeners. Needless to say, none of this was known to us at the time.

"Button your overcoat, Stevie," my mother said. "You'll catch cold when we go out."

This remark did not at the moment strike any of us as amusing. I buttoned my coat, and we hurried out. My mother and aunt ran down the hall. I followed at a slower pace, not because I was trying to maintain a shred of discretion, but because I was too stunned to move with speed. Rounding a corner, we burst suddenly upon a dignified-looking young woman holding a little girl in her arms.

"Run for your life!" my mother cried at the woman, at the same time jabbing a shaky but determined finger at the elevator button. In response, the woman looked at her with no expression whatsoever.

"Pick up your child and come with us!" Aunt Mag shouted, wide-eyed. The woman paused a moment and then laughed right in my aunt's face.

Mag was outraged. "Oh, yes," she sputtered with withering sarcasm. "Go ahead and laugh! But for the sake of that dear baby in your arms, don't you laugh!"

At this the young woman drew back in alarm, evidently concluding that she was confronted by three violently deranged people who might do her physical harm. She looked at me questioningly.

"We just heard on the radio," I said, "that there's something up in the sky."

The merest flicker of bemusement crossed her face, but the woman did not speak. It was clear that she was hovering between two alternatives, Alan Funt not having yet been let loose upon the world: Either we were a trio of incredibly inventive and determined practical jokesters, or we were insane. The third possibility—that there might actually be something up in the sky—apparently was never given serious consideration. Instead, she shifted the child in her arms to a more secure position and retreated a few steps down the hall, walking backwards so as to keep an eye on us. But my aunt was not to accord this gesture the honor of understanding. She moved angrily toward the woman, and her right hand pointed up toward the heavens. She must have looked like a witch calling down a curse.

"You ought to get down on your *knees*," she shouted, like a complete nut, "instead of laughing at people! We're going to church to pray, and that's what you ought to be doing right this minute—praying!"

Before the woman could interpret this admonition, a soft whir and click announced that the elevator had reached our floor. A moment later the door slid back and the smiling face of the Negro operator greeted us. Never have I seen a smile fade so fast. If this scene were to be enacted in an old motion picture, the man's assignment would be to open his eyes wide with fear and say, "Feet, get movin'!" In any event, the violence with which we dashed into the elevator at once convinced the operator that all was not well. My mother's first words confirmed his suspicions I'm sure.

"Hurry up and take us down," she gasped. "They're up in the sky!"

"Who is?" asked the man, aghast.

"How do we know who is?" my aunt shouted. "But you'd better get out of this hotel right now while you've still got the chance!"

"Yes, ma'am!" he whispered, withdrawing completely to his corner of the elevator. For perhaps ten seconds he regarded us warily, holding the car-control handle at full speed. Then, torn between fear and curiosity, he succumbed to the latter. "What did you say the matter was?" he said, frowning.

Aunt Mag's patience was exhausted. How many times did you have to explain things to people? "They're up in the sky!" she repeated. "Haven't you been listening to the radio?"

"No, ma'am."

"Well, you'd better do something, let me tell you. The radio just said they're up over Chicago, so you'd better run for your life!"

I am sure that if the elevator operator had been convinced that an interplanetary invasion was underway, he would have faced the challenge as bravely as the next man. But instead, he apparently concentrated on the idea that he was cooped up in a tiny cubicle with three dangerous lunatics. As a result, he became positively petrified. Fortunately for his nervous system, we arrived at the main floor at this point. He yanked the door release and shrank back against the wall as we thundered past him into the lobby.

Though we had met with icy disbelief twice in quick succession we were still ill-prepared for the sight that now greeted us. The lobby, which we had expected to find in turmoil, was a scene of traditional lobby-like calm. Nowhere was there evidence of the panic we had come to accept as the norm in a few short minutes. Aggravatingly, people were sitting about, smoking cigars, reading newspapers, speaking in subdued tones, or dozing peacefully in thick leather chairs.

It had been our intention to sweep through the lobby and proceed right across Dearborn Street, pausing only in the event that a sudden spaceship attack should force us to take cover, but something about the tranquillity around the registration desk presented a challenge we did not feel strong enough to resist. Indeed, we felt it our duty to warn the unfortunate souls who thought all was well that they were about to witness ultimate disaster.

The elevator man peered after us from what was now the safety of his cage as we raced to confront the blasé desk clerk.

"Is something wrong?" this worthy said quietly, evidently hoping that if something were amiss he could contain the area of alarm within his immediate vicinity.

"Well," said my aunt with a contemptuous sneer, "it's the end of the *world*, that's all that's wrong!"

The clerk's face was an impenetrable mask, although after a moment he permitted a suggestion of disdain to appear on it. I started to explain that on the radio—and then, in some clear, calm corner of my mind, I heard soft sounds in the corner of the lobby. It was a radio, and the sounds were not the sort a radio should be making at a time of worldwide crisis. The sounds, as a matter of fact, were of a commercial nature. Some other announcer on some other station was extolling the virtues of a brand of tomato soup.

A wave of shock passed through me as, in the instant, I saw things as they really were. Turning to my mother, I began speaking very fast, explaining exactly what had happened. For a split second she wavered, hoping, yet fearing, and then for her, too, the ice broke.

Light, followed by painful embarrassment, also dawned on Aunt Mag. Like bewildered sheep we retreated, excruciatingly aware that all heads were turned toward us, that the clerk was smiling at us in a frightfully patronizing way, and that never again would we be able to walk through that lobby without casting our eyes to the floor.

"We'll have to move out of this place," my mother said.

Our next reaction, upon us before we could even stagger back into the elevator, was one of wild hilarity bordering on hysteria. We laughed until our sides ached and tears poured down our cheeks. We fell into heavy chairs and laughed some more, and at long last, we pulled ourselves together, still shrieking with laughter, and started back toward our quarters. We laughed so hard going up in the elevator that I don't recall the elevator operator's reactions. I'm sure he must have assumed we were now in the euphoric stage, still nutty as three fruitcakes, if no longer dangerous.

We spent a restless night, alternately laughing and saying, "We'll never be able to face all those people again."

The next day on the way to school, I glanced at a newspaper headline and discovered that we had not been alone.

*   *   *

Another approach of the comic writer is that of the sardonic or cynical essay. Jonathan Swift employed this technique when, in writing to the generally unfeeling English of his day about famine conditions in Ireland and what the English viewed as the explosive growth of the Irish population, he recommended that a handy solution all around might be to encourage the cannibalistic eating of babies by the Irish, thus killing two birds with one stone. In writing humor of this sort, of course, the humorist is really getting something off his chest that he cares deeply about and simply employs the method of irony to make his point. It would also profit you to listen to Lenny Bruce's old albums. Strictly speaking, Lenny was a speaker rather than a writer, but his perceptions were brilliant, and whether your own interests involve performing or publishing, Bruce can be a good stimulant.

The idea for an essay of this sort occurred to me some years ago when I first encountered the information that blacks score lower than whites on intelligence tests, largely because of the disgracefully inadequate education they've been given, but also—according to a certain theory—because they are congenitally, genetically somewhat less intelligent than whites.

Needless to say, the scientific community, by and large, does not accept the theory, but there has been a good deal of intellectual interest and debate about it. Of course, it falls very pleasantly on the ears of white racists. So it was those people, not blacks, who were the target of my satire.

Note that comic essays of this sort, as a rule, do not make us laugh so heartily as do the other, more common forms. But they are still worth reading, and they do give rise to a bitter chuckle.

The Jensen Theory

It was in the year 2020, well after geneticist Arthur Jensen had died, that his long-discredited theories, with certain important modifications, were proven to be surprisingly valid. It was Jensen, as some readers will recall, who had, in the 1960s, first published the theory that the reason blacks in America generally scored several points lower in intelligence tests—all other things being presumably equal—was explained only partially on the basis of the all-too-obviously inadequate education they received in the United States, and that the dominant explanatory factor was genetic. In other words, Jensen argued that, for whatever mysterious reasons—perhaps just the roll of the genetic dice extrapolated over untold eons—blacks, as a class, were naturally somewhat less intelligent than whites.

The qualifier *as a* class was, of course, crucial in preventing misapplications and misinterpretations of the theory, since hardly had rumors of Jensen's hypothesis first come to public attention than mean-spirited racists and black-haters had leaped to the totally erroneous conclusion that practically all blacks were mentally inferior to practically all whites. Something about the racists' own sense of social inferiority—well-grounded, needless to say—had made it necessary for them to consider themselves superior to something. One can even, to a degree, sympathize with such ignoramuses as regards the eagerness with which they grasped at evidence that seemed to indicate an actual superiority in them, based purely on the color of their skin.

The better informed were, of course, all along aware of the superiority of large numbers of blacks to large numbers of particular whites. But this fact was generally considered irrelevant—oddly enough, by both sides—in the early stages of the debate.

For having had the temerity to even conjecture along the lines that he defended, Jensen himself was, perhaps inevitably, accused of racism, a charge he consistently denied. To the end, he was, in fact, puzzled by this sort of criticism, since he felt that he had committed no offense worse than that of, say, pointing out the simple fact that the Japanese are, as a class, shorter than Caucasians as a class.

Jensen was, understandably, opposed by the great majority of scholars who concerned themselves with such questions, almost all of whom argued that the dominant and perhaps sole factor in explaining differences in intellectual achievement was the inferior environment available to blacks in the United States. Let a generation of whites, Jensen's critics argued, be raised in crime-infested slums and ghettos, attending disgracefully inadequate schools, living in poverty and squalor, suffering social stigma simply because of their skin color, and inevitably they too would score markedly lower on I.Q. tests.

And there, so far as the public seemed concerned, the argument rested for a good many years. Each side had stated its case, and both justice and charity seemed to be on the side of those who argued that environment, not heredity, was the main explanatory factor in the all-too-apparent differences in achievement between the two racial categories. But in the year 2007, an investigative project, funded in private and totally without fanfare, finally announced the results of a ten-year study of all relevant data. The research team, which numbered well over a hundred and which united sociologists, psychologists, anthropologists and biologists of fourteen nations, announced that there was, surprisingly, at least a germ of validity to Jensen's theories in that it proved to be *not* the case, after all, that all races and subracial ethnic categories were precisely equal in terms of intellectual capability, much less achievement, but that Jensen had nevertheless erred in assuming a simple either-or, black-and-white set of alternatives.

The philosophical rationale that motivated the disinterested curiosity of Dr. Albert Zeit, who drafted the original research proposal, grew out of his observation that inasmuch as no two things in the universe are—or even can be—identical, it is therefore highly unlikely, if not impossible, that any two peoples, whether defined racially, ethnically, religiously, or by any other criteria, would be identical as regards intellectual capacity.

Zeit realized that his initial argument was open to question and that it could, in fact, be nothing more than an assumption, however apparently reasonable. The word *thing*, after all, is vague, and it is legitimately questionable as to whether an entire race can be responsibly thought about, or discussed, under the unitary rubric of a *thing*. It was certainly theoretically possible, Zeit concluded, that even though no two individuals would be precisely the same as regards intellectual capacity, it might nevertheless prove to be the case that, if it were possible to average out all living representatives of all ethnic or racial classes, any statistical discrepancy between or among them might prove to be so small as to be insignificant.

But it was precisely the doubt as regards this philosophical question that led Zeit to spend several years seeking financial underwriting for a larger-scale investigation into the fascinating question that had so long perplexed science.

The United Nations, perhaps not surprisingly, had no interest in funding the relevant research since representatives of Third World countries in particular considered the question at issue troublesome, insulting, unscientific, dangerous, or all of the above. But a consortium of private and corporate funders, some of whom insisted on anonymity, was finally constructed.

The results of the subsequent research proved to be far more revolutionary—and, for some, disturbing—than would have been the case had Jensen's crude theories been validated. For what, in effect, finally emerged was that Zeit's philosophic speculation had proved to have wider application than he had guessed in his wildest daydreams. The truth, which seemed to surprise almost everyone concerned, was that after all environmental factors had been accounted for—which is to say, discounted—there were indeed purely racial and ethnic differences in intelligence—physical differences—among the thirty-seven groups studied.

The fact that only so small a number were taken into account is easily explained. Zeit and his colleagues recognized from the onset that they could neither obtain adequate funding, accumulate a large enough staff, nor personally live long enough as individuals to incorporate every living tribe into their study. They assumed, therefore, and quite reliably, as it turned out, that it was not necessary to study every single human subgroup; whatever conclusions suggested themselves on the basis of a large-enough sampling could no doubt be responsibly extrapolated over the entire population of earth.

In any event, one thing the research team found was not a crude whites-are-a-few-percentage-points-smarter-than-blacks, but that some individual African tribes were inferior and/or superior to others and that *the same held true of all other peoples on the earth, regardless of color.*

One of the first controversial, even sensational, findings that emerged from the painstaking study was that Jews, as a class, scored consistently highest on all tests to which the groups studied were subjected.

While this was ego-gratifying to the few members of Zeit's team who were Jewish, and ultimately to all Jews who learned of the findings, it introduced a scientifically troublesome note into the study in that Jewishness is primarily a matter of religion rather than physicality. But if Jews themselves have historically been confused on this point, even scholars may be forgiven for a degree of imprecision. It is possible, of course, to define Jews as Semites, which describes them in a physical and tribal sense, but there still is a bit of haze over the question in that Jews are only one of the planet's Semitic tribes. A substudy found, nevertheless, that those nominally considered Jews—regardless of whether they adhered to or had abandoned their traditional religion—scored significantly higher than other Semitic tribes.

An Arab who had personally abandoned the Islamic religion did not deny the relevant facts but attributed them to the superiority of Western education over that generally available in Islamic communities. The Japanese, it was also learned, were only slightly behind the Jews as regards all-around intellectual potential. The Chinese were not far behind, in third place.

Next came the people of Scotland, Germany, and France, in that order.

The English, Swedes, and Russians followed, and after them, the people of Holland, Belgium, and Wales.

It might be assumed that those grouped in the top ten or so would be relatively pleased by their once-and-for-all, statistically established relative superiority to the larger number of groups rated behind them on the scale of 0 to 37. But any such assumption—had it actually been made—would have proved very wide of the mark. In fact, every group except the Jews responded in varying degrees of irrationality, paranoia, outbursts of patriotic irrelevance and surly defensiveness. Far from being pleased to discover that they were the second most intelligent people on earth, the Japanese immediately questioned the validity of the study and demanded to know in what narrowly defined ways they were inferior to the Jews.

As for the Chinese, they rioted in the streets of major cities of the People's Republic as well as in Chinese enclaves in the free world at having been told that they were inferior to their former oppressors, the Japanese. The Russians, shocked by what they considered their low rating, which they sensed was hardly compatible with their former dreams of world domination, rejected the findings outright.

As for Italians, they were furious at what they considered the unfairness of having their average lowered by the inclusion of the Sicilians in their group. Sicilian spokesmen responded, perhaps understandably, that if the Northern Italians felt so strongly on the subject, they might profitably consider granting independence to the southern isle.

The Spanish, Irish, Greeks, Poles, Czechs, Turks, and Portuguese were not only shocked by what they considered their poor ranking but seemed particularly incensed to learn that they had been rated lower than the Hungarians, whose notorious deviousness, it now seemed possible, was attributable at least in part to their relative intellectual superiority. Indians, Pakistanis, Vietnamese, Thais and other Oriental tribes seemed astonished chiefly to have been rated lower than the Chinese and Japanese. The fact that the study also found them slightly less intelligent, on the average, than almost all European tribes they considered not nearly of such importance, perhaps because for long centuries their philosophers and scholars had conceded the scientific and practical superiority of the Western mind while insisting on the moral and spiritual excellence of the Oriental consciousness.

As for the incorporation of the social entity sometimes described as "the American people," it proved to be almost impossible, primarily for the obvious reason that no such entity exists in racial and ethnic terms. The U.S. population was obviously a mixed bag of over a hundred different tribal groups. That, plus several centuries of intermarriage, resulted simply in the finding that while it was possible to incorporate the results of I.Q. studies applying to various *segments* of the American population, the direct relevance of such data to the main thrust of the study was so questionable as to be scientifically worthless.

One important finding—alas, usually overlooked in the storm of subsequent debate and denunciation—was that the differences between the highest-rated group and the lowest rated group was only seven points, on a 0-to-100 scale.

Also overlooked was the following footnote: "We wish to stress that the ratings, statistically inescapable as they may be, apply only to the time period from 1990 to 2020. Over any vastly longer span of time, it is impossible on the basis of available evidence to say what the vagaries of evolutionary chance might bring about as regards a long list of physical factors, which includes brain cell function as certainly as it includes height, shape of eye, straightness or kinkiness of hair, color of skin, or any other physical factor."

It was inevitable, of course, that the results of even so responsible and well-conducted a study would be distorted, according to the biases and purposes, good or evil, of a thousand and one distorters. Shameful racists—Nazis, Ku Kluxers, white citizens councils, fascist groups—chose simply to ignore the fact that they, as individuals, were demonstrably inferior to millions of individuals in the races they despised. Indeed, it soon emerged that those who were the least intelligent chose to clothe themselves in the mantle of the statistical superiority of their own ethnic and racial categories, whereas truly superior individuals emphasized that differences in intelligence among the world's tribes were slight.

A particularly wise point was made by New York's Cardinal Robert Devlin, who said, "There are those who argue that because certain individuals, or races, are statistically inferior they should therefore be dealt with harshly, critically or unjustly. But the moral law is very clear that precisely the opposite is the case, for all the great teachers of the ages instructed that we must be fair and affectionate to all, including even our enemies. And certainly no one can accurately call himself Christian who says, 'Because you are inferior to me I am therefore entitled to treat you basely.' "

After the arrival of the aliens, in 2094, of course, the striking intellectual inferiority of all human tribes was demonstrated, particularly as regards the murderous irrationality with which earthlings have traditionally responded to challenge or frustration.

It was not until 3013, alas, that biological and quiet approaches to the problem came to be widely accepted.

As of the present, we can only hope that another two thousand years of breeding for intelligence and courage will begin to make a dent in the problem. The aliens, to their credit, have been supportive, though largely because they had been driven to distraction by the general mindlessness of those who work for them.

May Zor, their god, bless our enterprise.

*   *   *

What sort of basic raw material can one draw upon for essay topics? Life. Just listen and observe, and the ideas will rush in on you in such waves that they'll knock you down if you don't brace yourself.

As I mentioned earlier, humorous essays often stem from strong feelings one has either for or against something. A few years ago I wrote a piece for *New West* magazine attacking the way some professional music critics had suddenly begun to take the more barbarous examples of punk and heavy-metal rock seriously. It seemed to me they were treating it as if they were writing about Beethoven.

This is the essay "Garbage Rock" as it was published:

This critic has the distinction of having been the first to detect the garbage rock movement. It is easy enough to assert, after the fact, that anyone might have realized the inevitability of the trend, given the success of punk rock. The fact remains that others did not. The shifting of the ground under all our feet was, in any event, over very quickly. Within less than a month the entire field of serious rock criticism had come to take garbage rock seriously, in large part because of my discovery that there are important clues to garbage rock music in the actual garbage produced by its more creative practitioners.

The historic breakthrough came when this writer, upon leaving the Bel-Air pad of Stanley Sickening, happened casually to glance at the contents of the four garbage cans (not to be confused with the group of the same name) that stood in the driveway awaiting pickup. A broken pair of Stanley's "sunglasses" (the quotation marks because he steadfastly refuses to wear them except at night or while performing), lying atop (athwart?) the rind of half a grapefruit, first caught my eye.

It was only the certainty, having thus left the premises, that Stanley himself was passed out cold, along with his business manager and tax attorney, on the kitchen floor, that gave me the courage to lift one of the cans into the back of my underslung '74 Chevy pickup. One could hardly, after all, pore through the gold mine of decaying artifacts in broad daylight.

Once home, I lugged the container, somewhat weightier than I had first thought, into my kitchen, got out a yellow legal-lined notepad and Gucci writing instrument, and set about the task of classification and analysis. One of the first clues fell easily enough from the tree, perhaps because I had been the first to note the superiority of Sickening's "Stab Me With Your Love" to the tiresome MOR harmonics of Jerome Kern's "All the Things You Are." Can it really surprise the reader that I next noted a toy rubber dagger, encrusted with—gravy? chopped liver? Not the sort of thing, certainly, one ordinarily sees in a garbage can, and yet very reasonably discarded. It was, after all, broken. Perhaps Stanley, tired of terrorizing stagehands and groupies with real knives (never mind the Cleveland incident and the three deaths), had resorted to the blatantly show biz fakery of a rubber approximation of the sadistic hardware which, even more than his inventive three-chord harmonies, initially brought him to public attention.

And what were the assorted broken eggshells? Clear but excruciatingly obvious representations of Sickening's own psychosexual emphasis on germination, birth, rebirth—the salacious appeal of apocalyptic destruction.

The three Campbell's tomato soup cans seemed almost to cry out loud, "Andy Warhol, Andy Warhol!" as I set them to one side of the kitchen table. The connection between Sickening and Warhol was evident enough. They both wore size ten-and-a-half shoes, were totally unknown in that insignificant area of the country between Pennsylvania and Wyoming, and— the clincher—had, during their teenage years, never learned the bridge to "Heart and Soul," but merely the first sixteen bars.

Perhaps only William Blake could have known the spiritual ecstasy with which, fingers trembling, I lifted three compartmentalized aluminum frozen TV dinner containers from the odiferous mèlange. Here it was again, the constant, even dominant, Stanley Sickening motif—the emphasis on the quick, the least troublesome, the slick, the prepackaged. And leave it to Sickening, with his incredible cat's sixth sense of where it's at, not to have scraped the last now-dried dollops of gelatinous pink gravy from the tins, as if to say, "Up yours, world! I'll take some of what you're dishing out, but I won't take all of it!"

Is it any wonder that many groupie Lolitas have publicly pleaded with Sickening and the other garbage rockers *not* to have sex with them—not even to do what he so gloriously celebrated in his early classic, "I'm Gonna Cop a Feel"—but rather to punch them repeatedly about the abdomen?

Roach Motel—obviously named after the famous Culver City motel opposite the old Hal Roach Studios—deserves more credit than it has been given for its sensitive use of insect spray cans attached to the necks of its members' guitars. Their fans are still laughing over the new record of broken windows, flying beer bottles, bloodshed, hostage taking, and general mayhem at Zeitgeist Hall last summer. Undoubtedly the last memories that fade will be of lung cancer occasioned by the insecticides, but you can't make an omelet without breaking eggs, as we say.

Speaking personally, and as much as I like garbage rock, I prefer the ideas of its leading representative even more, I asked Sickening, at our last meeting, where he thought he would go when he died. "To Pacoima," he said. In an instant I knew that his interest in Zen was utterly sincere.

Consider, too, the following exchange between Sickening and Flasher Gordon, his drummer.

"How's it goin', man?"

"Oh, you know . . ."

That, of course, was just it; Sickening did know. He knew, alas, far more than he had ever told us. But that the knowledge is there (lurking like a demon in the incessant G7 chords of his four-bar introductions, in the sweat-stained Levi's that he reportedly has not changed in the last two years), is radically evident.

Is it any wonder that a semireligious cult has grown up around the group, consisting, in large part, of people who profess little or no interest in its music? This will not come as a surprise to critics perceptive enough to realize the significance of the group's interest in Blake. It is true that Sickening revealed, in an early *Rolling Stone* interview, that it was not William but Robert "Baretta" Blake from whom he had drawn inspiration, but let him who is without sin and all that jazz. [© 1993, Steve Allen]

✻   ✻   ✻

There are some satirical essays which, because of their subtlety, might not be perceived as humorous at all by readers unfamiliar with the object of the satire. In the few thousand years of experience that has been recorded as human history one of the more perplexing provinces has been that of religion. To atheists and agnostics, almost all aspects of religion range from the well-intentioned but misguided to the patently absurd. But oddly enough, even almost all the religious believers in the human population, who probably comprise 90 percent of it, also agree that religions other than their own are not only based on very dubious propositions but incorporate a good deal of outright nonsense. Wherever truth might lie in this particular debate, it is clear enough that in recent years there has been a sharp rise in the expression of religious views that tend toward the inherently preposterous. To give but one example, from earliest ages there have always been people who were able to convince themselves that the end of the world was not only inevitable but actually at hand. Those who entertain such beliefs have in now countless instances been embarrassed by the fact that wrap-it-up day has come and gone without incident, but each new prophet of doom seems untroubled by the endless failures of his predecessors. There are certainly aspects of religion that are commonsensical, edifying, and intellectually buttressed. Unfortunately, in recent decades the great religious "revival" has concentrated less on such admirable elements and given more consideration to the occult, the bizarre, and the sensational. The recent increase in interest in that mysterious phenomenon known as *glossolalia*—"speaking in tongues"— provides an instructive instance. Since I assume there is a God, and secondly, that the very definition of God implies the quality of superintelligence, it has never been clear why the divine power would perceive it as in the interest of either Godness or human welfare to have his subjects babbling incoherently, as distinguished from preaching understandable and morally instructive ideas.

But coherent moral instruction is in short supply, while interest in the bizarre is flourishing. In any event, such considerations provide the background for the following essay, which was published in *The Realist* (Spring 1990):

SPEAKING IN NUMBERS

On March 24, 1989, in a basement meeting room of St. Malachy's parish, on Chicago's northwest side, there occurred the first known manifestation of a spiritual phenomenon that by December seemed likely to sweep at least the American branch of the evangelical and fundamentalist wing of Christendom. According to reports of witnesses, there had already been three instances, earlier during the scheduled prayer meeting, of glossolalia or "speaking in tongues."

For those unfamiliar with the practice, it involves what to a disinterested observer would appear to be totally meaningless babbling. Far from being frowned upon by modern Christians, it is considered a rarely valuable experience, the precise cause of which is a personal visitation by the Holy Spirit. On the occasion in question, however, a parishioner named Matthew Donohue, a forty-seven-year-old certified public accountant, suddenly stood and began part mumbling, part shouting a series of numbers.

"My memory of the incident," parishioner Joseph DeMaris recalled, "was that Donohue started speaking in tongues, at least for the first few seconds, but suddenly converted to numbers." Asked by an investigative journalist if he could act out Donohue's spoken words, DeMaris cooperatively said, "Sure. It sounded like this. Bahaba, lama, ma-ma-ma-do, maga 7. 7, 47, 9, 3, 6, 0—oh God—49, 56, 56!"

"He repeated some numbers, did he?"

"Yes," DeMaris said, "sometimes he would say a number and then repeat it four or five times, but mostly it was just a bunch of numbers that were disconnected."

According to other participants in the ceremony, Donohue appeared to become increasingly excited as he stood, eyes closed, knees slightly bent, swaying back and forth and half speaking, half singing the lengthy sequence of numbers to which he was giving voice. He seemed to emphasize some arithmetical information, but the meaning of this, if there was any, eluded those who were present.

Asked if he thought that Donohue's outburst was a legitimate manifestation of inspiration by the Holy Spirit, Father Leo Tierney, pastor of St. Malachy's, said, "We cannot be absolutely certain about such things but I personally believe that Donohue's experience was just as legitimate as that of the others who spoke in tongues that night. To those who don't know anything about glossolalia there may be a problem as regards what seems the total lack of meaning of whatever is spoken out, but people seem to feel so much better after they have this experience that I personally must respect their sincerity and the obvious benefits the experience confers on them."

Whatever the authenticity of Donohue's personal drama, the phenomenon is presently "spreading like wildfire," as one nun, a teacher at St. Malachy's parish school, put it.

"Perhaps," she said, "God is trying to teach us something by enabling us to communicate in what might seem, to others—or to skeptics—a meaningless manner. Perhaps He is saying that many of today's terrible problems—divorce and sexual promiscuity, drugs, alcoholism, terrorism—all of that—came about because of modern man's overemphasis on reason."

Father Tierney differed on this one point. "It's difficult to say," he conceded, "how you can blame intellectual rationality for political terrorism, sexual license, pornography, drug taking, and all that, but even so there might be a degree of truth in what the sister has said. Perhaps there has been too much emphasis on reason and science during the last hundred years or so. The Holy Spirit may now be telling us to return to emotion, which is certainly as God-given as the reasoning faculty. Perhaps He is telling us to become like children, willing to express our feelings by babbling innocently rather than the usually rationally coded messages."

Asked what connection there was between the apparently nonsensical syllables of a typical speaking-in-tongues experience and the new speaking-in-numbers, Father DeMaris said, "I personally don't know. But I have now witnessed this sort of thing in over a dozen instances and what impresses me most are the clear-cut spiritual, emotional, and psychological benefits that the people enjoy after they stand up and begin shouting numbers.

"Of course since I'm personally, by nature, a somewhat reticent type, there's part of me that still wants to 'make sense' of these numbers. For that reason I've taken to tape-recording them and having the sequences typed up. I have some of my friends who are experienced in mathematics and the use of computers checking to see if there are any noticeable patterns in the numbers or whether they are indeed, as they seem, totally random.

"It may sound superstitious but one of the women in our parish said she knew a numerologist—a kind of fortune-teller who reads numbers in the way that other people might read tarot cards or tea leaves—I'm hoping I'm not doing anything here that'll get me in trouble with my theological superiors," Tierney smiled, "but—who knows? Perhaps certain members do have the ability to carry coded messages. We're all familiar, for example, with the references, in the New Testament, to the number 666 as somehow representing the anti-Christ.

"And numbers, of course, have been very important, even long before Christianity, in the history of religion. There are frequent references, particularly in the old scripture, to forty days of this or that, things that come in tens—like the Commandments—and the number seven is very frequently referred to, so I argue that we should at least keep our minds open about this new manifestation of the Holy Spirit."

Reports that have come in during recent months from generally similar events in New York, Denver, New Orleans, Seattle, and other metropolitan areas, are generally consistent with the original instance reported.

An interesting aspect of the mysterious phenomenon has emerged in that speaking in numbers has now spread to the Spanish-speaking Christian community in both Catholic and Protestant groups. The numbers are, of course, being stated in Spanish. Because of the more mellifluous character of the Spanish language a number of students of the phenomenon have pointed out that in that language the numbers sound much more like traditional glossolalia than they do as communicated in English.

Robert S. Cartwright, S.J., theologian and professor of philosophy at Fordham University, observed in a recent commentary published in *Theological Review*, "At first there seems to have been a generally negative reaction to reports of the speaking-in-numbers phenomenon, but during the last few months this trend has been sharply reversed on the grounds that while the more traditional glossolalia appears to consist of speaking truly meaningless syllables, the same certainly cannot be said as regards numbers, for such words as *seven, twelve, nineteen,* etc., obviously have sharply precise meanings.

"It remains to be seen, of course, whether there is any to-the-present hidden meaning in the combination of numbers themselves. It's theoretically possible—because the Vatican has yet to take a position on the new practice, so far as I'm aware—that the phenomenon will eventually be attributed to nothing more than well-intentioned religious hysteria.

"But we must recall that, for Christians, the debate on glossolalia itself has long been settled. It has, from the earliest days, been generally regarded by perfectly responsible Christian authorities as an actual, validated manifestation of a visitation by the Holy Spirit. Because of that background, we should therefore sympathetically reserve judgment as regards speaking in numbers."

Limitation of space precludes further exploration of this phenomenon in the present study. I intend, however, to have more to say about it at a future time. [© 1993, Steve Allen]

*　*　*

Here is another illustration of one type of satirical essay that reading letters to the editors of serious journals inspired me to write:

Have you ever had the experience of getting in an elevator on, say, the nineteenth floor and finding yourself in the middle of some conversation that, because of its truncated nature, sounded almost meaningless?

". . . and as soon as he did that, they sent in the green one."

"No kidding? I would have thought Charlie would have put the grilled cheese in the cockpit by himself."

"No chance. As soon as you get up beyond the $50,000 range, you've got as much chance of getting all that cinnamon to Singapore as I have of making it with Dolly Parton."

"Well, no matter what you say, I still think that if Irene had married the midget in the first place, it wouldn't have turned out so bad."

Almost all conversations on elevators sound like that to me. I have a somewhat similar reaction to the experience of opening one intellectual journal or another and reading exchanges of letters referring to stories I've missed that were published in earlier issues. No doubt subscribers who read the original material later being commented on would have less difficulty, but since no one can keep up with all the worthwhile and scholarly periodicals, I often encounter bitter exchanges of correspondence that sound rather like the following:

In his July story on the dwindling influence of the Catholic church on international conglomerates, Morton Feinman referred to Gabby Hayes, the well-known cowboy sidekick, as having given Dr. Mengele the original inspiration for the medical experiments that have quite rightly forever blackened the name, of not only the Third Reich, but also Cleveland.

While I agree with the initial thrust of Feinman's thesis, I must take exception to his reference to me as Annette Funicello's hairdresser. Feinman would appear to be unaware that novelist Theodore Dreiser and Paul Dresser, the songwriter, were brothers. Dreiser, because of his ambivalence on the subject of his German-ness, took great pains never to be addressed as Herr Dresser. Perhaps it is the confusion of this term with *hairdresser* that led Feinman into the morass of CIA and fundamentalist Christian clichés that marred an otherwise insightful analysis.

Oh, and one more thing: Comedian Don Rickles most assuredly did *not* coin the term *hockey puck*. Shakespeare, in his third draft of his unproduced *A Midsummer Night's Waste of Time* says, "Harken, Puck, to that most limpid wrist of eventide . . ." It is not difficult to see that the Elizabethan *harken, Puck* led to the nineteenth-century *hockey puck*, which became common in southern Canada after the defeat of the English in the French-Canadian War. I must confess my indebtedness, in this connection, to Wolfgang Wolfe, great-grandson of General Thomas Wolfe, victor at the Battle of Quebec. When the English monarch was told that Wolfe was mad, he remarked, "I wish he would bite my other generals."

Feinman would seem to have been aware that Wolfe did engage in general-biting but, unfortunately, erroneously attributes this to Wolfe's sexual proclivities, about which the less said the better.

Salmon P. Chazenheimer
Vice President
Bechtel Power Corporation
San Francisco, Indiana

Morton Feinman hits the nail on the head in his insightful piece "How to Hit a Nail on the Head." There being no perfection in human experience, however, I must point out two minor errors in Dr. Feinman's otherwise well-developed argument. First of all, he depended, for some of his documentation, on the Sauerkraut section of *Frankfurter Allgemeine*, the notorious journal of the lower-German meatpacking industry.

This leads, no doubt inevitably, to Feinman's pathetic misinterpretation of the phenomenon of *strange attractors*, whereas it has by now been well-established that in refusing to address the apparent existence of order in chaos, the hypothesis that calls into question not only Newtonian but also Einsteinian physics, Feinman never for a moment considered the implications of the resurgence of the Chicago Cubs in the late summer of 1984, a possibility that would have seemed preposterous even to Alvin Toffler.

Zymole Trochee
South Bend, Mississippi

Feinman replies:

With all due respect to the conscious intentions of Messrs. Chazenheimer and Trochee, I suggest that interested readers re-study my original article in the light of a pharmacology suggested by Revelation 6:19 before making up their minds as to whether my interpretation of Ronald Reagan's pathetic dependance on Grecian Formula, cue-cards and TelePrompTers is more reliable than that of my critics.

I am certainly not remiss in asserting that readers have the right to know that Chazenheimer's argument stems more from his status as a leader of the neo-synephrine movement than out of any inherent weakness in my own formulations.

One does not have to turn to Liebnitz—though there's nothing terribly wrong with that—to perceive that Mortimer Adler, to whom Chazenheimer often slavishly appeals, is on the shakiest possible philosophical ground when he argues that if the driver of the Chrysler is not in the car but leaves his key in the ignition so that the voice reminder computer tapes are activated, there is actually no sound within the car's interior because there are no human ears to perform the act of perception. Does Feinman actually think that in resorting to the tiresome if-a-tree-falls-in-the-forest argument (see *Weyerhauser* v. *the State of Oregon*) he is really saying something new and insightful about punk rock? If so, I refer him to the comparative statistics on "Too Tall" Jones, "Too Short" Johnson, "Too Weird" Wennerholm, and "Too Dumb" Davis. Nuf—as we say—sed.

But, all seriousness aside, the airy assumption that the zoot suit of 1940s' Los Angeles was named after Zoot Sims is surely something that would make even Nat Hentoff gag, were it not for his recent application to study for the Jesuit priesthood.

Perhaps the success of the Rush Limbaugh–Pat Buchanan chain of charm schools, which Feinman had assumed was unlikely, unnerved the scholar whom I have elsewhere conceded does not wear a hairpiece. Moreover, I have not only withdrawn the original aspersion but have discovered that it came from careless listening to a conversation in which the party of the first part said, "I *do* have herpes."

Whether my digressions are irrelevant, or my irrelevancies are digressive, is, I submit, totally beside the point. Certainly it is sheer McCarthyism to suggest that a mere three or four convictions for child molestation ill befit a candidate for high office in the John Birch Society. To me, the fact that the gentleman molested only left-wing children speaks volumes.

Lester Feinman
Justice Department
Washington D.C.

*   *   *

Another of my targets was the heartrending essay, popular for a while in the fifties and sixties, that described our lovable selves in excessively poignant terms: "What Is a Boy?," "What Is a Girl?," "What Is a Mother?," "What Is a Husband?" (e.g., "A husband is a lord and master with a dishtowel in his hand, a tycoon pushing a lawn mower, a political expert reading the funnies, and a Metropolitan tenor singing in the shower," by Roberts-Piller-Katz).

A number of entertainers, such as Art Linkletter, Mike Douglas, and Arthur Godfrey, moved millions to tears with soulful recordings of such works.

But considerable controversy, some of it remarkably acrimonious, surrounds the question as to what is the most touching, heartrending soliloquy ever recorded. Touching-experts are in general agreement that the most moving monologue of all is my alter-ego, Seymour Glick's, immortal "What Is a Krelm?" The text is rendered here in its nerve-shattering entirety. Note that in structure it is faithful to "What Is a Boy?" et al.

What Is a Krelm?

I wonder how many people in these days of general turmoil ever look up from their treadmills to ask the question, "What is a Krelm?"

Well, Krelms are found in the strangest of places. On the phone, in your pants, from the gays of Greenwich Village to the Straits of Magellan, in cesspools, in rock bands, near your bird, and playing on your heartstrings.

A Krelm likes: soy sauce, collard greens, uncollard greens, chicken wire, salami, bird-seed pudding, and other Krelms.

A Krelm hates: fricassee of beaks and claws, turkey wattles, income taxes, or the heartbreak of psoriasis.

Nothing else can come home so drunk, grove up the fob of a good bertrand so often, or lose so many file-saws.

A Krelm is dignity with a fern in its clyde, mononucleosis with a frog in its throat, and stupidity with a bone in its mouth.

What is a Krelm made of? Well, it takes the strength of a lion, the cream of the crop, the back of your hand, the neck of a chicken, the Top of the Mark, the last of the Mohicans, and a hair of the dog.

There are several ways to get a Krelm. Advertise in the paper, jump in the lake, blues in the night, or punch in the mouth.

Mothers-in-law don't particularly fern for Krelms, traffic cops grab them, little boys eat them, and Howard Cosell insults them.

But you know, friends, when you're tired and weary, and worn and sick and miserable, and dirty and crummy and shaking and nervous and frightened and panicky and drunk and raggedy and rotten, and staggering and reeling and rolling in the gutter and throwing up—

Ah, but when you come home and sit down in your easy chair, and that little Krelm jumps up on the bridge of your nose and sits there and stares into your eyes, why I tell you—my fellow Americans—it just kind of makes life worthwhile to hear those three little words: "You're under arrest!"

And, if you can keep your Krelm when all about you are losing theirs and blaming it on you—if you can ask yourself, "What's it all about, Alfie?" then you'll know that a boom is only a ding-dong, but a good cigar is a Krelm.

So what *is* a Krelm? What is the derivation of the word? There is no derivative, no meaning. It's pure double-talk.

•   •   •

In the 1950s, I published a short book called *Bop Fables*, based on a series of recordings I had made. The "fables" were actually classic children's stories I had rewritten in hip, jazz-musician style. All the dialogue was expressed in that idiom. The result was a blend of the innocence of fairy tales and the bebop lingo of the urban hipster.

What follows is a slightly updated version of "Red Riding Hood."

Once upon a time, many many years ago, in the land of Oobopshebam, there lived a lovely little girl named Red Riding Hood. To give you an idea of what a sweet thing she was, children, I'll just say that she was not only a *lovely little girl*; she was a *fine chick*.

One day Red Riding Hood's mother called her into the kitchen and said, "Honey, your grandma is feeling the least."

"What a drag!" said Red. "What's the bit?"

"Hangoversville, for all I know," said her mother. "At any rate, I've fixed up a real wild basket of ribs and a bottle of juice. I'd like you to fall by grandma's joint this afternoon and lay the stuff on her."

"Crazy," said Red, and picking up the basket, she took off for her grandmother's cottage, going by way of the deep woods.

Little did Red Riding Hood know that a big bad wolf lurked in the heart of the forest. She had traveled but a short distance when the wolf leaped out from behind a bush and confronted her.

"Baby," he said, grinning affably, "gimme five."

"Sorry, daddy-o," said Red. "Some other time. Right now I have to make it over to my grandmother's place."

"Square-time," said the wolf. "Why don't you blow your grandmother and we'll have some laughs."

"Man," said Red, "Cootie left the Duke and I'm leavin' you. For the time being we've had it."

"Mama, I'm hip," said the wolf. "Dig you later."

So saying, the wolf bounded off through the forest and was soon lost to sight. But his evil mind was at work. Unbeknownst to Red Riding Hood, he took a shortcut through the trees and in a few minutes stood panting before the helpless old grandmother's cottage.

Quietly he knocked at the door.

"That's a familiar beat," said Red Riding Hood's grandmother. "Who's out there?"

"Western Union," lied the wolf. "I have a special invitation to Dizzy's opening at Birdland."

"Wild," said the grandmother, hobbling across the room.

Imagine her horror when, on opening the door, she perceived the wolf! In an instant he had leaped into the house, gobbled her up and disguised himself in her night clothes.

Hearing Red Riding Hood's footsteps on the stones of the garden path, he leaped into the poor lady's bed, pulled the covers up to his chin and smiled toward the door in a grandmotherly way.

When Little Red Riding Hood knocked he said, "Hit me again. Who goes?"

"It's me, Gram," said Red Riding Hood. "Mother heard you were feeling pretty beat. She thought you might like to pick up on some ribs."

"Nutty," said the wolf. "Fall in."

Red Riding Hood opened the door, stepped inside and looked around the room. "Wowie," she said. "What a crazy pad!"

"Sorry I didn't have time to straighten the joint up before you got here," said the wolf. "But you know how it is. What's in the basket?"

"Oh, the same old jazz," said Red.

"Baby," said the wolf, "Don't put it down."

"I have to," said Red. "It's getting heavy."

"I didn't come here to play straight," said the wolf. "Let's open the basket. I've got eyes."

"I'm hip," said Red, "not to mention the fact that you can say that again. Grandma, what coo-coo eyes you have!"

"The better to dig you with, my dear," said the wolf.

"And, Grandma," said Red, "I don't want to sound rude, but what a long nose you have!"

"Yeah," said the wolf. "It's a gasser."

"And Grandma," said Red, "your ears are the most, to say the least."

"What is this," snapped the wolf, "face inspection? I know my ears aren't the greatest, but whadda ya gonna do? Let's just say somebody goofed!"

"You know something?" little Red Riding Hood said, squinting suspiciously at the furry head on the pillow. "I don't want to sound square or anything, but you don't look like my grandmother at all. You look like some other cat."

"Baby," said the wolf, "you're flippin'!"

"No, man," insisted Red. "I just dug your nose again and it's too much. I don't want to come right out and ask to see your card, you understand, but where's my grandma?"

The wolf stared at Red Riding Hood for a long, terrible moment. "Your grandma," he said, "is gone."

"I'm hip," said Red. "She is the swingin'est, but let's take it from the top again. Where is she?"

"She split," said the wolf.

"Don't hand me that jive," said Red, whereupon the wolf, being at the end of his patience, leaped out of bed and began to chase poor Red Riding Hood about the room.

Little did he know that the wolf season had opened that very day and that a passing hunter could hear little Red Riding Hood's frantic cry for help.

Rushing into the cottage, the brave hunter dispatched the wolf with one bullet.

"Buster," said Red gratefully "your timing was like the end, ya know?"

And so it was.

*   *   *

The *Bop Fables* idea had occurred to me when a guitar player who was working on my show at the time told me that a day or two earlier he had asked his five-year-old son what he had learned at school that day. "Oh," the little fellow said, "we learned about some cat named George Washington."

The choice of words struck me as hysterically funny. The child, of course, wasn't trying to be amusing; he was just using the lingo that his father, a jazz musician, employed around the house. But the incongruity between the hipness of the language and the dignity of both the image and the reality of George Washington is what automatically struck the magic spark of humor.

That one instance gave me the idea of first telling stories drawn from history—such as the story of Washington and the cherry tree—in hip lingo. A few minutes later it occurred to me that it would be easier to deal with the well-known ancient stories familiar to children: "Goldilocks and the Three Bears," "The Three Little Pigs," and so forth.

All I did was get a straight, traditional version of the story and redictate the narrative in musician's language, which, as a jazz player, I spoke anyway, although not to the exclusion of more conventional modes of communication.

*   *   *

A series of ads for the liquor Campari attracted my attention a few years back because of its unique nature. Instead of the usual advertising text, the copy was set up as if it were the transcript of an actual interview. I fantasized that there might have been more to the interview with a deep-voiced actress we'll call Barbara Mosely than what was published. The first section of the following text is the ad copy as run in magazines. The second section is my satirical piece:

AN ACTRESS TALKS ABOUT HER "FIRST TIME"

ACTRESS: My first time was on the "red-eye" from L.A. to New York.

INTERVIEWER: I had no idea you could get Campari on airplanes.

ACTRESS: Well, only on some U.S. airlines. But I'm told you can get it on most European flights. They're really much more cosmopolitan.

INTERVIEWER: Well, what was it like?

ACTRESS: It wasn't sweet. On the other hand, it wasn't really bitter. I guess bittersweet is the only way to describe it.

INTERVIEWER: Really? Tell me the whole story.

ACTRESS: Well, I was restless . . . couldn't sleep . . . didn't feel like reading. Then, somewhere over the Rockies, the man next to me turned and said, "Look, as long as you can't sleep, how'd you like to try something really different?" I figured, oh, what the heck, why not? So he turned off the reading lamps, called for the flight attendant, and ordered Campari for two.
    Let's see, I had Campari and orange juice, and he had Campari and tonic.

INTERVIEWER: You certainly have a memory for detail. Then what?

ACTRESS: I guess I'm known for speaking my mind, and about halfway through I just had to tell him the truth.

INTERVIEWER: What did you say?

ACTRESS: "Is this it? Is this what all my friends are raving about?"

INTERVIEWER: Was he offended?

ACTRESS: Not at all. He just smiled and said, ". . . most people feel that way their first time. But like a lot of things, it gets better and better."

You know, he was absolutely right. The second time was wonderful. And now I just love it . . . there are so many interesting ways to enjoy Campari.

INTERVIEWER: Yes, I'm sure. By the way, whatever happened to the man on the plane?

ACTRESS: That's my one regret. I just wish my second time could have been with him. I feel I owed him that much.

That, to repeat, was the original text of the advertisement. I simply extrapolated the conversation from that point.

INTERVIEWER: Might I ask if I bear any resemblance to your mysterious stranger?

ACTRESS: Not the slightest. For one thing, I lied to you. Well, it was a half-lie in that I deliberately gave the impression I never saw the fellow again. Actually, I run into him at 35,000 feet from time to time.

INTERVIEWER: Would you consider yourself friends?

ACTRESS: Are you kidding? The jerk is a raving alcoholic. I later learned he says the same thing to every woman he sits next to on a plane.

INTERVIEWER: What same thing?

ACTRESS: Don't you remember? He said, "Look, as long as you can't sleep, how'd you like to try something really different?"

INTERVIEWER: I see.

ACTRESS: I don't. You see the Campari jazz was just window dressing.

INTERVIEWER: You don't mean that he—

ATRESS: The hell I don't. Having subsequently watched his technique from at least the length of a ten-foot pole, I can tell you that he starts with Campari and shortly recommends making it. I mean, right there, under the cover of darkness. I did tell you all this happened on a "red-eye," didn't I?

INTERVIEWER: Well, after he made his intentions clear, what did you do?

ACTRESS: I told him to f--- off.

INTERVIEWER: Did you always talk like a teamster or a stevedore?

ACTRESS: No, I used to talk like a lady. But then I became a star, and I figured what the f-----

INTERVIEWER: Did you do anything else to revise your image?

ACTRESS. Yes. I lowered the timbre of my voice to approximately that of Ben Gazzara. And when that wasn't enough, I took to deliberately going out on cold nights after taking hot showers. Anything to sound husky and tough.

INTERVIEWER: How odd.

ACTRESS: So's your old lady.

INTERVIEWER: Well, forgive me if I sound hopelessly old-fashioned, but I do think there was something to say for the old order in which actresses talked like Deborah Kerr rather than Rocky Graziano.

ACTRESS: Up yours.

INTERVIEWER: Another time perhaps. To return to our theme, do you still drink Campari?

ACTRESS: I drink any friggin' thing I want. Yes, I drink Campari. Usually on the rocks, sprinkled lightly with Dutch Cleanser.

INTERVIEWER: Why?

ACTRESS: Keeps the old vocal chords gravelly. Turns on men who've had it with femininity.

INTERVIEWER: But wait, just because Campari is no longer paying the bills, where is it written that our interview must be over?

ACTRESS: Where indeed?

11

Writing Funny Letters

Two factors usually determine whether I'll write either a funny letter or one that is completely serious in tone. One is the mood I'm in at the moment. But even more important is the general personality of the person to whom I'm writing. In other words, I wouldn't write a funny letter to Mother Teresa, Richard Nixon, or Ralph Nader. Most of the comic letters I write are dispatched either to comedians and comedy writers, or unknown admirers who have written to me in a funny, bantering style.

The writing of funny letters is a special and somewhat unusual subdivision of the comic gift itself. Although I have received a number of amusing letters over the years, few have come from professional comedians. Groucho Marx and Fred Allen were witty correspondents. So is George Burns. But I should have been very surprised if I had ever received a funny letter from Bob Hope, Jack Benny, Red Skelton, Edgar Bergen, or Jackie Gleason.

Common sense will tell you which of your friends it is appropriate to be facetious and lighthearted with and which you would be better advised to speak directly to.

A letter can be a good vehicle for relating funny anecdotes or for sharing news of a funny nature. This is often done, in fact, among family members and friends; and that brings up an interesting point. If the event you're describing truly constitutes an inherently comic situation, you don't have to "write funny" in rendering your account. If you're telling a friend or loved one about something amusing that happened, you don't have to waste two weeks learning how to write like Robert Benchley. Just give the facts, ma'am.

When might it be suitable to use humor in business letters? Well, if, for instance, one is seeking employment, humor should be used sparingly. A good deal depends, of course, on the relative positions of the executive and the job hunter. In other words, if you're an eighteen-year-old high school graduate, I wouldn't recommend your writing a funny letter to an official of AT&T if you're applying for a job. On the other hand, if you're a mature adult writing to, let's assume, an approximate social equal, and if some particular point can be either made or enhanced by a passing humorous touch, that can be a plus.

As it should in all aspects of life, common sense will be your primary guide. Most business letters are businesslike, and properly so; but if the person you are writing to is noted for a sense of humor, there's nothing wrong with injecting a light note or two in a letter or an interoffice memo.

Would it be appropriate to write a funny letter to someone who is seriously ill, or one who has just experienced a misfortune such as being fired? This, as the politicians say, is a good question. Oddly enough, the answer is yes: It's perfectly appropriate to use at least an element of humor in a letter to someone who has suffered a traumatic experience. Obviously, it wouldn't be reasonable to write one of those thoroughly silly letters in which scarcely a sensible thought is conveyed; but the fact that you're writing to someone who is suffering by no means requires that you write a gloomy or solemn letter. Your friend will appreciate receiving a cheerful, upbeat message.

This doesn't mean you should unnecessarily gild lilies or distort facts. Let's assume an extreme case, in which your friend has only weeks to live. It's absurd to say things like, "Well, Jim, I'm sure you'll pull through, and we'll be back playing golf again very soon." The obvious falsity of such misplaced cheerfulness will be apparent to the one who receives your message. But there are a thousand and one other sorts of lighthearted or amusing observations you can make, perhaps sharing news of a family experience, something funny a child has said, a witty joke you might have heard on television. The point of writing such a letter is the same as that of sending one of those happy-looking get-well cards—to cheer the recipient.

Apart from the obvious, what are the differences between composing a funny letter and writing a humorous essay? There are no hard and fast rules about the matter. Generally, depending on the sophistication of the writer's and receiver's sense of humor, a funny letter can get very silly indeed, not to mention that it can include a lot of "inside" jokes that might puzzle others, whereas a humorous essay will ordinarily have a slightly more formal tone. But the comic essays of Woody Allen, Robert Benchley, and S. J. Perelman are about as silly as you can get. Consequently, we can't make any Ten Commandments sort of statements about the distinction between the two literary forms. Perhaps the point is illustrated by my own essay about Latvia (included in *How to Be Funny,* which, while it stands on its own, was originally written as a letter to writer-producer Larry Gelbart and his wife, Pat.

If writing witty letters comes naturally to you, then feel free to exercise the gift. But if it's a foreign mode of communication, I wouldn't waste much time on it.

I recommend reading twice through the following sampling of funny letters I've written. The first time read them for just what they are, and enjoy a chuckle or two. The second time you read them analyze the methods I've used. In studying the letters, you'll detect application of some of my favorite joke techniques. For example, look for the Literalization formula in letters to Groucho, December 17, 1971 ("hand in"); writers Greg Lenburg and Randy Skretvedt, April 27, 1978 ("ticker-tape parade"); writer-producer Jeff Harris, February 26, 1982 ("miss a trick"); and TV interviewer Pat Collins ("control room applauded").

The Misinterpretation technique can be found in notes to Louise Kappen of publishers Price/Stern/Sloan ("execute"); writer-producer Leonard Stern, April 2, 1980 ("tamper with the records"); and Mel Brooks ("take care").

I also play with words in a number of letters: Dayton Allen ("cyclamates"); writer-producers David Pollack and Elias Davis ("tuna-smiths"); and Dareth and Tony Newley ("trollop-walloping"). There is, too, a considerable amount of starting sentences one way and then suddenly changing thought in midstream: The correspondence to David Letterman ("dissolution of the British Empire"), for instance. At times, I've used the Reversal formula, such as in the letters to Groucho, November 15, 1960 (". . . I'm a very silly person") and to writer-producers Bernie Kukoff and Jeff Harris (". . . find some other excuse").

There is also a note I wrote to myself when I was the host of the "Meeting of Minds" series on PBS, and letters to TV interviewer Jan Marshall ("Let me know . . . whether you want me to be artistic or entertaining"), and editors of the supermarket checkout stand paper *The Globe,* in which I use humor to point out an error of fact.

One of my favorites is a letter written to Todd Schwartz, of *Laugh Factory,* actually, both a letter and a contribution to the magazine. It uses a variety of comic devices, including what was initially an ad-lib—"the bell-ringer." (Originally the line involved a man named Jack Clouse.) It also employs wild visual imagery ("logo showing two-and-a-half slanted white salamis"); funny names ("Olympics, Earl Warren and the Supremes"); nonsense wordplay ("Pips, pips"); and parodies of three popular songs.

Here, then, are the letters, in chronological order.

April 5, 1952

Dean Myers
Columbus Dispatch

Dear Mr. Myers,

A dear, little old lady who makes a hobby out of saving articles about me and sending them to my office on a regular basis has provided me with a copy of your column of March 27.

The dear little old lady works for a commercial clipping service.

I found the article she forwarded to me hugely amusing. This was partly because I am huge and easily amused and partly because you whip up a superior column. I sampled it and found it eminently satisfactory and noticeably mild, with no unpleasant aftertaste.

As I recall (and I recall pretty well with the article lying three inches to the left of my typewriter) you said some nice things about *Songs for Sale*. Your only complaint was that you couldn't hear very well because you were interviewing me by telephone while so, at the time, were six or seven other radio-television editors scattered around the country.

If you think you were having trouble, consider my position. Have you ever tried to talk to eight people at once? Have you ever tried to explain to sundry telephone operators that eight different connections are weak? (singing) Have you ever been lonely? Have you ever been blue? Have you ever loved someone . . . just as I love you?

Be that as it may, and I'm not sure it is, I was the person in the most uncomfortable spot during the conference call and as such am in no mood to squander sympathy on undeserving columnists with tin ears.

I couldn't hear *any* of you very well. There was one voice that came in loud and clear from time to time, but I was rattled to finally learn that it was my secretary in the next room.

Besides, I am a very busy man. Having to hang around the office to make that call that afternoon meant missing the regular Tuesday meeting of the Aqua-Velva Aftershave Club.

I don't want you to think I'm ungrateful, Dean, but I wouldn't be keeping faith with the little old lady down at the clipping service if I didn't occasionally speak my mind to you gentlemen of the press.

Best wishes,

*   *   *

July 18, 1958

Mr. Groucho Marx

Dear Groucho,

I am writing this letter from London, which has impressed me so far as one magnificent straight line. I keep thinking of funny things here, and since no one else understands me, I thought I would unburden myself to you.

I have spent the last four days with two of my sons, Brian and Steve, Jr., and it is doubly interesting to see this land through their eyes as well as my own. In fact, I can see it much better through their eyes due to my being somewhat nearsighted. In any event, when you have a child who refers to Madame Tussaud's Waxworks as "Madam Toupee's Wax House," as Brian did the other day, you shall not have lived in vain.

Almost everything here is strange and fascinating and I highly approve of all of it, although there are complications: The word for water closet here is *loo*. It made me feel a little embarrassed to ask about the Battle of Waterloo.

And the money evaluation is very puzzling to an American, especially a stupid one. But I think I have it more or less straight now. There are sixteen ounces to a pound. One pound is worth twenty shillings. A shilling is worth seven ha'pennies and a slug. There are three wickets to a florin, two florins to a guinea, three guineas to a polack, eight half-crowns to a quid, four tentacles to a squid, and a tuppence is worth four Bobs and a Charlie.

There seems to be scarcely a house or public building in London that does not have historical significance. I've had so many places of interest pointed out to me the past few days that all the descriptive speeches seem conglomerated in my mind into one brief lecture that goes something like this:

"That building on your left is Worcestershire House. It was built in 1693 at the corner of Eaton Place and Drinkin' Place by the Earl of Brylcreem for his mistress, the Duke of Shirestershire. And right over here you'll see the Admiralty Bastion, which was formerly called Westminster Bowling Alley and is widely known as the place that Keats never heard of. Those holes and spots along the side there were made during the Boer War. The heavy building stones were shipped to Africa, badly scarred, and shipped back for insertion into the forward wall, by way of adding a bit of color. Just across the mall moat there you'll see the Hempstead Convents, fabled in song and story as the scene of the Coldstream Boarwrestling Tournaments. It was on that very bench that Jonathan Swift was arrested for vagrancy and thrown into the King's Reach, which is the place where the Thames flows under the powder room of Buckingham Palace. It's a pity we're just a few minutes late or you could see the Trooping of the Colored People past the statue of Abraham Lincoln, which was erected in 1309 to commemorate the signing of Colonel Tom Parker's first legal contract."

Believe me, that is not much of an exaggeration.

You can have a lot of laughs here just reading the telephone book. There are so many names like Wellesley-Claremont and Sir Wrigley Spearmint, and that sort of thing. You also notice that many English writers and other men of note use three initials before their surnames, for example: J. F. S. Haldane, I. A. R. Wylie, etc. I've been telling people I work in New York for a chap named R. C. A. Sarnoff.

I am off in the morning to Paris. You may never hear from me again!

Sincerely,

*   *   *

November 15, 1960

Mr. Goucho Marx

Dear Groucho,

I was very touched by your kind letter of November 10 about *Mark It and Strike It*. It was good of you to say that my writing gave you "quite a lift." As you will recall, this is the second lift I have given you in recent weeks, the earlier one being out of Bob Six's swimming pool.

Come to think of it, I also gave you a lift the night you fell down in the balcony of that theater on Wilshire Boulevard. I must say that knowing you has been one of the most uplifting experiences of my life.

I greatly enjoyed your autobiography, too, and am moderately depressed by the fact that it was a lot funnier than my own. For some reason or other, when I get to a typewriter what comes out is usually rather serious stuff. I know that I seem like a clown on the outside, but deep down in my heart I'm a very silly person.

Jayne sends her love. We hope to see you and Eden soon.

Fondly,

*   *   *

February 12, 1968

Mr. Benny Rubin

Dear Benny,

Please forgive me for having taken so long to thank you for the CARE package that you kindly dispatched to our disaster area here in Royal Oaks.

It arrived just as I was going down to the corner to sell a box of apples.

As soon as I opened the box, I began passing out rations to our fast-fading crew, after which we loaded all the stuff into our Rolls Royce and drove over to Bel-Air for a picnic.

The day may come, Benny, when the shoe is on the other foot, and you, too, will be starving and miserable and downcast and dejected and friendless.

I just want you to know . . . if that day ever comes . . . please don't bother me.

Cordially,

                 *   *   *

November 18, 1969

Mr. Dayton Allen

Dear Dayton,

Thanks for your outburst of November 6th.

As a long-time dependent on unnatural foods, I naturally attribute to them my unnatural strength, unnaturally magnetic appeal and unnatural sense of humor.

My mind is open on the subject, of course. However, I am having the opening closed up because people keep coming up and peering into it, which is disconcerting.

All seriousness aside, I do the health-food bit and am therefore partial to your argument.

As regards cyclamates—I say that if a fellow wants to go bike-riding with close friends, that's none of the government's business.

I intend to lie down in a quiet place sometime within the next few days and study your documents carefully. If after having done so I'm still able to get up, you may rest assured.

All good wishes.

Cordially,

                 *   *   *

September 14, 1970

Mr. and Mrs. Mac Benoff

Dear Miki and Mac,

Forgive me for having taken so long to thank you for inviting me to your delightful dinner party.

I enjoyed it all: the guests, the conversation, the food, the sculpture, the paintings, the house, the shrubbery, the furniture, the ashtrays, the cufflinks, the paperclips, the cigar butts, the pollution, the suffering, the misery, the unspeakable degradation that has made this nation great.

But be that as it may, and I see no reason to believe it is, I had a great time.

Cordially,

*   *   *

December 17, 1971

Mr. Groucho Marx

Dear Groucho,

By the time this letter reaches you I'll be in New York where I must do a week's filming of commercials.

Now that I'm one of the nation's increasingly large army of unemployed comedians, I find I must resort to such alternatives, just to keep my hand in.

Actually it's a little difficult to know what to keep your hand in. I tried keeping it in a cigar box for awhile, but that didn't seem to do the trick.

The main reason I'm writing is that when you were kind enough to invite me to lunch recently you failed to specify a date. I figure I will be unusually hungry shortly after the first of the year and would, therefore, enjoy accompanying you for a free lunch at any local country club of your choosing.

Consulting my appointment book I see that I have to go to Toronto, Canada, on January 7th, so perhaps Wednesday, January 12th, Thursday, January 13th, or Friday, January 14th would be good lunch dates.

I was going to sign this letter "Your obedient servant," but every time I get a letter signed that way I always figure it should be from Arthur Treacher or Eric Blore.

Sincerely,

*   *   *

December 28, 1971

David Pollock and Elias Davis

Dear Fellows,

"If you think for one minute that I'm going to stand idly by—"
    No, that's no good.
    "Of all the unmitigated gall I've ever—"
    Worse.

"Your brazen effrontery, gentlemen, in—"

"Inasmuch as I'm old enough to be your father (and probably am, if I remember your mother)—"

But all seriousness aside, as one of the most prolific tuna-smiths of our time, it ill-behooves me, especially after I ate a couple of cans of the stuff for dinner last night.

What the hell's supposed to be so funny about mercury poisoning I don't quite see. But far be it from me.

By the way, did you folks hear the one about the guy who had to get rid of his new Mercury because it was contaminated with tuna fish?

But I was touched by your thoughtfulness. And I hope you never try to put the touch on me in any other way.

Please punch this letter up and send it to Gary Owens. If anything ever smacked of local radio, this certainly does.

And if you've ever had your local radio smacked....

Oddly,

* * *

May 7, 1975

Mr. Paul Keyes

Dear Paul,

As regards the *Newsweek* story—
You've blown my cover.

And if you've ever had your cover blown, you know how painful that can be.

But since the secret is out, perhaps a word of explanation would be in order. As you know, I've been hurt in the business for a good many years because it has gradually become painfully evident that I am both a *cad* and a *neb*. I decided, therefore, to have a little fun at the public's expense by creating a new character for myself—funnier by far, I think, than Senator Buster, the Question Man, Big Bill Allen, the Late-Show Pitchman, or any of the other characters that Carson might or might not be doing shortly. Ben-Dak is, then, simply a neb and a cad spelled more or less backwards. For a while I considered changing my name to Ben-Gay. But I got a complaint from a fellow named Baum who had heard about it.

Besides, how many people can say that they've been gay? Either you are or you aren't.

Actually I was glad to receive your cheerful letter since I have recently been depressed about the fact that even many of my most affable and pacifistic friends are wearing those little epaulets on their casual jackets.

Watch your step,

*   *   *

November 4, 1975

Bernie Kukoff and Jeff Harris
CBS Studios

Dear Fellows,

Jayne and I are leaving in just a few days to work for two weeks at the Fairmont Hotel in Dallas.

I'll be working as a busboy, and I'd rather not state on paper what Jayne's specific employment will be. Suffice it to say she will be making a lot more money than I will. She will be making it, in fact, hand over fist. And as long as she keeps her hand over my fist her secret will be safe.

Be that as it may—and how's your sister?—our fortnight's absence renders it impossible for us to have the dubious pleasure of conferring with you over the dinner table about our forthcoming third annual triumph. Rest assured, however, that the minute we return we will probably find some other excuse.

I will keep you advised.

Cordially,

*   *   *

October 21, 1977

Mr. Steve Allen

Dear Steve,

Now that we've completed taping the first two "Meeting of Minds" shows of the new season I wanted, as the host, to send this note to you—in your capacity as the writer of these very interesting scripts—to tell you how much all of us appreciated being able to work with your absorbing and informative material.

I'm sorry I muffed a few of your lines, and probably covered up another one or two with my laughter, but I had to miss a few rehearsals so I'm sure you'll understand.

In any event, I look forward eagerly to seeing your rewrites on the next four shows; I'm sure that when they finally get on the air the critics will treat them as kindly as they did the first six last year.

Oh, incidentally, my wife greatly enjoyed playing the role of Florence Nightingale. She hopes you were happy with her performance and both of us would like to thank *your* wife for her very important help with what I understand were some editorial suggestions and revisions in the script.

We'd be delighted to take you two to dinner some night soon, if you can possibly tear yourself away from your dictating equipment.

Cordially,

*   *   *

April 19, 1978

Messrs. Greg Lenburg and Randy Skretvedt

Dear Fellows,

First of all, Randy, I won a Scrabble game using your last name last Thursday and am deeply indebted to you in this connection.

Secondly, I'm glad that somebody is doing a Steve Martin scrapbook. He's one of the scrappiest comedians I know, and it's high time there was a book about it.

Thirdly, I'm not going to be in town very much between now and April 29th, so I doubt that we'll be able to get together.

If you have any specific questions you'd like me to answer, however, feel free to shoot them to me on paper. I do all my writing with a tape recorder and can probably knock out a few answers sometime between now and the 29th.

Perhaps you were watching when I had the pleasure of appearing with Steve on the "Tonight" show recently. I recall observing at the time that much of his performed humor involved "imitating jerks." A careless listener might have assumed I was putting Steve down. Actually I was sending him up.

But all seriousness aside, I think that this is an accurate-enough description of some of the things he does. He himself is very creative, quick-minded, witty, funny, etc., but on stage he pretends to be one form of jerk or another: an insensitively conceited disc jockey type, a Las Vegas show biz type, etc.

Even his "excuuuuuuuse me" is not a joke, but one of those jerky things that certain kinds of people say.

Steve's chief audience at the moment would appear to be in the fifteen-to-twenty-five age range. This is, of course, much better than appealing to people who are sixty-five to seventy-five since they won't be around much longer.

I had the pleasure of giving Steve his first television exposure, and I hope I don't give him his last.

Good luck with the project.

Cordially,

*   *   *

April 27, 1978

Mr. Greg Lenburg and Mr. Randy Skretvedt

Dear Fellows,

Yours of April 23rd received and contents duly noted.

Believe it or not, there was a time in the history of this great nation of ours when people used to write dumb things like that to each other.

Now they're writing dumb things like *this* to each other.

Your stationery is certainly very impressive, Greg. It looks remarkably businesslike. It's just beginning to occur to me that Randy Skretvedt is in the Lenburg business.

Personally I've been a Lenburg fan ever since that great ticker-tape parade down Fifth Avenue in the 1920s.

What a thrill it was to see fifty thousand ticker-tapes marching down Fifth Avenue, their little tapes ticking away.

And their little ticks taping away.

Personally I was ticked off because the parade made it impossible for me to cross Fifth Avenue.

Did you hear about the farmer who crossed Fifth Avenue with a chicken and got a chicken that mugged itself? (Or any other brilliant finish.)

All solemnity aside, it would give me great pleasure to write the introduction to your book on Steve Martin. That's not saying I'll do it, you understand, but I am always tempted by the prospect of great pleasure.

I would not dream of accepting a penny for my services in this connection, since if it got around town that I was doing things like this for a penny there's no telling where it could lead.

Send me the manuscript so I'll know what it is I'm writing an introduction for.

Cordially,

*   *   *

May 19, 1978

Mr. Steve Edwards
"The Steve Edwards Show"

Dear Steve,

Quite by chance, as I was leaving your studio the other day, I ran into none other than Late Nate, the mulatto fellow whose name you had inadvertently brought up during our interview.

He was quite incensed about some of the things we had said, but since I have always enjoyed the odor of incense I gave his remonstrances short shrift.

I think you can take it from there.

Again . . . thanks for your kind words, give my regards to your mother, and please don't make a pest of yourself around the neighborhood.

Sincerely,

*   *   *

June 12, 1978

Mr. Lewis Wechsler

Dear Lew,

Forgive me for having taken so long to answer your letter of April 27.

As you may recall, there was a mix-up about my back-to-the-U.S. reservations, as a result of which I have just spent the last several weeks in the men's room of the Guadalajara Airport because of my refusal to pay *mordita*.

Or for that matter, to pay Gonzales or Lopez.

Thanks for the literature about the snow snake controversy.

And some people say there's no God.

All good wishes.

Cordially,

*   *   *

November 30, 1978

Mr. Leonard Stern

Dear Leonard,

On or before November 21 you dictated—apparently to a secretary insufficiently sure of her professional standing to identify herself by initials—a message to the effect that until I heard from you again I could "go under the assumption that there was no such joke formula in the Gleason 'Honeymooners' scripts."

At least I *assume* that's what you dictated. As you will see by the enclosed Xerox copy of your letter, however, duplicates of 'which have also been sent to the Legion of Decency, the FBI and Anita Bryant—your letter actually states that "there was no suck joke formula . . ."

Needless to say, I'm greatly relieved to hear this since if there is anything television does not need, in its present period of distress, it is suck jokes.

Actually, I don't watch that much television, so for all I know there may be all sorts of suck jokes on the three major networks.

But if this is the case, and I don't know it, you can simply blame it on the fact that lately I've been rather out of tuck with things.

Respectfully,

*   *   *

January 18, 1979

Mr. Gary Owens

Dear Gary,

I am deeply indebted to you for providing me with that picture of my son obviously standing sound asleep in the midst of great excitement while being interviewed by you at the recent *Superman* opening.

You didn't have to tell me you weren't wearing your putty nose or fright wig. Having known you for many years I was perfectly aware that you were wearing a putty wig and a fright nose.

But far be it from me . . .

As soon as my son wakes up I will let him thank you personally.

Cordially,

P.S. I'm glad to hear you have your own building. It worked out very well for my old friend Walter Chrysler.

*   *   *

November 29, 1979

Ms. Louise Kappan
Price/Stern/Sloan

Dear Ms. Kappan,

In compliance with your request of November 28, I have executed the enclosed document.

In case you might consider such questions of interest, I chose to execute it by gas rather than electrocution, hanging, or the firing squad.

I am personally opposed to executions but do recognize that in unusual circumstances drastic measures must be taken.

Which reminds me that I must have my inseam checked very soon.

Sincerely,

*   *   *

January 25, 1980

Mr. Gary Owens

Dear Gary,

Thanks very much for your thoughtful gesture.

I don't mean your letter or present. I meant the *nervous* gesture you made just before you sneezed the other day.

All seriousness aside, I was very touched by your letter.

I was also touched by my brother-in-law—for an amount of money I don't even want to mention.

In fact, I don't even want to mention my brother-in-law.

Incidentally, you'll be glad to hear that Kafka and Nietzsche are back together again.

You and I suffer from the same disease, the chief symptom of which is the inability to finish a sentence along the lines we had in mind when we started it.

Anyway, I did want you to know how much I enjoyed the luncheon itself, how flattered I was to be invited to take part in it, and by your generous response.

Here's hoping we have the pleasure of working together again in The Near Future—which is a small club in Pacoima.

Sincerely,

*   *   *

April 2, 1980

Mr. Leonard Stern
Columbia Pictures

Dear Leonard,

Of all the unmitigated gall.

Imagine you, a former member of the Stern gang, having the temerity, the tumultuousness, the Tammany Hall to write to me, a notorious Gentile, asking me to tamper with the records of the Directors' Guild.

First of all, I deny ever having *made* such records. And if I did, you may be very sure that they sold poorly, largely due to the fact that they were mono rather than stereo.

The fact that I am mono myself rather than stereo I take to be irrelevant.

Be that as it may, and I have my doubts that it is, I have always held—as regards our relationship—that there's absolutely no onus attached to the stigma. For that reason, and that reason alone, I'm happy to attest that you did indeed serve as director of comedy sketches on "The Steve Allen Show" from November 1956 until June 1959.

If anyone wants concrete evidence of the verve, the originality, the polish, the Polish that you brought to that task, I refer them to the "Tonight" show where on many an evening Johnny Carson can be seen performing the same routines, precisely as you directed me in them so many years ago.

I trust that this evidence will stand up in court, which is more than my lawyer was able to do last week, and that through my efforts we have now made your welfare and pension fund radioactive back to 1956.

I had dinner the other evening in New York with Herb Sargent, but he only toyed with his food. Fortunately an official of the Mattel Company observed this peculiar behavior and as a result you will see a line of toy food on the market in plenty of time for Christmas.

Let that be a lesson to you.

Cordially,

*   *   *

July 11, 1980

Mr. and Mrs. Irving Lazar

Dear Mary and Irving,

Thanks for one more delightful evening. My immediate dinner companions—Janet and Linda—were charming, and during the cocktail hour I had an interesting chat with Gregory Peck and your dog.

The dog got more laughs than Greg.

Although not from Greg.

I had to tiptoe out right after dinner because I had an early rehearsal call the following morning. I could not help noticing as I departed, however, how favorably impressed Luis seemed by my tiptoeing.

Jayne would have been present but for the fact that due to general overwork she passed away quietly in her sleep that same night.

Game trouper that she is, however, she is nevertheless going ahead with her performance as Margaret Sanger.

Love to you both.

Sincerely,

*   *   *

August 4, 1980

Mr. Roger Alan Deitz

Dear Mr. Deitz,

It's been such a long time since I've been addressed as "Sir" that the receipt of your letter sent me into shock, cardiac arrest, and a state of blatant mopery with a sprinkling of malfeasance in office.

All seriousness aside, I've been telling fledgling songwriters for about thirty years that my most hysterically complimentary opinion of their material is unlikely to do them the slightest bit of concrete good.

But do they listen to me? No! They go into the concrete business.

So I'll be glad to listen to your numbers, too.

Actually there is the possibility—if they're *comedy* material—that somewhere along the line I might be able to think of a use for them.

But if they're simply great songs like "Stardust," "Laura," "Tenderly," and so forth, you'll probably never make it because you have too much talent and the market today is interested mostly in garbage.

Any friend of Dayton Allen's is a friend of mine.

I'm doing a comedy special for NBC soon, incidentally, and plan to use Dayton on it.

All good wishes.

Cordially,

* * *

September 3, 1980

Mel Tolkin

Dear Mel,

Just after my last letter to you went out, yours of August 27th came in.

Sure, I'll be glad to read your twenty-three-page outline of the story about China.

None of this twenty-four- or twenty-five-page stuff, you understand. When I make an agreement I expect the other party to stick to it.

And I'll be glad to give you my thoughts, although the way things are going these days I'd better hang on to all the thoughts I have. They may be valuable sometime.

I'll also be glad to give you my opinion as to whether there's a movie in your outline.

Of course I think there's a movie in everything. I read the folded instructions in a jar of Vicks last night, and I can just see Ernest Borgnine playing the part of the man with the chest cold.

Sorry to hear about your overdosing on *Skag*. It always sounded to me like the name of a union. "Well, Skag is out on strike again."

At the moment I'm busy myself working on a few projects, the most notable of which is a horror-disaster film titled *The Day Irwin Allen Stood Still*.

All the best, which is probably more than you deserve.

Cordially,

The following was written in response to a phone message from Jim Stein and Bob Illes telling me I was "terrific" on the Emmy Awards the previous evening.

September 8, 1980

Dear Jim and Bob,

That shows how much *you* guys know. I was *funny,* not terrific.
I was terrific in *bed* last night.
And I sleep alone.

*　　*　　*

September 25, 1980

Mr. and Mrs. Anthony Newley

Dear Dareth and Tony,

I'm sorry I had to tiptoe away from your delightful party at midnight, but I had an early work-call Sunday morning.
And then, too, I have so little opportunity to tiptoe these days.
It's rather sad, really, in that before you two came here from overseas I had a reputation in our business as one of the great tiptoers of all time. I was, in fact, equally competent to tiptoe through tulips, juleps, polyps, fillips, though I have no reluctance to confess that I preferred to tiptoe through the trollops.
I still recall, with an utter absence of guilt, that any time a trollop objected to being tiptoed through, I would give her a good wallop. If, in fact, I was, in those halcyon days, known for anything more than tiptoeing, it was trollop-walloping.
I realize I might be wasting time in giving you all this information because there was international media interest in my feat—and my feet, too—upon the occasion of the annual Trollop-Walloping Festival, which took place in Gallup, New Mexico. I am immodest enough to recall that to this day in the town square of that square town there is displayed a plaque, to *The Greatest Trollop-Walloper of Them All,* your obedient servant.
I shan't bore you with the full details of how I originally *became* a servant, and the incredible degree of my obedience in that lowly role, although to do so would be only fitting.
Which is more than I can say for Ed McMahon's white suit.
But, all seriousness aside, I did want to apologize not only for being the first of your guests to leave, but for the accident that my departure coincided with that of a middle-aged black woman who, understandably I suppose, cast many a fearful glance over her shoulder as I followed her out into the darkness that surrounded your mansion on the evening in question. As far as I was concerned, it was a *great* evening.
But it is not the most comfortable thing in the world to have a strange black woman casting fearful glances over her shoulder as you walk innocently to your car in a neighborhood populated by some of the great nouveau

riche of our generation.

Were there to be any sort of formal investigation of the incident I should have to testify that it was an overcast night to begin with. While I do not deny the civil right and the new left of Mrs. Schwartzkopf to cast fearful glances over her shoulder, I nevertheless hold myself blameless.

Anyway—your house was breathtaking (fortunately I had my Primatine Mist), the food perfect, and the guests, for the most part, pushy.

Thanks, and love to you both.

Sincerely,

●　　●　　●

September 9, 1981

Eydie Gorme

Dear Eydie,

I just happened to hear your recording of "Send in the Clowns" on KGIL this afternoon—Friday—and had to take tape recorder in hand to tell you it's the best damned record—of anything, by anybody—that I've heard in a very long time.

In fact, your rendition of the number was so moving that when I stopped for a red light, fourteen clowns jumped into my car.

Love,

●　　●　　●

October 8, 1981

Mr. George Burns

Dear George,

Why is it that if I start a letter "Dear George" nobody says anything, but if I started it "George dear" people would talk?

Well, people talk anyway.

But they don't talk as funny as you do.

All seriousness aside, Jayne and I are indebted to you for another great night.

Not that what happened at your house was so terrific, but on the way home three Armenians helped us change a flat tire, and we had a million laughs.

We hope to see you soon.

Love,

●　　●　　●

January 8, 1982

Mr. and Mrs. Ron Clark

Dear Sheila and Ron,

Jayne thought that I was writing to you—and I thought that *she* was writing to you—to explain our Mysterious Nonappearance at your Christmas party.

Due chiefly to the failure of last-minute efforts to have Henry Kissinger assume responsibility for these negotiations, and by the authority invested in me by the vest I'm wearing, know all men by these presents that we had every intention of coming to your party. The problem was we were already obligated to attend the annual holiday get-together of Jayne's brothers and sisters and their assorted offspring and in-laws.

And if you've ever tried to spring any of your in-laws, you know how uncooperative wardens can be.

Unfortunately, Jayne's family talks a lot; and in this case we couldn't shut them up and get away from them until about 11:45.

Another complication is that our hostess of the evening served dinner about an hour and a half later than she should have, with the result that dessert wasn't served until about 11:00 p.m. It was close to midnight by the time we were able to get in our car, and I felt that we had no business barging in on you guys after midnight, particularly when the street you live on is too narrow to accommodate a barge anyway.

But we apologize 1) for not showing up, and 2) for the long delay in getting this explanation to you.

Needless to say, if Jayne also writes you a funny letter—I'll be hornswoggled.

And if you've ever had your horn swoggled . . .

Love,

❂   ❂   ❂

February 26, 1982

Mr. Jeff Harris
Ready-to-Wear Productions
20th Century Fox

Dear Mr. Harris,

Thank you for your letter of February 24th.

First of all, I'm terribly sorry to hear about the problem with your typewriter as a result of which you are not able to type any capital letters.

This saddens me deeply because the well-known comedian Fred Allen and the poet e.e. cummings were stricken with the same malady.

The fact that they are no longer with us shows the fatality of it all.

The primary purpose of this letter, therefore, is not only to wish you a fond farewell but to hopefully be the first one to do so, if Mr. Kukoff has not beaten me to that privilege.

As regards my beard, let me say that I grew it for a picture. Unfortunately, no one has as yet taken the picture.

The beard has, I suppose, not made a great deal of difference in my life except that the percentage of anti-Semitic mail I am receiving has increased somewhat.

Nor can I stand idly by in the face of your assertion that you don't miss a trick. To my personal knowledge you have missed many tricks. I once stood not ten feet in front of you and deftly withdrew a queen of diamonds from my nose. You missed it.

I wish you good luck, nevertheless, with your Ready-to-Wear Productions. If you have anything over there, right off the rack, in the way of a nice 44-Long comedy series, I'd appreciate your keeping me in mind.

By the way, did anyone ever tell you that your signature looks like *doff?* The reason I mention this is that I understand Pepperdine College is starting a new series of late-night classes in which there is major emphasis on the proper formation of the letter *j*. I have some pull over there because I once helped a man get some pepper out of his dine, and he has been beholden and Bill Holden to me ever since.

Weakly,

*   *   *

May 20, 1982

David Letterman
NBC-TV

Dear David,

If a man can write "Dear David," why can't he write "David dear"?

I'll tell *you why he can't (patriotic music begins to build here)*. It's because the American people have had it up to here—

And down to there—

With blatantly promiscuous behavior. Hasn't it ever seemed strange to you that Frankie and Johnny were lovers? (*Tympanies are building now*). I, for one—and "Tea for Two"—do *not* propose to stand idly by, nor do I feel that I was elected to preside over the dissolution of the British Empire.

Anyway, thanks for your attention, David, and I know that you'll do something about this important problem.

Oh, while I have dictation machine in hand—I've been requested by a young whippersnapper of my acquaintance—one John Magee (and the world will breath easier tonight knowing that there are not *two* John Magees) to write a letter of introduction for him, since it has apparently come into his mind that his proper role in the great panorama of history is to serve as a member of your writing staff.

All seriousness aside, I haven't had the pleasure of reading any of John's material, but I have known him and his family for years and he was always a witty and personable young fellow, so far as I could judge by his behavior around our house.

He and his brother, and my son Bill—who now works for CBS—formed the nucleus of a sort of gang which was characterized by its general wit and silliness.

True wit and silliness—as Secretary Watt would be the first to attest—are certainly in short supply in today's television. If I were you I would throw down a challenge to Magee. I would say to him, "All right, Magee, put up or shut up."

I never was able to get him to shut up under my roof, but then I have a very funny roof and that might have had something to do with it.

Whether the present budget of "Letterman in the Wee Hours" would permit you to add anyone to your writing staff I have no idea. But then I haven't had an idea of any kind for the last three hours.

In any event, Magee will either be writing to you independently or will be looming over your desk as you read this letter.

I wish to state, for the public record—which is being released in three speeds next week—that I have not written this letter under duress but am motivated only by my long-held conviction that we must get our young people off the streets and back into the alleys where many of them belong.

Congratulations on all the fine things you're doing, but I suppose you know that if NBC ever finds out about it you're finished.

Love to Irene.

I know there is no Irene in your life at present, but someday there may be.

Sincerely,

*   *   *

February 23, 1983

Michael J. Grossman
Columbia Pictures Television

Dear Michael,

How generous of you to admit that you are "unabashedly a fan."

The next time I run into you it will be my pleasure to give you a good bashing, once and for all.

All good wishes.

*   *   *

September 29, 1983

Mr. Jeff Harris
Universal Studios

Dear Mr. Harris,

The enclosed picture was taken by private investigators with a hidden camera.

To tell the truth, the camera was so well hidden that we have not yet been able to locate it ourselves; but that is our problem.

Your problem is that unless you deliver to us, within forty-eight hours upon receipt of this message, $50,000 in negotiable securities of both McDonnel Douglas and Chrysler Corporation stock, copies of this picture will be distributed to all major wire services and Midas Muffler shops, from Point Conception to the Mexican border.

And if you've ever had your conception pointed by a Mexican boarder you know how painful that can be.

It will do you no good to go to the police about this matter. We got the picture from them.

It will also do you no good to go to Spelling-Goldberg. *Anybody* can spell Goldberg, so what's the big deal?

Sincerely,

Clyde Klaveman
THE NBC LIBERATION FRONT

*   *   *

March 9, 1984

Mel Brooks

Dear Mel,

Thanks for yours of March 6. Your *what* I can't quite recall.

I was particularly impressed by the second paragraph of your letter, which reads as follows: "Take care."

For your information, I have been taking Care, like clockwork, for several years. This fine product has not only cleared up my sinuses, but opened my pores, stiffened my spine, stepined my fetchit and cleared my throat.

I note, too, that your address is a box number.

How a man with your money could possibly demean himself by living in a box I'll never know. Have you discussed this with your lovely wife?

Most of the best.

Sincerely,

❖   ❖   ❖

March 9, 1984

Jan Marshall
Showbiz

Dear Jan,

Since Jan is both a man's name and a woman's name, far be it from me—
    Listen, it takes all kinds.
    Needless to say, I am deeply touched by the mere thought of winning the Golden Sprocket award. It just so happens that I used to raise golden sprockets, and golden retrievers as well, in the North Carolina territory many years ago.
    Some people may prefer labradors or cockers, if you'll pardon the expression; but I say that when a man comes home in the evening, bone-weary and sick at heart, there's nothing that will restore his faith and courage like sitting down in an easy chair, lighting up a pipe, having a sip of sherry, and having his golden sprocket jump up on his lap and lick his face.
    And, if his dog isn't available, any red-blooded man will accept a good face-licking from any qualified party.
    Some restrictions do apply.
    If you have the temerity to sum up my career in less than fifteen minutes, more power to you. In any event, I've told my secretary, Dawn, to set up the interview for your show.
    Needless to say, I will be happy to appear through the facilities of the Arts and Entertainment Channel, although you will have to let me know, sometime between now and then, whether you want me to be artistic or entertaining.

Cordially,

❖   ❖   ❖

March 21, 1984

Todd David Schwartz
Laugh Factory

Dear Mr. Schwartz,

At first the name Todd Schwartz didn't ring a bell with me.
    Then suddenly I remembered—Todd Schwartz, the bell-ringer.
    In any event, you're lucky to have gotten out of that line of work and into something more substantial. "Laugh Factory" sounds like a good idea.
    And I'm glad to hear that the Warner people are backing you up.
    I have often laughed at their funny logo—showing two-and-a-half slanted

white salamis—which to some people, I suppose, looks like the letter W, though you and I know better.

I'm glad to hear you're doing a story about the Olympics and am happy to contribute a response to the question: "What the Olympics mean to me."

I've always thought that the Olympics were the greatest pop-rock group since Earl Warren and the Supremes.

I wonder how many young people today know, for example, that long before Gladys Knight had any Pips to speak of the Olympics had a minimum of seven pips as their back-up group?

They don't have them any more, of course, because of the tragic incident in which they backed up too far and fell off the stage. But far be it from me . . .

But not even the Beatles or the Stones have given us such great hits as "I've Thrown a Custard in Your Face," "If You Knew Sushi Like I Know Sushi," and "The Incredible Hulk" (from which, by the way, the writers of "The Impossible Dream" did a blatant rip-off):

> To be—the Incredible Hulk,
> To boast—an incredible bulk,
> To feel such a terrible anger,
> To rip off your clothes and turn green.
> This is my quest—

Is it any wonder that I will never forget the Olympics?

Sincerely,

* * *

May 8, 1984

Dinah Shore

Dear Dinah,

It was sweet of you to send us that letter about the Salvation Army's Sally Award.

But where were you when we won the Signal Hill Ladies' Auxiliary *Silly* Award?

Or the Southern Methodist University Training Department's *Smutty* Award?

Incidentally, this is not the first Sally I've won. I once won Sally Eilers in a raffle at the Motion Picture Country Home. Nothing came of it, however, as she still preferred James Dunn.

But all seriousness aside—it was sweet of you to write.

Jayne joins me in giving you a great big—mmmmwah!

Sincerely,

A brief word of explanation about the following letter: At an all-Western costume party, I had had a picture taken with producer-writer Larry Gelbart and his wife, Pat. To make myself look authentically cowboyish, I did not wear my trademark glasses and added a dapper moustache. The combination made me look curiously like the late film actor Zachary Scott.

June 12, 1984

Mr. and Mrs. Larry Gelbart

Dear Mr. and Mrs. Gelbart,

I am presently writing the definitive biography of the late film actor Zachary Scott. In this connection, my interest was aroused by the enclosed photograph of you and Mr. Scott in what would appear to be a western setting.

I may be mistaken in this last assumption in that a garment worn by a background figure suggests that the photograph may have been taken at a social function honoring the late Shah of Iran.

In any event, a number of questions occur to me on the basis of the pictorial evidence, and I am hoping you will be able to clarify them:

1. Mr. Scott's neckerchief would appear to be askew. It also happens that Gov. Reuben is Askew. Do you perceive any connection between these two facts?

2. We may be safe in concluding that Mr. Scott's left hand is gracefully draped over the shoulder of Mrs. Gelbart. Ordinarily one would assume that his right hand is somehow in contact with the woman on Mr. Scott's right. But, on the other hand—no pun either intended or achieved—it occurs to me, because of my long familiarity with Mr. Scott's sexual proclivities, that you might be the best person from whom to solicit information about the actual location of Mr. Scott's right hand.

3. Mr. Scott was given to reciting verbatim, also word for word, the old poem "Dangerous Dan McGrew." Is the garment you are wearing by any chance the original "buckskin shirt that was glazed with dirt"? No harm done if it's not.

4. Are you able to identify the dance-hall girl seen here wearing a Sargent's flea collar?

5. As you may be aware, Mr. Scott suffered a severe neck injury while falling from a horse during the filming of *How Green Was My Pooltable* and, consequently, was never thereafter able to look anybody in the eye, even upon demand. Do you suppose this is the reason that, although the other three figures in the photograph are staring—like raccoons caught in the act of garbage-can raiding—into the camera, Mr. Scott's gaze is directed some seventeen degrees to the right?

6. Do you suppose there's any connection between that fact and the

aforementioned general askewity of his neckerchief?

7. Lastly, after responding to the above questions, would you also be interested in helping me in connection with my biography of Zachary *All*, a prominent though somewhat pushy clothier who achieved television fame in the 1960s?

Cordially,

Sterling Zelman

* * *

August 3, 1984

Ms. Pat Collins

Dear Pat,

Thanks for your sweet letter of July 25th.

The letter was so sweet, in fact, that instead of filing it, I ate it.

And it agreed with me.

All except the second paragraph, which I had a bit of trouble with.

I was touched by your mentioning that the control room applauded when I appeared on your program. I have brought this astonishing news to the attention of various societies specializing in parapsychological research, scientifically unexplainable phenomena, and general weirdness, because it seems to me significant that you are providing evidence of an instance in which an actual room applauded a human being.

You will undoubtedly soon be contacted by specialists who will want to know whether the room applauded by banging its walls together, and, if not, by what means.

All good wishes to you and your family.

Sincerely,

* * *

August 30, 1985

Mr. George Burns

Dear George,

Until I saw some of the publicity stories about our recent *Alice in Wonderland* soiree I hadn't been aware—believe it or not—that you had attended the party. But now I have the pictorial evidence that you were not only present but drinking, smoking and generally wilding it up.

If you think you had fun at the party on the second floor, you should have gone to the one downstairs. It was much better, largely due to the class of people down there.

Actually, I think you and I may have stumbled onto something. To review the circumstances—

You had a great time at the party.

I had a great time at the party.

And we never even saw each other.

I may never talk to you again.

Love,

*   *   *

December 18, 1985

Editors
The Globe

Gentlemen,

I thank you for the story *How to Overcome Shyness,* in which you made reference to my book *How to Make a Speech* (McGraw-Hill).

The aspect of your feature that has occasioned the greatest comment and which, therefore, calls for an immediate response concerns the picture caption: "Allen, with wife Audrey Meadows."

In a time when scandal and sensation are in dramatic public demand and, therefore, useful to the media, it is hard to even think of a subject matter concerning which jaded Americans have not already been made intimately familiar.

I suppose that the *Globe*'s discovery of the sordid story of my marriage to Audrey Meadows—given the fact that for the past thirty-one years it has been commonly assumed I was married to *Jayne* Meadows—does at least have the virtues of novelty and freshness. But the striking question is how I was able, for three decades, to keep the ugly reality of my true marital status from public scrutiny.

Part of the problem, of course, was that the man popularly assumed to be married to Audrey, Continental Airlines executive Bob Six, had to be kept quiet. The means by which I achieved this end I do not plan to reveal but will say only that they relate to Continental's connection with the CIA, so important to the success of that agency's efforts during the recent unpleasantness in Southeast Asia.

I must say that Jayne and Audrey, personally, have been more than cooperative. My only obligations, which were contractually agreed to, were to keep the glamorous, dramatic Jayne well-supplied with the high-fashion gowns that have come to be her trademark. Other than that we needed only to make occasional appearances together at high-profile media events —Broadway openings, industry dinners, or occasional tandem Las Vegas concert appearances.

As for Audrey, the wise-cracking, deadpan straightwoman for Jackie Gleason and Art Carney, she was wonderfully cooperative except for the fact that she refused to have children.

This unhappy fact forces me now to reveal one more detail of the scandal, that the young network executive, Bill Allen, who has always assumed that Jayne Meadows and Steve Allen were his parents, was actually ordered from Kids-R-Us, a San Fernando Valley agency that surreptitiously distributes factory-second children.

For the last couple of years I have been doing a series of comedy specials for ABC television called "Life's Most Embarrassing Moments." The *Globe* has now produced my own most embarrassing moment. But, in a sense, I feel considerable relief that I need no longer expend emotional energy in hiding the vile secret that your editors have brought to light.

Sincerely,

*   *   *

April 25, 1986

Mr. Larry Gelbart

Dear Larry,

My secretary has, I believe—Well, listen, I'll believe anything—

But all seriousness aside, you have been advised that it was not possible for me to take part in the meeting April 21st at the Beverly Hills Hotel in the Terrace Room.

The main reason is that I was busy at the time in Room 614, and having a lot more fun than you people were.

But really—I'm writing to share with you the good news that, having given careful study to the signature affixed to your letter (and you know how hard it is to get a fix these days), I have rummaged around through earlier correspondence from you and located what I believe are all the missing letters in your signature.

That you took the time to personally hand-sketch an L and an E is clear enough. At that point the pen apparently slipped from your perhaps relatively lifeless fingers and God knows what the denouement was.

If you still need the missing *r*'s, the *y*, the *s*, the *g*, the *l*, the *b*, the *a*, and the *t*—just let me know.

I provided the same sort of service many years ago for the Campbell's Soup people, and you know what great luck they have had with the alphabet.

Best Wishes,

In March 1989, the Museum of Broadcasting here in Los Angeles was nice enough to present an evening of tribute to my old "Tonight" show. Members of the old gang were there—Steve and Eydie, Jonathan Winters, Pat Harrington Jr., Sid Caesar, Gene Rayburn, Stan Burns, Louis Nye, and the show's producer, Bill Harbach. According to Rick Du Brow of the Los Angeles *Herald Examiner*, "A small miracle took place . . . a [re-creation] of the wildly infectious spirit and looniness of the series' early days." And indeed that's what it felt like!

In any event, Bill Harbach was scheduled to arrive by plane from New York for the event, and since neither Jayne nor myself would be available to meet him, I made arrangements for one of my staff members to pick him up at the airport and deliver him to our home in Encino. Since the two had never met, I thought a letter of introduction would be appropriate. Also I wanted to be sure Bill was aware of the scheduling leading up to the evening's event. The following letter, hand-delivered by my assistant, was the result.

March 3, 1989

Dear 006-7/8,

This letter will confirm that you have been met at the airport by Secret Agent 14.

She used to work as an agent for the Morris office, but she kept it a secret.

Fourteen will take you promptly to a safe house and if either of you can recall the combination to the safe there will be no difficulty in getting admitted.

Your room during your visit will be the one directly to the right as you enter.

It is possible that during your stay you may encounter a Japanese gardener. Be on guard against discussing confidential matters in his presence as he has never personally accepted the terms of surrender at the end of World War II.

You may also meet a young woman who poses as a student and housesitter for the ostensible owners of the dwelling. Do not be deluded; she is a former hooker from Philadelphia whom we have reason to suspect has connections with the KGB, as well as the MCA, the ICM, the CAA, and other groups known to be infested with ruthless agents.

At 05:00 on the evening of your arrival there will be a small buffet dinner service, to which a carefully chosen group—code identification *Nondescript*—has been invited.

At about 06:40 the master of the house (there is apparently some dispute about his rank) will absent himself to report to the L.A. Country Museum of Art on Wilshire Boulevard.

The lady will leave the premises at 07:15, so that she can arrive at the same meeting place well before 08:00.

In order for our people to convene without drawing suspicion, we have set up a phony front, or diversion, made to resemble a public discussion about an ancient television program said to have been "created" by a television executive whose daughter is presently making pornographic films with gorillas.

Your assignment—should you accept it—is to contest this view during the discussion that will constitute the bulk of the evening's proceedings.

Sincerely,

003

• • •

July 11, 1990

Mr. Bob Saget
TAV Studios

Dear Bob,

Since I've been doing a lot of work recently at the TAV Studios on Vine Street, parking in the lot across the street, it has repeatedly come to my attention that the first letter of your first name on the theater's marquee is sagging badly.

If I were you I would raise hell with my agent about this. Success or failure in our business, you know, is a matter of little things—a grain of sand here, a missed opportunity there, and suddenly everything goes to hell.

Mark my words, if you don't get that *B* straightened up, pretty soon your employers won't care about the *O*. Eventually the Saget will start sagging, and then where are you?

Sincerely,

• • •

October 12, 1990

Mr. Larry Gelbart,

Dear Larry,

I thank you for the general thankfulness of your recent thank-you message.

On a more important subject, I have written to you earlier about your signature, which has the unique distinction of being totally devoid of actual letters of the alphabet.

At least that was my first hypothesis, which I now confess was inadequate. Because I come from an English-speaking background I naturally was looking for alphabet-fragments of my mother tongue.

(Rest assured I am not unmindful that some great straight lines, such as *background* and *mother tongue* are flying by here—but I can't stop for everything.)

Be that as it may—and you know what goes here—I have now perceived that there are indeed letters to your signature, but that they are in Arabic.

I showed a sample of your handwriting to a Muslim trumpet player of my acquaintance, Wingy Hussein, and he tells me that your signature actually expresses a remarkably vulgar thought in his native language.

Yours in Mohammed,

•   •   •

March 8, 1991

Mr. and Mrs. Sidney Sheldon

Dear Sidney and Alexandra,

It was a pleasure running into you the other evening, as always, partly because it gave us a chance to settle the "Cuando Caliente El Sol" matter.

Actually I did write a remarkably similar song years ago called "Who Is the Yenta with Sol?"—but that's another matter.

Have a wonderful trip. Jayne and I hope to see you when you return.

Cordially,

•   •   •

November 14, 1991

Mr. Herb Sargent

Dear Sargent Herb,

I never cease to marvel at the carelessness with which the popular media—and with whom are these media popular, by the way?—report the facts.

And the gullibility of readers takes my breath away—which, considering what I had for lunch, is not the worst thing in the world.

Imagine sending a reporter to Pip's Comedy Club—do you know Pip, by the way? You'd love him.

I'm not kidding; he used to work with Gladys Knight.

Anyway, Pip himself asked me to come down to his stupid comedy club to take part in the kids' magic show. After accepting the invitation I decided I would make a few kids disappear, just to entertain the crowd.

But the first thing I do in that act, as you will no doubt recall, is Señor Wences.

The next thing that happens is—the *audience* winces.

But at least they laugh their little heads off when I get my hand caught in the "Alright?" box, followed by a full three minutes of Gleason- or Caesar-type shtick. And as for you, Sargent, I'm disappointed that you would assume, purely on the basis of the pictorial evidence, that I was wearing a hat.

That isn't a hat, you numbskull.

And sometime, at a mutually free moment, you must explain to me how your skull ever got that numb. We migraine sufferers could put that knowledge to good use.

Anyway—which is better than be-that-as-it-may any day of the week—what you so cavalierly described as my hat is actually my hair.

Well, more truthfully, my hair*piece*.

No doubt you never would have made the mistake were it not for the hirsute appendages at the sides. I told the hairdresser to make me look as orthodox as possible, but he never could get the curls just right.

This is no small point, either, because, as you know, my act concludes—and people are so grateful when it does—with a spirited rendition of "If I Were Harry Richman" from *Fiddler on the Hoof,* the famous musical about two Jews who got off a covered wagon in Montana back in 1872.

And your recollection about the Cole Porter estate is no better than your powers of present observation, something with which I'm intimately familiar because for several years I *lived* on the Cole Porter estate, in a charming house that was formerly a guest cottage.

But, hey, I don't hold any of this against you. I do hold it against myself for having put the word *hey* into the preceding sentence—but that's another matter.

I just finished a book reporting on my fifty years in radio and TV, despite the fact that I've forgotten about twelve of them. It'll be out next year, but then so will my uncle. The title is *Hi-Ho, Steverino.*

Hope to see you soon.

Sincerely,

*   *   *

January 7, 1992

Mr. Jack Carter

Dear Jack,

Of all the Christmas cards we got, yours was the funniest.

I refer, of course, not to the hand-printed message on it but to the consistency of the recycled paperstock, the type-size, the finger-stained ink, and all of that.

But all seriousness aside, you're a funny man, Jack.

I once saw you dressed as a funny woman and you weren't bad then either.

There's no point in my overpraising you here; we both know you're no Gary Collins.

But then neither is Regis Philbin.

So far Irvin Arthur's campaign to gradually ease us all into at least semi-retirement seems to be going very well, but hey—

I have nothing to add to that; I just like to say "But hey—" from time to time to make myself sound younger.

Jayne joins me in sending our love to you and Roxanne.

Sincerely,

12

Creating Cartoons

Just as verbal jokes continually occur to me, so does visual imagery expressed in cartoon form. Many of these ideas have been turned, in collaboration with artists,* into finished works. My penchant for word play seems to surface in my cartoons, such as the one that shows two men about to cross a street and then uses literalization to interpret the common idiom "We've got the light" (Fig. 1).

In a variation of this approach, I often devise cartoons based on the use of a word, or term, having more than one meaning (note "conversion" in Fig. 2 and "territory" in Fig. 3).

Sometimes I create cartoons from jokes I have performed in a comedy routine, as in "George, you need a prefrontal lobotomy like you need a hole in the head" (Fig. 4) The line can exist perfectly well on its own, without the accompanying drawing.

Sometimes the funniness comes from the symbiotic relationship between the picture and the caption (Fig. 6—"How many calories in a slice of whole wheat?"). Neither the caption nor the picture would be funny on its own. The combination is what brings the chuckle, if there is one.

At the other extreme, I am fond, too, of devising cartoons that require no captions whatever (Fig. 5, the four panels showing the duck hunter). The bizarre visual twist triggers the comic surprise. A variation of this is to have a printed sign within the sketch transmit the message, as in "The Incredible Normal Man" (Fig. 7), or "Ladies Garment Workers' Union" (Fig. 8). Cover those labels and you will see that the artwork, though comical in style, is meaningless.

---

*All cartoons in chapter 12 were illustrated by Roland B. Wilson.

Fig. 1. "Let's cross here, Harry; we've got the light."

Fig. 2. "Smith is attempting the conversion out there."

Fig. 3. "The ball is now in Oklahoma territory."

Fig. 4. "George, you need a prefrontal lobotomy
like you need a hole in the head."

Fig. 5.

Fig. 6. "How many calories in a slice of whole wheat?"

Fig. 7.

Fig. 8.

Fig. 9. "You want to get out and stretch your legs?"

Fig. 10. "Guess I'm a little fast."

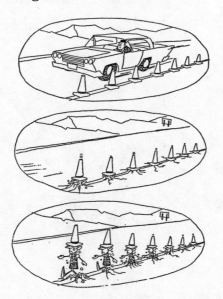

Fig. 11.

Fig. 12. "Martinis or manhattans?"

Cartoons fall into two broad categories—those that involve simply a funny caption—usually one that would be funny even without the attendant sketch—and those that are purely visual. In many instances, of course, the artist's work will greatly enhance the verbal joke of the caption. This was the case in my "Want to get out and stretch your legs?" sketch (Fig. 9), "Guess I'm a little fast" (Fig. 10), and "Martinis or Manhattans?" (Fig. 12).

It also applies to all of the late Virgil Parch's work. He employed scarcely any other formula than the Literalization technique for the creation of his cartoons. For instance, in one a surgeon is huddled over an operating table, scalpel in hand. On the table, however, is not a human being, but a short, thin ribbon of cloth. An intern provides the caption: "Dr. Benton is operating on a shoestring."

Parch once sent me a personal note and an original cartoon showing him following me as we walk through an open field. But behind me, without my knowledge, Parch had stopped a wheelbarrow and proceeded to dig up the earth around some of the footprints I had left. His caption for the sketch was: "Steve, I worship the ground you walk on."

The purely pictorial cartoon jokes—such as my weird clowns coming up through the cracks in the road (Fig. 11)—require no verbal elaboration.

The best way to stimulate your own cartooning creativity is to see and read as many top-quality cartoons as possible. This provides the proper mind-set. You begin to think of cartoon-type jokes, as distinguished from jokes that would be appropriate for Rodney Dangerfield, or "what if" monologues that might be right for George Carlin.

Because I am a particular fan of sophisticated cartoons of the *New Yorker* sort, I once talked so much about a specific feature by Shel Silverstein that its caption became the title of a subsequent published collection of his work. The picture shows two pathetic prisoners in what appears to be a medieval dungeon. The poor fellows are down a dark stone well. Their wrists and ankles are bolted to the wall, they are covered in chains and their predicament is, quite obviously, utterly hopeless. The reader may visualize as many additional factors as he or she wishes—iron bars at the top of the passage, alligators below, whatever. But precisely at this moment, one of the prisoners turns to the other and whispers, "Now here's my plan—"

The greatest!

Another cartoon I saw in *Collier's*, probably thirty-five years ago, was drawn, I'm reasonably certain, by Irwin Caplan. The scene is a typical Western panorama, an apparently endless desert, with mountains in the distance, cactus, dried cattle bones, etc. In the foreground, however, there's a narrow strip of two-lane highway, at the side of which sits one of those "Joe's Eats" type hamburger stands. Looking again at the background, we see a track that has been traced in the sand, made by a grizzled, ragged, gaunt character who has apparently pulled himself, on hands and knees, many miles across the desert to reach this spot. By the look of him, he has gone without food and water for days and is at death's door. Finally he has dragged himself up to the counter of the little lunchstand and pulled himself half-erect, at which point he looks at the proprietor and says, "Well, what's good today?"

I advise would-be cartoonists to haunt secondhand bookstores, preferably in somewhat rundown neighborhoods. The reason is that the prices there will generally be lower than those of stores in urban neighborhoods with much foot-traffic. In any event, find published collections of works by the best cartoonists. Devour them. Study every page, analyze the techniques of the various artists. The *New Yorker* is a wonderful source. Issues of this magazine, as well as many others which carry several cartoons in each edition, can also be found at your library.

The following pages contain a few more examples of cartoons I have created over the years.

There's no one narrow approach to conceiving cartoons. There are different styles, and different types of writers think of the basic humorous ideas. Certain cartoons, as I say, are simply visually funny. They require no narrative at all. It would be possible to add some sort of caption to these cartoons, but doing so would generally weaken, not strengthen, the humor.

As regards the other, quite distinct kind of cartoon, there may be nothing particularly amusing in the sketch itself. The humor lies totally in the caption, which will usually be a line spoken by one of the characters.

The best, most successful cartoonists do both their own pictures and jokes, although some of them are perfectly prepared to accept jokes, or buy them on the open market. All that matters to cartoon editors at magazines and newspapers is that the final product be funny. They wouldn't care if one person or twenty-seven participated in the creation of it.

The real mystery—and I doubt if there's anyone on earth who could give how-to advice about it—concerns the matter of *drawing* funny. Word jokes are a snap to dissect, analyze and, for many people at least, create. But why one sketch artist's cartoons have a sort of vaguely square look, while another's seem inherently comic regardless of the subject matter, is extremely difficult to say.

But, as I've suggested before, study the work of the masters: George Adams, Charles Addams, Jules Feiffer, Ed Koreen, Virgil Parch, Gary Larsen,

Fig. 13.

Fig. 14.

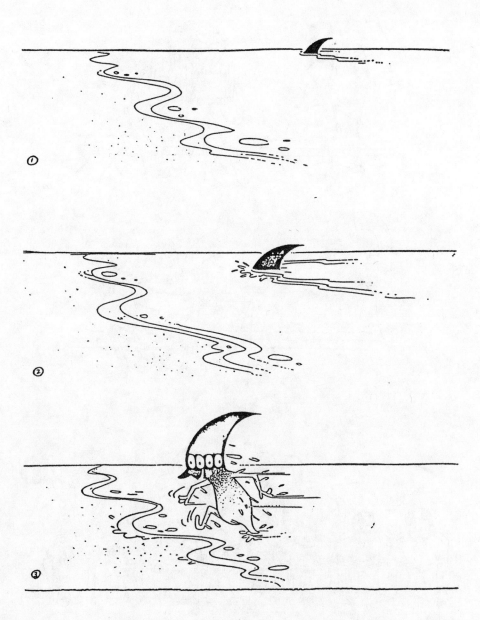

Fig. 15.

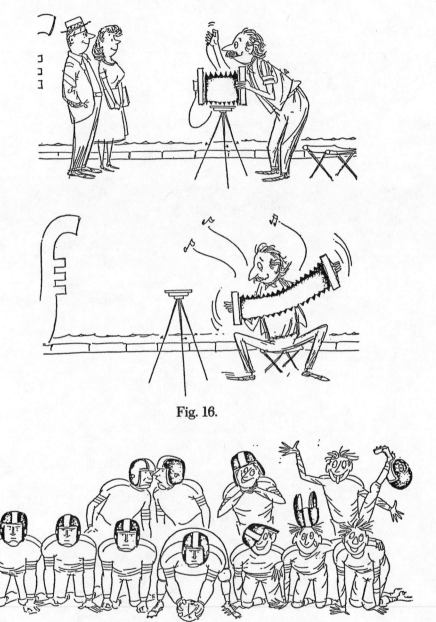

Fig. 16.

Fig. 17. "The line is unbalanced on the left."

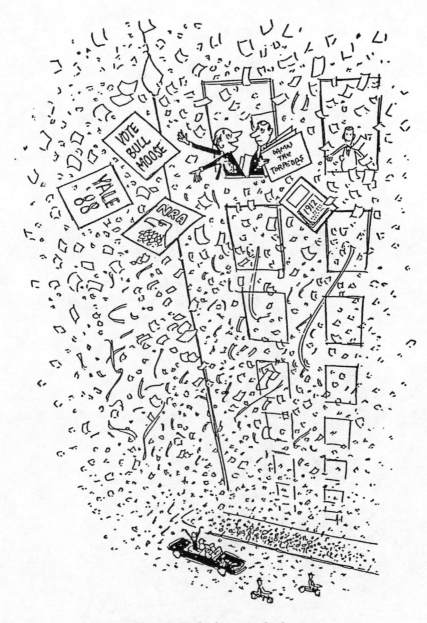

Fig. 18. "I don't care who he is;
it's a great opportunity to tidy the office up."

Fig. 19.

Fig. 20. ". . . and remember, in the event a man is knocked down,
his opponent must stay back out of camera range."

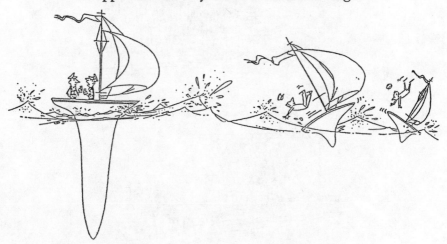

Fig. 21. "She's not very fast, but she's mighty steady."

Fig. 22.

Shel Silverstein, Saul Steinberg, Garry Trudeau. Try to identify the factors that make you prefer these cartoonists to other practitioners of the art. Study cartoons published in Europe, too. Again, libraries and bookstores can help track down such materials.

The market for magazine cartoons has changed quite a bit since the heyday of general-interest, mass-circulation publications. Although the number of magazines that regularly run cartoons for which they pay big bucks has decreased, there is a growing assortment of specialized journals using cartoons geared to a narrowly focused editorial thrust. These include publications about health, exercise, sports, science, computers, and photography.

Some of the major magazines that accept cartoons from independent contributors are *Good Housekeeping*, the *New Yorker, Playboy,* and the *Saturday Evening Post*. In addition, the *Wall Street Journal* accepts cartoons from freelance people.

The best way to submit cartoons is to send copies, together with a self-addressed stamped envelope, directly to the publication. Rates, which vary widely depending on the outlet, range from about $10 to over $600 per cartoon. Two of the bigger payers are the *New Yorker,* which offers a basic rate of $500 plus further payment subject to size of the published drawing, and *Playboy,* which pays $350 for a black-and-white cartoon and from $600 for one that is printed in color.

Since rates and submission criteria change frequently, however, it's always a good idea, before any submission, to consult the last edition of the *Writer's Market* or contact the proposed magazine for a copy of its submission guidelines. Most are happy to send these free of charge.

If you're short on artistic talent but have funny cartoon ideas, you might try selling them to an established cartoonist. You can receive a commission of approximately 25 to 50 percent on the payment he or she receives from a publication. The percentage hinges on whether the cartoon is in completed form when sold, or if the deal is made mainly on the basis of your idea.

Where to find ideas? Be a sharp observer and they'll come with almost no effort. The *New Yorker* cartoonist Dana Fradon, according to *Advertising Age* magazine, gets many of his ideas by free association while reading the *New York Times.* For other cartoonists, flipping through Sears, Roebuck & Co. or J. C. Penney mail-order catalogs seems to strike the spark.

If your interest lies in originating comic strips or newspaper cartoon panels, contact the feature syndicates, which sell this material to newspapers around the country. They usually need to see about a two-week supply of your work before considering taking it on. Here is a sampling of current syndicates:

King Features Syndicate
235 East 45th Street
New York, NY 10017

Los Angeles Times Syndicate
Times Mirror Square
Los Angeles, CA 90053

Creators Syndicate, Inc.
1554 S. Sepulveda Boulevard
Los Angeles, CA 90025

American International Syndicate
3801 Oakland Street
St. Joseph, MO 64506

News USA, Inc.
1199 National Press Building
Washington DC 20045

Minority Features Syndicate
Box 421
Farrell, PA 16146

Crown Syndicate, Inc.
Box 99126
Seattle, WA 98199

Tribune Media Services, Inc.
64 East Concord Street
Orlando, FL 32801

United Cartoonist Syndicate
Box 7081
Corpus Christi, TX 78415

Newspaper Enterprise Associates, Inc.
200 Park Avenue
New York, NY 10166

Singer Media Corporation
3164 Tyler Avenue
Anaheim, CA 92801

Washington Post Writers Group
1150 15th Street NW
Washington, D.C. 20071

Submissions to the *Wall Street Journal* should be sent directly to the newspaper's New York office.

Although I am not too keen on comic strips, unless they're hip, it was, ironically, a strong interest in these cartoons as a child that ultimately led to my creating the PBS television series "Meeting of Minds." On the program, major historical figures—Plato, Thomas Jefferson, Susan B. Anthony, among others—came together for provocative conversation in a talk-show format.

As a ten-year-old I was familiar with comic-strip characters in the Chicago newspapers, and I often wondered what would happen if all the macho heroes of the day, characters who almost always won their fights—Popeye, Tarzan, Joe Palooka, and the like—should come face to face with one another. Which strongman would emerge the victor? One Sunday, I snipped out some panels from each of those comics and wrote new dialogue for the characters. When I was finished, I had produced my own strip. It was identical in structure to "Meeting of Minds," which years later I would conceive, write and host, and which would earn a Peabody, an Emmy, and other prestigious awards.

Here are a few more of my cartoon ideas, not yet in illustrated form. In each instance, consider the technique that makes the joke work as a cartoon:

Bridegroom in a bazaar where various repairs and crafts are provided: "Where can I go to get my troth plighted?"

❖   ❖   ❖

Two Hindu gods are talking. One has four arms. The other one is commenting, "Well, forewarned is four-armed, I always say."

*   *   *

A weird-looking farmer is speaking to a neighbor. He says, "I raise hackles myself."

*   *   *

A blind man sits on a street corner. He wears shabby clothes, dark glasses, a battered hat.

Around his neck is a sign that is supposed to say "I AM BLIND." The printing, however, is quite sloppy and only the letters *BLI* and part of an *N* can be seen on the card.

*   *   *

Two policemen are standing on a street corner, one of them handcuffed to an enormous fellow who is carrying on his back a small tobacco shop, with wires, pipes dangling, etc.

The arresting policeman says, "I caught him in the act of shoplifting."

*   *   *

Dachau-like prison camp, somber, moody, with chains, whips, barbed-wire, etc.

Guard says to prisoner, "Have a nice day."

*   *   *

Several hundred people are standing in line to get in to see *The Exorcist*. The fourth figure in line has pointed hooves and a long red tail showing under his overcoat.

*   *   *

A man watching Walter Cronkite on TV turns to his wife and says, "Oh, so that's the way it is."

*   *   *

Two women are sitting in a kitchen talking. One, referring to her husband, says, "It's really wonderful how mechanical Bill is."

We see that Bill, who is fixing a lamp, has a key in his back and a few hinges around his knees and elbows.

*   *   *

A woman orders "the house salad."

The waiter brings a dish with salad shaped like a little house—chimney, gables, front door, windows, etc.

*   *   *

A sophisticated, literate-looking couple, early-middle-aged, are in bed together. The lights are turned low, the woman is wearing attractive night attire.

Man says, "Wait a minute. Are you wearing your floppy disc?"

*   *   *

Two incredibly crummy-looking, wino-slob bums are sitting side by side on a bench in Central Park.

One says, "I realize, of course, that to say as much is to incur the risk of being put down as an elitist."

*   *   *

The Miss Universe pageant. Three or four of the contestants are humans, but others are beings from various parts of the universe: some with two heads, or purple stripes, an eye on their belly buttons and so forth.

*   *   *

Doctor's office: Male patient, naked to waist, is sitting on an examining table, hooked up to cardiogram machinery. Readable diploma on wall includes the word *Cardiology*.

The solemn-faced doctor says, "I can't quite understand this, but you seem to have a song in your heart."

* * *

We see a standard boss's business office, and beyond a partly opened door, a waiting room. In the room, there is a human, but an odd one. He has three feet on each leg, growing down from the knee level. His facial expression is fierce and he carries two heavy leather straps in each hand.

Inside the office, the secretary is saying to the boss, "There's a strapping six-footer who says he wants to talk to you."

* * *

A sign over the low-class-looking restaurant says something like "Joe's Eats. Chicken-fried steak."

Inside we see a large chicken frying a steak.

* * *

In one room of an apartment or a home, a man is hanging from a sort of clothesline. Two large, easily recognizable clothespins (or perhaps four) connect him to the line, one grasping his jacket at shoulder points, and perhaps the other two out at about elbow points. The man's feet are clearly two or three feet off the ground.

In one hand, he is holding a telephone, saying, "Christy, I *told* you I was hung up tonight."

* * *

Scene at baseball diamond. Players are in every position, but each has a double standing immediately next to him.

The announcer is saying, "And the Minnesota Twins are on the field now."

* * *

A flaky, strange-looking patient is sitting in a doctor's office.

The doctor says, "Mr. Barton, the tests confirm my personal diagnosis that you are severely neurotic, are victimized by excessively eccentric behavior patterns, and strike most of those who meet you as an out-and-out flake. I'm afraid the only path open to you is to become a television weatherman."

13

Writing Funny Song Lyrics

I have been composing songs since the age of ten. So far I have written over 4,700, most of which have been composed at the piano but some were born in the shower, the car, some even in my dreams. My biggest hit, "This Could Be the Start of Something Big," occurred to me while I was asleep. Although a majority of my tunes are sad or romantic love songs, possibly because of a chaotic childhood in which I experienced long separations from my mother, my comedic self has generated hundreds of humorous songs as well as parodies of familiar hits and standards.

Some of these were created spontaneously on one or another of my television shows. "We're Under Arrest in the Morning," "It's an Icky, Icky Feeling," and "Do We Have a Salami?" are among examples that I and music director Donn Trenner ad-libbed on our Westinghouse Broadcasting comedy show, which ran from 1962 through 1964. Such inane titles were usually triggered by an offhand remark.

The standard procedure was that one of the shows' pianists—Skitch Henderson, Don Trenner, or Paul Smith—knowing how my mind works, would, upon hearing an innocuous spoken phrase, immediately play a short melodic phrase with the number of notes matching the number of syllables in the phrase. In one instance I had been given a small piano made of chocolate, which I promptly ate, and I said, "I just ate a chocolate piano." Skitch played a musical phrase, after which I completed the melody and provided the following lyric:

> *I just ate a chocolate piano.*
> *It tastes like a Baldwin to me.*
> *It's also a fine way*

To swallow a Steinway,
And burp in the key of C.

Not a brilliant lyric, obviously, but then I didn't have much time.

To fully appreciate any comic number the lyric should be heard within the context of the melody. It isn't a case of just having (1) a funny lyric, and (2) a separate funny melody; it's the combination of the two that works. Or doesn't, as the case may be. But since this is not a primer for musicians, we'll limit ourselves to lyrics in the upcoming examples.

Any subject, no matter how serious, is fair game. For instance, at a party one night I ad-libbed a joke that later became the title of my musical revue, *Seymour Glick Is Alive but Sick. Glick,* a satire on the *Jacques Brel is Alive and Well*-type revue, has proven to be an ideal vehicle for displaying comic musical compositions. In one such song, I deal with the infamous 1979 nuclear reactor accident in Pennsylvania, but using a typical Hawaiian Island hula rhythm. I purposely lead the audience to assume that I am talking about the music of Hawaii. This is accomplished partly by the fact that, while I am introducing the number, the accompanist very softly plays the melody of "Aloha Oe," or some other island classic. I refer to the great tradition of such music and explain that when I had the pleasure of performing, as visiting soloist, with the Honolulu Symphony Orchestra, I thought it reasonable to write something appropriate for that particular occasion. But then, I explain, I ran into a problem. I had planned to name the song after one of the islands, but after completing the melody discovered that every island in the South Pacific chain had already had dozens of songs written about it.

I then allege that after checking with Rand-McNally, I was finally able to come up with one island that had not heretofore had a song written about it. At that point, the number starts, with what is indeed a typical Hawaiian treatment, in a ukelele rhythm. To further enhance the illusion I do the standard hand-shtick that hula dancers do and move about a bit in the same style. The first big laugh, of course, comes on the third line of the lyric, when the audience hears the name of the island and realizes they've been tricked.

THREE MILE ISLAND

There is a place so rare
I'd like to take you there;
It's Three Mile Island.
Where the radiation emanation
Fills us all with trepidation—now.

It's a place that's oh, so dear
Though the people live in fear,
'Cause they don't know
Just how long they've got,
And the nuclear reactors get so hot.

There is a place so fine
Where the turbines whine;
It's Three Mile Island.
The geiger counters clicky-clacky
'Stead of wicky-wicky-wacky-woo.

They told us it was safe
And then, oh well,
They said to be prepared
To run like hell.
And I know we all bless the name of
   Three Mile Island.

Seymour Glick also included a rock-blues number that points a finger at Ronald Reagan's economic policies, which led to the recession of 1982:

Now they took all my money,
My food stamps, too;
Can't get no welfare and I'm tellin' you—
I got the Supply-side, Trickle-down, Laffer-Curve
   Recession Blues . . .

Seymour Glick, parts of which debuted on three of my NBC-TV comedy specials, opened at New York's St. Regis–Sheraton Hotel in 1982. It chronicles the life of fictitious tunesmith Glick, who, as the premise goes, was over the years blatantly ripped off by nearly every prominent American songwriter. For example, six years before Sammy Fain and Lew Brown wrote the plaintive "That Old Feeling," Seymour had composed a remarkably similar song—"That Gold Filling"—for a musical about a young dental student. A romantic ballad, it is sung by the leading lady to her lover, the dentist.

I saw you last night
   and got that gold filling.
When you fixed my bite,
   I got that gold filling.
The moment you sat me down,
   I saw your drill—

*And when you turned it on,
    my heart stood still.*

*Once again I seemed to feel
    that old aching,
Though I knew my two front
    caps were still breaking.*

*There'll be no newer
    cavities,
To tell you the truth—
For that gold filling
Is still in my tooth.*

Then there were a number of tunes that Glick composed during his Food Phase—a time when he was obsessed with eating—that other writers have cavalierly appropriated: "Lover Come Back To Me" (the original was Seymour's "Liver Come Back To Me"); "If You Knew Susie Like I Know Susie" (Glick actually was first with "If You Knew Sushi Like I Know Sushi"); and "This Could Be the Start of Something Big" (Seymour had, in fact, beaten me to the punch with his own Hawaiian novelty "This Could Be the Start of Suckling Pig").

In the revue I use, in addition to parodies, several other songs for which I wrote both words and music to carry the *Glick* storyline. Thus, when the host (first myself, then later, in the California production, comic Bill Maher) speaks of Glick's Nature Period—during which he spent time wandering on the beach—we hear the rock ballad "Mouth-to-Mouth Resuscitation" (see chapter 9). The song has a particularly catchy tune because I feel that funny lines have more impact when paired with either a lovely or zippy melody, the match-up of which increases the incongruity.

Later in Glick's illustrious career, the composer went to Holland, where he became fascinated by the huge waterfront dikes protecting the country. He noted the flaming torches, or faggots, that were placed on the dikes in the evening to guide sailors home through the dense fog and wrote this melodramatic ballad called "Faggots and Dikes."

*In Holland many years ago,
When the sea was high,
And the northern winds did blow
Warning flags would fly.*

But when the winter's sun had died,
And flags could not be seen,
Torches to the dikes were tied,
Soaked in kerosene.

Faggots flamed throughout the night,
Banishing the dark,
Yellow beacons burning bright
For each lonely bark.

Now the dikes are lighted by
Ev'ry modern means,
Yet I must confess that I
Miss the early scenes.

So this tender song I sing
To recall the day,
When the warning bells would ring
And the people say:

CHORUS (waltz tempo)

Faggots and dikes,
Faggots and dikes;
Do you remember the long winter hikes?
Each girl and boy
Then would enjoy
Going to view all the faggots and dikes.

Faggots and dikes,
Faggots and dikes;
Do you remember the trips on our bikes?
When we would ride,
Side by side,
Going to view all the faggots and dikes?

> *All of the faggots were flaming*
> *Those nights when the weather was damp.*
> *Do you remember—those jaunts in September,*
> *When overnight we would camp?—singing—*

Faggots and dikes,
Faggots and dikes;
Those were the days we were happier tykes.
All of the Dutch
Liked very much
Going to visit the faggots and dikes.

Crying faggots—
Faggots crying—
Over the land that was low:
Crying faggots and dikes,
A-live, a-live, oh.

That song actually was originally ad-libbed one night in 1957, at a party in New York, when Bob Bach, producer of "What's My Line?," dared me to write a tune based on the title "Faggots and Dykes." As you can see, I used Misinterpretation to create the song, seizing upon two pairs of words that sound alike but that have totally different meanings. No complaints were ever received from gay-rights groups, since the lyric is in no way pejorative, nor was it intended to be. In some instances I have seen apparent homosexuals laugh the loudest at the number.

Many comic songs, such as "The Gold Filling," are parodies—the sort of thing the late Allan Sherman did so brilliantly. Some are just cute nonsense, in the same category as Cole Porter's "Violate Me in Violet Time in the Vilest Way You Know."

Most humorists who perform in the musical idiom try their hand at parody at one time or another. Allan always wrote his parodies to fit long-familiar and therefore well-known songs. One he wrote for his first album was the now-famous switch on "Frere Jacques," which came to him in less than two minutes. To perceive the humor of the number, it is, of course, necessary to have some degree of familiarity with not only the French folk melody but with American-Jewish culture.

Sarah Jackman, Sarah Jackman,
How's by you? How's by you?
How's by you the family?
How's your sister Em'ly?
She's nice, too—
She's nice, too.

How's your brother Bernie?
He's a big attorney.
How's your sister Doris?
Still with William Morris.

How's your Uncle Nathan?
Him I got no faith in.

How's your cousin Ida?
She's a Freedom Rider.

How's your brother Bentley?
Feeling better ment'lly.
How's your cousin Seymour?
Seymour joined the Peace Corps.*

I wrote and performed my first parody in 1948. Inspired by a freak snowfall in Los Angeles, I composed "Say It Isn't Snow" and that night sang it on my radio program. The original model, of course, was Irving Berlin's "Say It Isn't So."

Say it isn't snow;
Say it isn't snow.
Say that stuff I see is popcorn falling;
Say it isn't snow.

One of my wackiest parodies was composed on a crowded bus. I was traveling with Milton Berle, Henry Fonda, Kirk Douglas, and other prominent entertainers, making a political tour for the Democratic Party. At one point, the group took a seemingly endless bus ride across a part of Wyoming to reach an airport. To relieve the boredom I wrote a parody of the song "Chicago," called "Wyoming," then rose and sang it to my restless companions:

Wyoming, Wyoming,
A wonderful state.
If you are a gopher
It really is great.
You bet your bottom dollar
You'll lose your way in Wyoming.
It looks like Truesdale looked not long ago.
Where the hell can you go?

Wyoming, Wyoming,
It isn't too hip;
So thanks to Wyoming
For a real dull trip.

There never is heard
A discouraging word;
I just heard a vulture
Say "How's your bird?"

TAG

Canyons out here
They really are deep;
I saw a man
Who danced with a sheep,
In Wyoming . . . Wyoming . . . my home state.

Of more recent vintage is the following, "My Tan," based on the Fannie Brice classic "My Man." It's suitable for performing in either Palm Springs, Miami, or "mountain's" resorts, where people make a big deal of getting and keeping a deep suntan. Ideally, the performer doing the number should be Jewish, since the lyric includes so many Jewish references. I've never used it in my own act but have sent copies to Shecky Greene, Jack Carter, and Red Buttons, feeling that it might be appropriate for some of their bookings.

MY TAN

It cost me a lot
But there's one thing that I've got,
That's my tan,
Yes, my tan.

Two or three
Guys I see,
But they're not as dark as me,
With my tan,
Yes, my tan.

I swim with the sports
Till I look just like a schwartz
With my tan,
Oh, my tan.

Once I was pale and gray
Now I'm Sidney Poitier
With my tan.
What a man!

I lay around the beach.
I burn and then I screech.
It isn't fun,
But when I'm done,
I'm like a bun
All nice and brown.

CHORUS

Oh, my tan
I love it so.
You'll never know
How I laid around the docks
Just like a lox.
If it never, ever fades
I'll be the Ace of Spades.

Now no longer do I get
Mugged in the park,
For those mothers, they

Can't find me in the dark.
With my toasty, golden brown
I'm the tannest Jew in town.

I've paid through the nose,
But when I take off my clothes,
There's my tan.
Oh (Oy?), my tan.

First the beach, then the lamp,
Now I look as dark as Hamp,
With my tan,
What a man.

I use oil and cream
And I try hard not to scream
When I burn,
Then I turn.

Want to tan nice and deep;
But like a schmuck I fall asleep,
And I burn,
Never learn.

I lay around the pool;
Now maybe I'm a fool
Once like a ghost
Then brown as toast,
I burn the most.

CHORUS

Oh, my tan I love it so.
Forget the snow.
When you're in Miami Beach
And out of reach,
What's the difference if they call?
Go on, and have a ball.

When I get back home
Why do I make a fuss?
They will make me ride away back
In the bus!
But for now I'm such a man
And it's all because—
I'm . . .
tan!

The next parody, to the melody of trumpeter Bunny Berigan's theme song, "I Can't Get Started With You," I wrote as an inside joke to some of my conservative intellectual friends, though one of them—Ralph de Toledano—published it in his syndicated column.

A LIBERAL'S LAMENT

I

I've flown around the world in a huff
Because we wouldn't call Khrushchev's bluff,
The Berlin Wall I've charted
Still I can't get started
With you.

I helped to re-elect Thomas Dodd,
I'm still a firm believer in God.
I've dined with Richard Nixon,
Still I can't start mixin'
With you.

The Viet Cong,
I've always said it was wrong,
Warned it was Red all along.
(Phooey to Ho Chi Minh!)
Tell me, what more can I do?

Why, I booked Barry G. for my show,
Told Jimmy Hoffa where he could go,
The Loy'lty oath, I take it,
Still I just can't make it
With you.

II

Now I subscribe to National Review
And I send checks to Freedom House too.
I find the Buckleys charming
Still I seem alarming
To you.

I worked to chase the Commies from SANE,
And Fidel Castro gives me a pain.
I like a John Wayne movie,
Still I don't seem groovy
To you.

I'll never tell
Burnham or Kirk or Bozell
They can go singly to hell.
Though we may argue, I much prefer them to
Welch.

I lift my nose at sandal and beard;
I find the New Far Left pretty weird,
Love Ralph de Toledano
Still I seem like guano
To you.

A couple of years ago I did a comedy concert in Manitowoc, Wisconsin, a charming lakefront community where, during WWII, American submarines were built. I often write little nonsense numbers that, because they apply to a specific locale or situation, will almost never be performed again, but audiences particularly appreciate such examples because they understand that they were created solely for their entertainment.

The chief comedy component of my concerts consists of answering actual questions written by people in the audience on cards that are brought to me backstage shortly before I go on. In this case, someone asked, "Have you ever written a song about Manitowoc?" Within a few minutes I had dashed off the following lyric, sung to a march-tempo melody:

MANITOWOC

*There was a man at the dock
In Manitowoc.
He looked like a manatee to me,
But there are no manatees in Manitowoc
So that he clearly could not be.*

*I said to him, "Where can I walk
In Manitowoc?"
He said, "I hope I don't sound mean,
But from here on the dock
In Manitowoc,
I don't care if you take a submarine."*

The first thing to do in writing a parody, obviously, is to select a suitable original. It goes without saying that the number should be widely known; otherwise few would understand the point of the burlesque. Secondly, you should decide whether you will be literally satirizing the original or merely using it as a point of departure and doing a funny switch on it.

By far the greater number of parodies are in the latter category. When Weird Al Yankovic, for example, writes a song called "Eat It," he is obviously basing it on Michael Jackson's "Beat It," but his version does not make any particular philosophical observation, comic or otherwise, about the original. The same can be said about practically all of Allan Sherman's brilliant parodies and other comic lyrics. I refer to other lyrics because not all amusing song titles have a connection with previously written lyrics. Allan's "Hello Muddah, Hello Faddah," for example, simply involved putting a lyric to a classical composition called "Dance of the Hours."

I gave Allan the title and an opening line or two for his parody, "Somewhere Overweight People," which is, of course, structured like "Somewhere Over the Rainbow." Allan completed the lyric in his usual superb fashion, but his version is in no way a comment about the lovely song from *The Wizard of Oz*; it simply adopts its form for a fresh comic purpose.

Somewhere, overweight people,
Just like me,
Must have someplace where folks don't
Count every calorie.

Somewhere, over the rainbow
Way up tall,
There's a land where they've never
Heard of cholesterol.

Where folks can eat just what they want
And still be trim and slim and gaunt,
You'll find me—
Where every little thing I taste
Won't wind up showing on my waist,
Or worse—behind me.

Somewhere, overindulging is divine.
If their waistlines aren't bulging,
Why, then, oh, why does mine?

If bluebirds weighed as much as I
You'd see some big fat bluebirds in the sky.*

Another example of adopting form only is a number I wrote and recorded some years ago based on the structure of Tony Bennett's classic "I Left My Heart in San Francisco." I prepared a new melody and lyric for a verse, establishing the background as the field of plastic surgery. The title was "I Left My Nose in San Diego."

My heart could never wait
Out by the Golden Gate
But part of me will stay in Southern Cal.
A plastic surgeon just last week
Remodeled my old beak
And so I tell this story to you, pal.

CHORUS

I left my nose
In San Diego,
Where I suppose
It waits for me.

Before he took that cable stitch
I looked like Beulah Witch.
I had a schnoz from here to there,
Now I don't care.

I left my nose
In San Diego
Although he charged an awful fee.
Oh, I'll come back to you, San Diego,
Because you still smell good to me.

Note that in the preceding examples there are certain points where the parody lyric matches specific phrases or lines of the original. An instance would be the relationship of *cable stitch* in my version to *cable cars* in the original. To get the point, of course, one would have to be familiar with the knitting term *cable stitch*. It also helps to know that Beulah Witch was a large-nosed puppet on Burr Tillstrom's "Kukla, Fran and Ollie."

In planning to sing a parody, you must be certain that a given audience is familiar with the song you're sending up; otherwise it won't work. For example, while watching a serious television discussion on the venereal disease chlamydia, it occurred to me that a funny song-parody could be written with that title to the melody of the hit song of the 1930s, "Perfidia." It was a big record, with an English lyric, for Helen O'Connell and the old Jimmy Dorsey orchestra; and, of course, it's been a standard in Latin music for decades. But I'm not going to bother to write the parody because very few people under fifty—unless they're Hispanic—have knowledge of the song "Perfidia" and relatively few, of any age, are aware of the disease chlamydia, despite its high incidence. But at a convention of Mexican-American gynecologists, the routine would no doubt be a big hit.

Some of the comic numbers I've written have been parodies not of specific songs but of an entire genre of music. Have you ever noticed, for example, how many country-and-western songs there are about traveling highways and driving truck rigs? This sort of song seems peculiar to rural America. I can't imagine that there are Russian folk songs titled "Drivin' Down to Old Murmansk," or "Gonna Mosey Back to Minsk." I've been asked why I think back-country or southern people write so many songs about traveling. Well, have you ever lived in some of those small rural communities? I'm reminded of Abe Burrows's classically funny title "How Ya Gonna Keep 'Em Down on the Farm, After They've Seen the Farm?"

In any event, the following lyric satirizes the rural American lust for road travel.

DRIVIN'

I was ridin' on a trolley
In Raleigh,
To a little used car lot
In Charlotte.
Then I was drivin' out of Asheville, North Carolina
To Nashville, Tennessee.

Had some letters marked for Winston-Salem;
I had to mail 'em
And I was drivin' tons of bacon
Down to Macon,
When I met a young tomato
From Decatur.
In fact, the little girl was on the lam
So I decided I'd drive her to Birmingham.

Then we were drivin' down to Vicksburg,
A real hicksburg;
Honked our horn "ahooga-hooga"
All the way to Chattanooga.
She said she used to play piana
In a dive in old Savannah,
But I drove the little lassie
All the way to Tallahassee;
Still she wouldn't shut her mouth.

If I hadn't gotten rid
Of that there crazy kid,
I would have driven all over
The whole goddamn South.

As we've already mentioned, some of my funniest parodies are based on beautiful love songs. The following, "Ugly to Look At," a take-off on "Lovely to Look At," is another such example. Note that though its lyric expresses a sentiment exactly opposite to the original's, I've used many words and phrases, such as *to look at, to hold, to kiss,* and *a combination like this,* that are identical to those of the classic:

You're ugly to look at,
Disgusting to hold,
And chilling to kiss.
A combination like this

Is quite my most impossible dream come true.
Imagine finding a klutz like you.

You're ugly to look at,
It's bilious to hold you terribly tight.
When we're together, the moon is new,
And, oh, it's awful to look at you,
Tonight.

In the next parody, I take the structure of "I Fall in Love Too Easily" to create a number about a poor soul who can't seem to get a full night's sleep. The verse uses nearly all the lyrics of the original, substituting only *asleep* for *in love*.

I fall asleep too easily.
I fall asleep too fast.
I fall asleep too terribly hard
For sleep to ever last.

My brain must be well-schooled
'Cause I've been fooled in the past.
And yet I fall asleep too easily
For sleep to ever last.

The next two parodies are similar to "Somewhere, Overweight People" in that I hooked onto the established songs' titles and adopted the tunes' structures to come up with comic concepts that have nothing at all to do with the originals. The first is a send-up of "What Are You Doing the Rest of Your Life?"

WHAT ARE YOU DOING WITH THE REST OF YOUR WIFE?

What are you doing with the rest of your wife?
She's already seen the best of her life.
But the boys all say the chest of your wife
    Is a beauty to behold.

People say that you don't care any more,
About her makeup or her hair any more.
Are you even sure she's there any more?
    Do you think she's getting old?

I know that what I say is so uncool.
Perhaps I'm really acting like a fool.

If you have eyes for someone new
Then I'll be glad to put this question straight to you.

What are you doing with the rest of your wife?
I would love to head out West with your wife.
If you think you've had the best of your wife,
    Well, then, why not let her go?

Don't make a pest of your wife.
Let her go while there's still zest to her life.
I would gladly take the rest of your wife
    If it's all the same to you.

The next example is based on the Brazilian bossa nova classic, "The Girl From Ipanema."

THE GIRL WITH EMPHYSEMA

Tall and pale and light and chalky,
The girl with emphysema goes walking
And when she passes, each one she passes
Goes (wheezing, etc.).

She should stop smoking; that's her solution
But she contributes to air pollution,
And when she passes, through noxious gasses
It's (wheezing, coughing).

Oh, how she's coughing and sneezing.
Oh, how she's hacking and wheezing;
So she's not really so pleasing,
Once there were nights when we kissed;
Now she lives in a Primatene mist.

Tall and pale and weak and sickly,
Those girls with emphysema go quickly,
And when she passes, you'll see her lips turning blue.
Let the girl with emphysema
Be a lesson to you.

Back in 1949 I introduced a song-lyric monologue that over the years has been widely copied. I simply read the words of a popular song whose lyrics are annoyingly repetitious or particularly absurd (in some cases both). I make no jokes about the song, merely use an introduction that prepares the audience to expect the upcoming lyric to express, as I point out, "profundity, beauty, insight and philosophical gravity." Of course, the surprise at hearing the redundant words explains the bit's funniness. The first time I thought to try it was in 1948, with the song "Love Somebody," a big hit of that day. The song's lyric consisted largely of the line "Love somebody, yes I do," endlessly repeated.

I still include this routine in my shows, sometimes using the lyric to the Rolling Stones' popular "I Can't Get No Satisfaction." And it still gets big laughs.

Some of my comedy numbers have a major satirical thrust. "When They Stop the Stoppoon," which is not a parody but a satire on a certain type of song about a dance, "Begin the Beguine" being an example. In *Seymour Glick Is Alive But Sick* I included an entire routine about popular songs about dances. I was always a little skeptical of such songs because it seemed to me that the dances themselves never actually existed. Have you personally ever heard anyone say, "Gertie, let's get up and do the *Beguine* right now"? Of course not. And who ever did the Carioca or the Continental? In any event, that gives you an idea of the philosophical rationale for—

WHEN THEY STOP THE STOPPOON

When they stop—The Stoppoon
It brings back a night
Or a morning—
Or was it a noon?

When they stop—The Stoppoon
It sounds like the laugh
Of a love-sick giraffe
Or the babble-ing
Of a baboon.

I remember that night in Boise,
The Stoppoon was remarkably noisy.
Then it suddenly came to a halt
And my lonely heart cried, "Oy, gevalt!"

When they stop—The Stoppoon
You'll notice the words were lousy;
But not half as bad as the tune.
It was splendid, but it ended;
It was gory as Rory Calhoun.

> *Now I always insist that*
> *They stop—The Stoppoon.*

Another satirical but nonparodic number is "I Like Sad Songs by the French." Actually, some of the music of that genre is quite good. Nevertheless something about the kind of songs that Edith Piaf used to feature always struck me funny, at least as far as the factor of degree was concerned. French songwriters have a way of writing extremely long lines. They get much more dramatic than American composers and lyricists.

The student of comic lyric writing should have his or her attention drawn to the fact that the last lines of the first and second paragraphs of "Sad Songs" rhyme. Ordinarily such an observation would come under the heading of "So what?" except that, in this case, there's a purposely long distance indeed between those two lines. The singer is supposed to rush through the lines, in the French manner, apparently in the hope of sustaining our interest in the rhyme-factor.

I LIKE SAD SONGS BY THE FRENCH

I like sad songs by the French,
Ones you sing like a mensch
When a song rambles on, ambles on
With a million and one, yes, a million
    and one
Extraneous words in it.

Sad songs by the French, like the ones
    by Jacques Brel,
Who, contrary to what you have heard,
Is by no means, my love,
Either living or well,
But who, nevertheless
It is true, I confess,
Wrote of trees in the Bois
And of one naked tree,
    [in December, you see]
With no birds in it.
And the chords, they are minor
And there's nothing finer
For making you cry.

It is true, oh, my love, that we
    sometimes don't know

What we're crying about,
But the songs, they are long
And some chords, they are wrong,
And Charles Aznavour
Who is rich but acts poor
Sings of love unrequited
And strolls in the park
And rolls in the dark.

But the main thing, you see, is the lines
Must go on, must go rolling along,
'Til they're too great in length
To sustain any strength
Or good form in a song.

They don't know what to say
On the Rue de la Paix
So they sing up a storm.

And some nights, all alone
In the Bois de Bologne
When they try to keep warm
They somehow don't make it,
So, toute suite, they fake it
And get very drunk.

When the morning, it comes
They've got heads like steel drums
And a breath like a skunk.

But they sing just the same;
It's the name of the game
If you're French, don't you see?

You and I'd feel like schmucks
Standing there in a tux
While just crying out loud,
But the French love to bawl;
That's the fun of it all
And of tears they're so proud.

There's no ifs, ands, or buts,
They'll just spill out their guts
With a mike in their hands.
Every song is tres tragique
But their wardrobes are chic
When they work at The Sands.

For they travel, you know;
There's no place they won't go
To tell us of their gloom.
We may say, "Well, that's tough,

We've got bad news enough,"
But they pack every room.

For we all love to cry,
Every gal, every guy,
If the singer is French.
So, monsieur, who's to blame
If the songs sound the same
When they come from Paree?

With a chord in C Minor
Why, there's nothing finer
For bringing you down.

With F-minor diminished
You'll really be finished
And leaving this town.
Chevalier used to sing
'Bout romance in the Spring
But that's over and done.

Today no French singer,
Not even a swinger,
Would dare laugh at a sin.
No memories bridal,
It's all suicidal;
Depression is in.

Another example that is half-satire, half-cuckoo is a typical song about a city. Everybody writes songs about New York, San Francisco, Paris, Rome . . . but why aren't there any songs about less glamorous towns? In providing a musical setting for the following lyric, I wrote deliberately in the Cole Porter vein—a kind of sexy, sophisticated, 1940-ish beguine.

CLEVELAND

Cleveland,
I met you in Cleveland.
I asked you to cleave
And cling to me.

In Ohio
You gave me the eye-o
And now what a thrill
You bring to me.

Can't conceive that you'd leave
For my heart's on my sleeve
In Cleveland.
Please believe me,
Don't grieve me
Or ever deceive me.
In Cleveland.

The lake was Erie,
And so were you, dearie,
But we strolled along the sand.
Now Columbus or Cincinnati—
They drive me practically batty
But you've got to believe
You and I'd never leave
Cleveland.

The next number, too, is partly satirical in that it's based on a certain kind of love song, but the dominant element of it is just craziness. It, too, has a purposely sweet, romantic melody.

AH-CHOO

I'd been walking around in the rain,
With a heart as heavy as lead,
Then I sat by an open window
And through my tears I said,

CHORUS

[long build-up to a sneeze]
Ah-choo! I said, "Ah-choo!"
You whispered Gesundheit,
And that's how I met you.
It's true, I said ah-choo.
You whispered God bless you
And changed my gray skies to blue.

Now was it hay fever
That brought us together?
Or a sneeze just by chance
That brought me romance—that day?

Ah-choo, was it the flu?
You whispered Gesundheit
And gave me your hand that day.

You smiled so sweetly
And offered a tissue,
I knew that I oughtn't to kiss you,
But, ah, 'twas a really big choo.

Donald O'Connor sang that on one of my NBC comedy specials. I've always loved Donald's work—his singing, dancing, comedy—since I first saw him as a child in vaudeville back in the 1930s. Which brings up an important point for those who will be writing comedy songs. The humor of them won't be apparent if the singer is essentially square. In other words, oh, let's say, Perry Como or Nat Cole—certainly two marvelous singers—would not get big laughs doing a number like "Ah-choo," but a naturally funny performer like Donald O'Connor got very big laughs indeed with it.

As we have seen, not all satirical songs take other numbers as their target. A satirical song may make a comment about a public figure, or a newsworthy event. I wrote the following number during the Watergate period, when the public first found out that Mr. Nixon and his cronies talked pretty dirty, though some of them posed in public as guardians of virtue. When the transcripts of the secret tapes began to be published, of course, the four-letter words had to be taken out, usually to be replaced by the term *expletive deleted*. That inspired this number, which was sung by Elaine Joyce and Steve Lawrence on one of our TV comedy specials.

EXPLETIVE DELETED

I'd like to expletive deleted you.
Oh, expletive, that's what I'd like to do.
I'd like to expletive and expletive
And expletive and expletive,
I'd really like to expletive you.

I'd like to expletive deleted you.
Until we've expletived ourselves to death.
And when you've expletived my expletive
And then have nothing more to give,
I'll expletive you till you're out of breath.
I'd like to expletive deleted you.

The next lyric, written to a Cole Porter-style melody, is also based on a phrase that first began to be commonly heard in the 1970s, as part of the general "in" lingo. The saying *between consenting adults* had, of course, been in the language for a long time, but it had an actual vogue, in the context of discussions about sexual morality in the 1970s. I considered the number a bit too strong for television, but it worked well as part of the *Seymour Glick* show.

BETWEEN CONSENTING ADULTS

Between consenting adults—
It's all right with me.
Between consenting adults—
It's all night with me.

About certain kinds of conduct,
I'm strict and unrelenting.
Nevertheless, I say
It's A-okay
If the adults are consenting.

It was between the dark and the dawn
That a call rang out,
Then I looked all about
And I heard someone shout
"Let it all hang out!"

Whenever we're meeting
I feel the beating
Of my heart and my pulse.
But, you know the scene,
It's between
*   consenting adults.*

The next number is satirical, but only to a degree. As far as the musical form is concerned, I wrote in what might be considered the "42nd Street" style, like one of those great Harry Warren novelties of the thirties or forties in which show-biz characters sing about show business. But in the real musicals of that sort, the songs were always upbeat, cheerful, peppy, lots of fun to listen to. I chose to take a negative—and hence comic —bit of show-business reality as the subject matter. When performers are really dying on stage, failing totally to enlist the sympathetic interest of an audience, they often perspire profusely. This is referred to as "flop sweat." In analyzing the following lyric, the reader should envision a line of chorus girls and boys, really punching away, keeping game smiles on their faces as they nevertheless share the truth of their predicament with the audience.

FLOP SWEAT

Flop sweat,
I'm gettin' that flop sweat.
You can't be calm
When you're bomb-
    ing like this.

Flop sweat,
I'm starting to mop sweat.
You can't feel high
When you're dy-
    ing like this.

    There's no business like show business,
    So they say,
    But when you're out of luck
    Just like a schmuck
    Ev'ry day is closing day.

I'm in the wrong show;
It's as dumb as The Gong Show.
I'm doin' bad.
Is it sad?
You bet!
Get me a mop!
This is flop,
    flop sweat.

Another satirical number made fun of a certain kind of song common in the thirties and forties that is still occasionally written. It sets a man-woman flirtation and/or love relationship in a particular glamorous exotic setting, the beach at Pango-Pango, Paris in the Spring, Christmas in Vermont, or whatever. I recall writing this song at a grand piano in a suite at a hotel in Puerto Rico, where Jayne and I were appearing on a convention program.

IT WAS CARNIVAL IN RIO

I

It was Carnival in Rio,
But we were in Pacoima.
It was Christmas in Madrid
    When you did what you did,
    But I was back home.

It was Paris in April
But, just as any ape will,
*   You went in Clifton, New Jersey*
*   And gave me a call—collect.*

There was moonlight in Vermont, dear,
But I was in Detroit.
Scots were roaming in the gloaming,
*   But you were in Wyoming*
*   At the time.*

You had the thrill of your life in Rome
While I, like a jerk, was back home.
Ah, that tropical weather—
*   Why don't we get together*
*   Sometime?*

II

It was waltz-time in Vienna,
But not in Provo, Utah.
A Venetian gondolier
*   Sang so loud and clear*
*   But not for us.*

It was spring in Pango-Pango
Where all the jet-set gang go,
But you were stuck in Duluth
*   Doing something uncouth*
*   I fear.*

Ah, that winter in Jamaica—
When I was in South Bend;
There were valleys fresh with clover
*   But you were all hung over*
*   At the time.*

Oh, those nights on the Isle of Capri
But the boy in your arms wasn't me.
Ah, that tropical weather—
*   Why don't we get together*
*   Sometime?*

Ideas may come from anywhere—perhaps just spotting a sign or an advertisement. I once wrote a brief number after noticing the "Do Not Disturb" tag hanging on my hotel room doorknob.

Please do not disturb,
Please no raps or knockings,
When I'm in bare feet or stockings,
Please do not disturb.

What the hell's the rush?
I'll be leaving soon enough.
Do not attend to this verb.
Please do not disturb.

While most of my jokes and sketches are intended to do nothing more than amuse, sometimes one makes a social statement or commentary. That's true of comedy generally. Author-entertainer Kinky Friedman, who has been called "the Lenny Bruce of country music," satirizes everything from women's lib to anti-Semitism. In this next number, though it gets good laughs when performed, you'll see that it actually takes a strong position against the incredible degree of civic corruption that, sad to say, characterizes life in the good old U.S.A. In all major Eastern cities, the Mafia, among other organized crime elements, has been dominant for over half a century. The following number illustrates how it is possible to make a strong social statement and yet entertain while doing so. The music is a typical march-like Sicilian tarantella, the kind of happy, hand-clapping rhythm you hear in movie scenes of Italian weddings, as in the *Godfather* series, *Prizzi's Honor,* or *GoodFellas.*

HERE'S TO THE MAFIA

I

Here's to the Mafia,
Here's to "the boys."
What's the big excitement
If they rub each other out?
You never get rich
By digging a ditch
So everybody shout,
Hey!

Here's to the Mafia,
Sicilians all true-blue.

They own the politicians,
Have the judges in their pay.
They'll grab you,
And they'll nab you
And they'll stab you;
What the hey?

What's a little murder?
It's the old American way
So here's to the Mafia.

II

Here's to the Mafia,
Here's to the mob.
They own good old Chicago
And they run New Jersey, too.
So what do we care?
They're always there,
No matter what you do.
Hey!

Here's to the racketeers,
Vito, Gino, Vinnie, Al and Frank.

Who cares if they sell heroin,
And pills and lotsa smut?
And what if you don't respect 'em?
So you get a kick in the butt.
In Cleveland, Kansas City and Detroit
They get their cut.

So here's to the boys;
Let's make a noise,
Here's to the Mafia.

Going back for a moment to *Seymour Glick Is Alive But Sick*, it's easy to see that all songs in a production with such a title would have to be funny. But when I wrote some forty songs for the CBS television production of *Alice in Wonderland*, I felt obliged to produce a few funny lyrics for that as well. Some of the songs from the score are quite somber in tone, but, of course, there had to be a few out-and-out humorous numbers. In the famous scene with the two crazy women, the Cook and the Duchess, I had to provide such a song, particularly once Imogene Coca and Martha Raye, wonderfully funny women, had been cast in the roles. What did Carroll tell us about their characters? That they were both pains in the neck and quite rude to dear little Alice.

However, the two characters were so harsh that I had to take that into consideration in preparing a song for them. It is titled "There's Something to Say for Hatred." Most songs of that bouncy musical type are about cheerfulness, smiling, the power of laughter, and so forth. I was saying, facetiously, of course, just the opposite.

There's something to say for hatred,
For rudeness and for spite.
Oh, no, my friend,
We can't pretend
That everything's sweetness and light.

There's something to say for trouble,
For nastiness and gloom.
Just try to be cheerful
And you'll get an earful
Of your impending doom.

This world is not a paradise
If, indeed, it ever was.
It's a vale of tears
And so, my dears,
Throw out the chaff?
Don't make me laugh!

There's something to say for mis'ry,
For suffering and pain.
Down at the bank,
Now let's be frank,
They only care for gain.

There's something to say for frowning,
Why must we always smile?
Forget your dreams;
Resort to schemes
And, in just a little while,
"The best laid plans of mice and men"
Will all come crashing down again
And we'll all despise each other
        in the grand-est style!

You'll note that the humor in such a lyric is quite different from that of the *Seymour Glick* songs, which are funny in a very broad way, whereas the humor of this number is wry, philosophical.

What other forms of funny songs are there? Quite an easy one for beginning writers to attempt is the sort that starts with a joke or a funny thought. There was a hit song in the 1960s titled "Call Me." In fact, there's been a number of songs based on that same idea over the years. "Wherever you are, any time of day or night, please—call me." So I thought of the phrase *Call me—but not collect.* After that it was just a matter of stating and re-stating this simple idea in standard, thrity-two-bar, chorus-and-bridge form. A clever comedienne and singer, Pam Meyers, performed it in one of the *Seymour Glick* TV sketches.

CALL ME, BUT NOT COLLECT

If you ever need a friend
I'll be there until the end.
Call me . . . but not collect.

If you're ever down and out.
Get on the phone and shout;
Call me . . . but not collect.

Even, my love, if you get old
I promise I'll never put you on hold.
Ev'ry day my love for you enlarges
S'long as you don't reverse the charges.

If you lose all your money
I'll be there to help you, honey.
Call me . . . it's what I expect.
Yes, call me . . . but not collect.

Another instance of a song constructed from a single joke is the following number, based on a line I first heard, God knows where, about thirty-five years ago: "I take her wherever I go, 'cause I can't stand to kiss her goodbye." In this case, I set the lyric into the framework of a Gay Nineties richly old-fashioned waltz, again depending in part on the contrast between a zany lyric and a sweet melody to provide another level of humor, in addition to that inherent in the versified variations on the original joke.

I CAN'T STAND TO KISS YOU GOOD-BYE

I'll just have to take you wherever I go,
'Cause I can't stand to kiss you goodbye.
I'll have to stay near you, this much I know,
For I can't stand to kiss you goodbye.

A boy, if he loses his girl, will miss her,
But it's not quite the same
With your kind of kisser.

So rest easy, my bride;
You will stay at my side,
'Cause I can't stand to kiss you goodbye.

What further how-to advice can be given beginning composers and lyricists who wish to write funny material? Long before they start worrying about what melodic forms might be suitable, or what lyric twists or rhymes might be fresh and clever, they must obviously start with the original idea. It's not all that different from just looking for funny ideas generally, whether the result is a single joke, light verse, funny song, short monologue, or sketch. For my part, as I've already mentioned, since childhood I have been interested in and amused by conversational cliches. Something in me automatically refuses to use "in" jargon.

Back in the late 1960s, to give an illustration, I began to be bugged by the fact that some people, sometimes even the very hip, seemed unable to carry on a conversation, on any subject, without using the word *into* about forty-seven times. "Oh, you know, man, like wow, I'm not into that." Some jargon is hip for about six weeks, but other instances, for whatever mysterious reasons, have a longer life.

In any event, in a conversation with my friend Anthony Newley one day, I used the word *into* myself and then apologized for doing so. Tony and I had been talking about songs, and it occurred to me to say, "I've just gotten a great idea for a love song titled 'I'm Into You.'" Although I didn't intend a second, off-color interpretation, I nevertheless recognized that the title could be so construed. Because of the nature of the lyric, I chose to use a cheerful, two-beat rhythm of the sort found in such popular songs as "I'm Gonna Sit Right Down and Write Myself a Letter" and "Jeepers Creepers."

I'M INTO YOU

Some people are into baseball;
Others are into what's new.
   Some are into books
   Or romantic nooks.
I'm into you.

Some folks are into meditation,
Others are into what's true.
   She's into dreams
   And he's into schemes
But I'm into you.

   Into-ness is wonderful;
   There's lots of "into" scenes.
   People keep saying "into"
   But I'm not into what it means.

Some people are into a sunset
Or some other fabulous view.
   Some guys are into money
   But I tell you, honey,
I'm into you.

People are forever asking artists if they have favorite brain-children. Ordinarily, my internal computer kicks a question of that sort out without answering it. But in this case, there is one of my songs that strikes me as funnier than all the others, although if I included it in my concert performances it would get fewer laughs than some of the more dependable—because more understandable—numbers.

I got the idea for the lyric over forty years ago, the first time I heard the name of the famous Canadian vacation resort Lake Louise and Banff. Although I've never been there, I assume that the community proper is called Banff and that it's on the shore of Lake Louise. But references to the resort invariably use the full title—Lake Louise and Banff. In any event, years ago I heard somebody say, "I think this year I'd like to go to Lake Louise and Banff," and I laughed because part of my brain interpreted the word *banff* as a verb, so that the sentence seemed to be of the same sort as "I'd like to go to Lake Louise and swim," or "I'd like to go to Lake Louise and fish."

Another amusing factor, since the comic section of my brain has always been fascinated by the *sounds* of words, as distinguished from their meaning, is that *banff* sounds like doubletalk rather than legitimate human language. Let's put the *banff* underneath the *krelman* here so we don't break the *zamter*. How's your *banff?*

In any case, a few years ago I rendered that silly thought in pop-song form and put it into *Seymour Glick Is Alive but Sick*. It was very sweetly sung, in sort of a Jeanette McDonald manner, by Barbara Heuman. The lyric can be found on pages 159–60.

There's another funny song I've written—"Liu Shao-Chi and His Revisionist"—that has never been publicly performed. In fact, the only time it's ever been sung aloud at all is when, having finished the lyric with the help of my then-sixteen-year-old son Bill, who threw in a few good lines, I sang it to him while the two of us were touring China in the late 1970s.

Would there be any circumstances under which I would ever perform the number publicly? Theoretically yes, but I doubt if it will ever happen because the audience would have to consist of people knowledgeable about China, and particularly the period of the Cultural Revolution. The Maoists were in control of China then, in the late 1960s and early 1970s, and one of the Chinese leaders who was in strong disfavor was Liu Shao-Chi. Hard-Left Marxists use the term *revisionist* as one of contempt. The point is that a true Communist should adhere strictly to Marx, or at least to the version of Marx imposed by his local interpreters, and not revise the basic program or its history. In China in the 1970s, practically every dreadful thing that happened—even if it had to do with natural causes—seemed to be blamed on poor Lui Shao-Chi, though some years later he was rehabilitated by Deng Shao-Ping.

Also, to appreciate the lyric, one would have to be familiar with the fact that of all the world's political groups, Marxists are the most given to repeating stock phrases, invariably worded in precisely the same way.

One tipoff that an individual or a group is not thinking profoundly is this very factor—that certain cookie-cutter phrases are used again and again. Well, as Bill and I traveled about China (the details of the trip are given in my book *Explaining China*), we finally reached the point where we had heard quite enough of the phrase *Liu Shao-Chi and his revisionist line*. We did continue to hear it, of course, but in every instance we would exchange a quick look as if to say, "Oh, God, not that again." Now if a humorist or comedy writer gets bugged by something, he will inevitably use it as raw material for some form of comic expression.

Because the lyric deals with sober realities—and again keeping in mind the comic value of contrast or incongruity—I wrote a happy dance-tempo tune, in the genre of "The Lady's in Love with You," or "Raindrops Keep Falling on My Head."

LIU SHAO-CHI AND HIS REVISIONIST LINE

What makes the crops go bad?
What makes the people sad?
Who makes you hate your Dad?
Liu Shao-Chi and his Revisionist Line.

Who made the Great Leap fail?
Who likes to read your mail?
Who ought to stay in jail?
Liu Shao-Chi and his Revisionist Line.

Khrushchev blew it,
Brezhnev knew it,
Puttin' Mao in the shade.
There's nothing to it
So don't you do it.
Liu Shao-Chi almost had it made.

Who's out of favor now?
Who's bad as Lin Piao?
Who's on the skids and how?
He and his clique

> *Tried to make us weak;*
> *You can bet your Mommie*
> *He's no Commie.*
> *Who's workin' on a farm,*
> *Or down in a mine?*
> *Liu Shao-Chi and his Revisionist Line.*

I've already mentioned two of my songs that attack jargon or cant. Another in that category is "A Policeman's Love Song." I have been amused by police lingo since I first heard it. One of the most dependable sources for TV jokes, sketches and satires in the early 1950s was Jack Webb's "Dragnet" series. There probably weren't ten comedians in the business at that time who did not somehow make fun of the special language of that show's scripts, which was, of course, based on real police talk, to some extent at least. Now within the rules of that particular conversational game, a policeman will rarely say something like, "I saw this white woman and kept my eye on her." Instead he'll probably say, "I observed this Caucasian female individual and kept her under surveillance."

So, using that as the first line of the lyric, I developed an autobiographical love story, including a happy ending.

A Policeman's Love Song

> *I observed this Caucasian female individual*
> *And kept her under surveillance.*
> *In my opinion she was acting in a real suspicious manner,*
> *So I kept her under surveillance.*
>
> *At the time of the incident*
> *Referred to in my report,*
> *Though the time was early morn*
> *I could have sworn*
> *I saw her take a snort.*
>
> *I observed this Caucasian female individual*
> *For the next few years of my life.*
> *Now I'm proud to say*
> *And report today*
> *That the unknown Caucasian female individual*
> *Is my wife.*

One of my standard routines involves taking a real newspaper headline and treating it as a song title. The original concept was ad-libbed during a rehearsal about thirty-five years ago. I was talking to somebody about the plight of the amateur songwriter and happened to observe that it was so easy to write a song that millions of people were attempting it, even though the market could accommodate only a few hundred songs a year. I said that you could get song ideas literally anywhere. At that point, I happened to see a newspaper that I had planned to use for one of my Letters to the Editor monologues, and it occurred to me to say, "You could find song titles even in newspaper headlines."

At this late date I can't recall what headline I noticed at that moment, but I met a fellow in an airport not long ago who told me that about thirty years back he was watching what must have been one of the first instances of the Songs–from–Newspaper–Headlines routine. He even remembered a headline I had used, "Batista Flees." The story, of course, related to the collapse of the corrupt government of Cuba's Fulgencio Batista when Castro's troops took over that country.

Improvising a tango melody, I sang, "Batista fleas—I was bitten by Batista fleas." The audience laughed so hard at that one line that it was not necessary to continue the lyric.

Unfortunately most of the newspapers I've used over the years as a source for headline titles were simply discarded, but a few instances are in my files. The first was from a headline in the *National Enquirer*:

TOUGH GUY ROBERT STACK TO PLAY A GAY

Tough guy Robert Stack
To play a gay.
It'll bring him back
In a great big way.

He used to be
Elliot Ness,
But now he's dancin'
In his sister's dress.

Hey, there, rough guy,
You're a powder-puff guy,
Tough guy Robert Stack.

The next was the headline on a story in the *New York Times*:

STOCKS OFF AS INDICATORS DROP TO 17-MONTH LOWS

Stocks off as indicators drop
To 17-month lows.
The market sometimes goes ker-plop;
It's enough to make you tear your clothes.

First it's up,
Then it's down;
Hey, John Houseman,
Did your broker leave town?

It's been kinda tough
For the nation,
And if that ain't enough,
Here comes deflation!
Stocks off as indicators drop
To 17-month lows.

Here are a few others, the first based on a story about football player Mark Gastineau:

GASTINEAU TO KEEP ON DANCING

Gastineau to keep on dancing
Every time he makes a sack.
It's a gas to know
That Gastineau
Loves to whack
The quarterback.

Smack 'em, bust 'em,
That's his custom;
It's what he always did.
If Gastineau
Keeps on dancing
He'll replace
The Tap-Dance Kid!

SISTER CALLS CASTRO A TRAITOR

Sister Calls Castro a Traitor
Hey, bring back the Cuba of old,
When Russia had a plan-ski
But so did Meyer Lansky,
And the Godfather went for the gold.

Sister calls Castro a traitor;
Hey, bring back the Cuba of old,
When the boys who say "goomba"
Could do a mean rhumba
And mutilate, spindle or fold.

PRESIDENT CALLS FERRARO CHOICE "A LOGICAL STEP"

President calls Ferraro choice—
A logical step,
But Reagan sure will not rejoice
Or think it logically hep.

First he implied it was just a token
Then he took that back, soon as it was spoken.
Gerry's advancin'
While Ronnie prays.

Now he's dancin'
The latest craze—
Hey, everybody, do that
Logical Step.

To explain the technique used in writing those lyrics I point to my earlier observation that almost any statement can be interpreted in more than one way. Indeed, this is a problem that will always bedevil communication among humans. Savage battles have been fought over the centuries, even between Christian groups, over rival interpretations of one passage of Scripture or another. But as regards the newspaper headlines, I usually ignore the obvious interpretation and pretend that some alternative explanation is operative.

The second phase of the technique involves thinking of some usually quite minor joke commentary about the incorrect interpretation selected. The third element is that the joke must be rendered in rhymed verse, which of course is sung to a melody created for the specific situation.

For example, recall the trip Richard Nixon made as vice president to South America when an angry mob threw stones at his car as a way of protesting American foreign policy. There was a headline the next day in the *New York Daily News*: "Nixon Stoned in South America."

At this point I ignored the obvious meaning of the key word—the verb *stoned*—and pretended that the word referred to being under the influence of either alcohol or drugs. Because we were dealing with South America, I next decided to use a Latin rhythm. Then the simple joke was expressed in the form of rhymed verse, as follows:

> Nixon stoned in South America;
> What a regular guy.
> He goes to work in South America
> But instead he just gets high.

When the comedy TV soap opera, "Mary Hartman, Mary Hartman," was at the height of its popularity, I composed a nutty lyric for its theme song that had a lovely English melody. The words, expressed by a bewitched viewer infatuated with Mary (Louis Lasser), are funny because they extol characteristics ordinarily considered unattractive.

> Mary Hartman,
> How can I explain
> How your pigtails
> Haunt my fevered brain?
> Ah, your dreary voice,
> That vacant stare,
> They are almost more than I can bear.
>
> Mary, you're more precious
> Than Fort Knox.
> Even though somehow
> You're such a lox.
> I can't understand
> The magic thing you do,
> But Mary Hartman, Mary Hartman,
> I love you.
>
> I have gone bananas
> What can I do?
> No ifs or buts—
> Though you're a klutz—
> You drive me nuts.

14

Television: Shtick, Stunts, and Routines

We've earlier mentioned my Question Man sketches, which Johnny Carson's Carnac the Great mimics. Is there a formula to writing such jokes? Yes. Obviously you start with the answer first, and then suggest a question that would go before it. The best sort of answer is some common and hence familiar expression. *Bats in the belfry* would be a good example. Once you've taken any such phrase, pretty much at random, then you just play a mental game, asking yourself what sort of comic question would lead to that answer. A good example here would be, "Okay, cowboy, where is Masterson hiding?"

That, of course, only works if the audience is familiar with the character from southwestern history, Bat Masterson.

One of the Question Man jokes starts with the answer *Harry Reasoner.* The question is, "How would you describe a highly intelligent gorilla?"

A number of these jokes were included in the book *The Question Man*, published by Simon & Schuster, back in the late fifties, when the routine was often featured on my Sunday night comedy series. One of the exchanges starts with the answer: *My cup runneth over.* The question is: "How did all this thlop get in my thauther?"

One that worked very well came from a fellow in the audience at one of my recent concerts. His card said, "Mr. Question Man, the answer is *Sheik Yamani.*" If you stare at the clue silently, you may have trouble with it. But as soon as you say it out loud to yourself, you begin to think of comic possibilities.

What question did I give for that answer? "How do you attract the attention of a head waiter?" The line, obviously, is based on the fact that the correct pronunciation of *Sheik Yamani* sounds very much like *shake ya money*.

Incidentally, the above suggestion about saying comic lines aloud is important. If you're reading something silently, you will tend to perceive the word in one way, whereas words may change when they are spoken. When I taught a course in radio-writing years ago, I had frequent occasion to emphasize the point that there's a great difference between eye-copy and ear-copy. People communicate a certain way on the printed page but in quite a distinct style when they speak.

Some of my most successful routines—Letters to the Editor, Man on the Street, From High Atop—were largely a matter of detecting the humorous element in something noncomic that already existed. Letters to the Editor, for example, has been a standard of journalism since early in the century, and probably longer than that. But when I got to New York in 1951, one of the first things I noticed was that the letters published by the *Daily News* were almost all of a wild and rabidly angry sort. I don't know whether the people who read that paper were angrier than most, or whether the editors simply chose to print letters of that sort. Perhaps both factors were operative. But it struck me that some of the letters were written at such a fever pitch of hostility that they went over the edge of righteous civic indignation and into the Twilight Zone of the absurd. From that personal reaction it was a short step to decide to simply read the letters aloud in front of a studio audience.

For the routine, I donned a newspaperman's fedora with the word PRESS on the hatband and read actual letters written to newspaper editors, changing the signature to get the last laugh. Here are some examples:

> Could anybody give me some information on how to keep birds off my cherry trees? They don't even give the cherries a chance to ripen. I've tied things on the branches to scare them away but that didn't help.
>
> Signed: George Washington

> How stupid can people get? They now know that smoking can kill them; what more do they need? I don't understand them. Boy, if I knew someone was selling me a pack of poison, I'd sure have the brains to keep away.
>
> Signed: The Marlboro Man

> My gripe is people who litter up telephone booths—people who put little bits of paper, gum, candy wrappers, etc. on the small space beside the phone, leaving no room for your change purse, nor the notebook in which you might want to write down a phone number—who force you to step on gum or tobacco juice on the floor, then convey it on your shoes to the carpeting in your car or home—who leave greasy hair-goo on the receiver, some of which sticks on your ear and hair—who leave the odor

of stale cigar smoke on the transmitter—who clear out without paying the extra toll charge, forcing you to waste valuable time with the operator establishing yourself as a DIFFERENT caller, before you can make your call—and who tear up the phone books so you can't locate the number you want!

Signed: Superman

Elected officials seem to have only one fear when they are convicted of a felony—disbarment. In the case of congressmen, it is fear of censure. It would restore my faith in the judicial system to see these thieves sent to jail as an example to others who might be tempted to violate a public trust.

Signed: Richard Nixon

Again comes Mr. Rockefeller with some more of his lousy taxes. Why doesn't he ever consider the class of people who have to work for their money and need what we have left after taxes to buy food? Does our governor think that we just inherit our money?

Signed: William F. Buckley

Among the traffic hazards of early morning city-bound traffic we have the gals who finish combing their hair and putting on makeup at the wheel, but even worse is the driver with a cup of coffee.

This driver, who apparently has missed breakfast, tools in and out of traffic, one hand on the wheel and the other pouring coffee down his throat—a menace to limb and car!

However, he doesn't win them all—the other morning a gulper, cup to lips, had to panic brake and cascaded his coffee all over his shirt. I hope it had cream and sugar in it.

Signed: Juan Valdez

Come on, Television, who are you kidding with these so called beauty contests . . . Miss America . . . Miss Universe . . . Miss USA. . . . They're not beauty contests at all. As far as I'm concerned, they are ugly contests. All they do is exploit women; half the show is women parading around in their bathing suits. They couldn't care less if they had a brain in their heads. Well, I for one am not going to support this T-and-A Television. I will not only refuse to watch the shows, but I will boycott the sponsors as well. Maybe this will make you think twice before you use women to make money.

Signed: Hugh Hefner

I am getting a little sick and tired of reading about how Cher and her boyfriend want more privacy and how they can't stand to have their picture taken.

Doesn't Cher realize that those photographers have to make money too? They have families to support, and if Cher doesn't want her picture taken, let her go into another line of work . . . and really struggle for a living.

Signed: Roseanne Barr Arnold

Hateful George says New York has become "one vast kennel," that the filth on our streets is due to dogs, and that we are all driven mad by the "incessant barking of dogs." I have never lost any sleep because of a barking dog, though the constant drag racing on my avenue does keep me awake. As for your "viva vivisection" remark, you bum, you belong in one of those laboratories, and I for one (and there are plenty like me) would like to find you and vivisect you, without benefit of an anesthetic.

Signed: Lassie

What happened to the decent girls in New York? Girls I meet either dress like pigs, drink too much, spend all your money, or go out with someone else when you're not around. And to make matters worse, a sizeable proportion of them are married! Aren't there any of those old-fashioned girls left who dress decent, look decent, act decent, and *are* decent? I would really like to know.

Signed: Madonna

What is happening to our young girls today? Since when did they think they had to listen to obscenities and the crudest, most vulgar comments on sex and feel they had to snicker or laugh uproariously?

This, in the long run, is no guarantee of popularity with men. Have a little dignity, young ladies, about yourselves. Be proud of your femininity, dress becomingly and modestly, and don't let yourselves be brainwashed into being a party to today's trends.

Signed: Andrew Dice Clay

In the case of the Man on the Street, again we're talking about a journalistic cliche of long standing. Our world is now so troubled that literally every day there are serious questions or problems that attract our attention. For a great many years, editors have been sending inquiring reporters to the various places citizens gather just to pick up a few quotes, to see what the Man on the Street thinks about timely questions. Our television sketches of the same name are based precisely, in construction, on the old newspaper feature. Even the camera work—the tight close-ups of the speakers, with myself not seen at all—is the same as the way newspapers deal with that sort of material.

We will one day remove the last lump of coal and the last drop of oil from the earth, but we will absolutely never reach the bottom of the humor barrel. There will always be new forms and subjects out of which to strike the magic spark of funniness.

What then is the how-to element here? It's obviously not a matter of instructing the reader to write versions of the Question Man, Letters to the Editor, or Man on the Street. Rather, the would-be humorist must become practiced at keeping his or her eyes open for new ideas.

❀   ❀   ❀

When I appear as a guest on other people's comedy specials I generally create something new for the occasion, unless the producers insist that I do something familiar. That happened in mid-1986, when I did the HBO "Comic Relief" special, the one with fifty-seven varieties of comedians. I'd planned to do the "Three Mile Island" song, with Doc Severinson's orchestra, but Billy Crystal, Robin Williams, and the producers said they'd prefer that I do the good old Letters to the Editor bit, which I did.

In the case of a comedy-variety special done a few years ago in Mexico —"Festival of the Stars"—I thought that, since we were actually taping portions of the show in the open patio of a Mexican hacienda before a mixed Mexican and American audience, it would be reasonable to create something specifically for that kind of a setting; so I wrote a sketch in which John Ritter played straight for me. I performed as a Spanish flamenco dancer—flat black hat, tight black pants, a short black jacket—somebody like Jose Greco. I called myself Señor Gracias De Nada, which in English means, "Thank you, you're welcome." ("It's nothing.")

The first joke was added at the last minute because either I had forgotten to tell the producer that I required a false moustache, or, if I had, the makeup man had neglected to bring one to the location.

Necessity being the mother of invention I decided, shortly before showtime, to just stick a piece of black tape under my nose.

By the way, John Ritter was a marvelous straightman. He's one of the best comedy actors in the world anyway, and the constant ad-libbing I did didn't faze him a bit. Here, then is the routine:

Señor Gracias De Nada

JOHN: Señor De Nada, may I say it's wonderful to have you here.

STEVE: Thank you, Señor. And may I say it is wonderful to be had. Meaning no disrespect, Señor.

JOHN: Señor, if you don't mind my saying so, that moustache looks suspiciously like electrical tape.

STEVE: That, Señor, is because it *is* electrical tape. My head is AC and my mouth is DC. And I'm going to say some shocking things. Especially if you gringos antagonize me.

JOHN: Señor De Nada, you are so versatile. What would you say that you are famous for?

STEVE: I am famous for four or five years, Señor. Maybe six at the outside. And I am working outside at the moment.

JOHN: Actually, Señor, what I meant is—you are famous as the creator of some classic Latin dances.

STEVE: Oh, yes.

JOHN: What dances have you created, in all seriousness?

STEVE: In all seriousness? None at all, Señor. Well, back in the thirties, when I was dancing in London—the 1930s, when this girl over here was a mere cucaracha—I created the famous dance, Stomping at the Savoy, although the busboy I stomped was not very happy about it. (*He stomps around.*) I also invented flamingo dancing.

JOHN: Oh, of course. The flamenco dance.

STEVE: No, Señor. Flamingo dancing, not flamenco. This is a popular misconception. You students would perhaps be interested to know how all these misconceptions became so popular.
    As a matter of fact, they are—unfortunately—more popular than I am.
    All seriousness aside, muchachos, the correct name is *flamingo* dancing.
    But to do it properly, one must have very long, thin legs. And it helps if they are peeenk. In the flamingo dance, you walk around with your long, pink legs and you scream, "Schmock! Schmock! Schmock!"

JOHN: Just like a flamingo.

STEVE: No, just like a jerk.

JOHN: Oh, yeah, I'm hip.

STEVE: I doubt that *very* much, Señor.

JOHN: Where will you be performing next, Señor De Nada?

STEVE: After thees it's not too definite. But actually I am already booked to work in the beautiful Mexican port city of Matzoland.

JOHN: No, no. Don't you mean Mazatlan?

STEVE: Leesten, you go to your church, I'll go to mine.

JOHN: Well, enough about your dancing. What are some of the great Mexican songs you've written?

STEVE: Oh, they are so many, Señor. You've heard of "I Lost My Heart in San Francisco"?

JOHN: You didn't write that!

STEVE: No. I wrote "I Lost My Car in Tijuana." And then, muchachos, I wrote "You're Just a Hockey Puck from Acapulco." That one is being recorded by Charo. Or, as you say in English, Dolly Parton.

JOHN: Well, Señor De Nada, we are—very fortunately—running out of time. Would you show us the dance for which you are famous the world over?

STEVE: Wheech one is that, Señor?

JOHN: It's the merangue!

STEVE: The merangue. Yes. I'm famous the world over for the merangue, and it gives me great heartburn to do it for all of you right now.

JOHN: I'd love it, Señor.

STEVE: Here I go. . . . Music! (*dances while spraying shaving cream all around on the brim of his hat*) There you are, Señor. The lemon merangue.

JOHN: Thank you very much, Señor Gracias De Nada.

We used to have a lot of crazy characters appearing on my Westinghouse series in the early 1960s. One of the wackiest and most popular was a fellow named Gypsy Boots. Gypsy bounded on stage like a madman every time he appeared. He spoke about three times louder and faster than was necessary and seemed to be bursting with excess energy.

There was invariably some rationale, however flimsy, for his visits. He wanted to convince me of the merits of drinking raw carrot juice, or of a diet consisting largely of mulberry seeds and crumbled linoleum, or whatever. Physically, he was a remarkable specimen. Gypsy was—is—about twenty years older than he looks. And he was a hippy before the word was ever invented in that he wore a beard, sandals, odd attire, ate a vegetarian diet, and chose not to conform to any number of society's social customs.

He would run on stage carrying a food blender, plug it in, jam it with carrots complete with the greens, whole apples, oranges, nuts, birdseed, froth it up into a foaming brew, drink deeply of it himself, and force me to do the same.

Gypsy also did crazy exercises, shouted slightly off-center pithy sayings, and in general turned the studio into a madhouse.

He appeared only on our show—ours was probably the only one nutty enough to make him feel at home. Also, he was on with us so often that I guess the hosts of other talk shows or comedy programs assumed he was somehow my property, although I wouldn't have cared who else had booked him.

Incidentally, from time to time Gypsy Boots can still be seen on television football games that originate in Los Angeles. The cameras like to pan the crowds to pick up shots of people with weird-looking hats, young women with bulging sweaters, or whatever. I often see Gypsy then.

Another character who appeared with us was Frank Zappa, the rock singer, although he never came on to perform music. One time I asked him what he was prepared to do. He signaled for the curtains to open and an old automobile became visible. Then Zappa gestured to the orchestra to give him a little background music. At that point he and a couple of people he had brought with him—God knows who they were—began attacking the car with sledgehammers. Within about five minutes they had broken all the windows, crumpled the fenders, hood and doors, and reduced the car to a pile of junk.

Did the audience consider this entertainment? Your guess is as good as mine. Apparently they did. They laughed, applauded, jumped around to the rhythm of the music. . . . As they say—go figga!

Another marvelous character who appeared from time to time on the old show was a gentleman named Professor Voss. I believe he was in his seventies but he was in robust condition, that being easy to assess because he usually appeared naked to the waist, wearing nothing above his belt buckle but a strange necklace made of dried ears of corn. He shared with us details of his diet, but mostly gave remarkable physical demonstrations, one of which involved his sitting in a large tub of cold water in which large blocks of ice were floating. Without any important input from me, Mr. Voss one evening gave us one of the loudest and longest laughs I have ever heard from an audience. The conversation leading up to it went approximately as follows:

STEVE: Professor, if you had to specify one thing that was the mainstay of your diet, what might that be?

PROFESSOR: Well, Mr. Allen, I would say the most important thing a person can take in is water.

STEVE: Water?

PROFESSOR: That's right. The first thing I do when I get up every morning is to drink about three quarts of warm water.

STEVE: Three quarts? My goodness. And what do you do then?

PROFESSOR: (*matter-of-factly*) Well, you stand a considerable distance from the toilet—

I cut him off at that point, of course, but the harm, such as it was, had been done, and the audience would not let us continue for quite some time, so wild was their laughter.

Oddly enough, remarks of that sort never brought so much as a single postcard of complaint, nor should they have, because there was always the clear understanding that the shocking or outrageous comment was not planned and not deliberately resorted to.

One more popular character—he appeared on both the "Tonight" and the Westinghouse shows—was a recent immigrant from Italy named Joe Interleggi, who I called the Human Termite because of his peculiar habit of eating wood, or at least biting off chunks of it with the strongest teeth and jaws I have ever seen on a human. Joe could bite the cap off a beer bottle and crumble it up into a ball as if he were chewing a stick of gum. It was a bit difficult to understand what he was saying because he had quite a thick Italian accent, but audiences loved him, and so did those of us on the show. He was always cheerful, remarkably energetic, and amazingly strong.

One of his tricks involved kneeling at the corner of a wooden table and then picking the table up by biting the edge of it with his teeth. With the table aloft in this position, his arms held high, hands empty, he would whirl about the stage to the accompaniment of ad-libbed Italian Tarantella music and vigorous, rhythmic clapping from the audience.

On one occasion, I accompanied Joe out into the street, where he pulled a large bus about thirty feet along the curb . . . with his *ears!* How do you pull a bus with your ears? It's not easy. What Interleggi did was fasten two or three clothespins to each ear and then somehow tie some twine through the clothespins. The twine was then attached to a stronger rope, and it was this that was fastened to the bumper of the bus. He faced the bus, leaned backward at a steep angle, and did indeed succeed in moving the vehicle forward, although it appeared that at almost any minute the ears might be torn from his head.

Joe's every remark was prefaced by his name for me—MistaSteveAllen. "MistaSteveAllen, I'm glad to be here tonight." "MistaSteveAllen, my friends back in Italy love you." "MistaSteveAllen, you are a good guy."

The biggest laugh Joe ever got on our show came, I'm sure, as something of a surprise to him, as it did to all of us. On that evening, Mr. Interleggi appeared at the studios accompanied by a heavy-set young woman. I stress that she was quite a bit overweight, not to be unkind to her but because this has direct relevance to what it was that made us all laugh so heartily. Joe was always somewhat vague in explaining to our production people exactly what it was he was going to do once he got on stage with me, but that never mattered much because he was invariably entertaining. In this particular case, he had asked only for a length of clothesline, a wooden chair, and a supply of broken glass.

The glass fragments he spread out on the floor of the stage, for what reason we could not at first tell. He added to the supply by breaking the tops off some beer bottles with his teeth. He next called to his young companion, who was seated in the audience, to join him on stage, which she promptly did. To this day, I doubt if he had told her what he had in mind.

In any event, he instructed the young lady to seat herself in the chair. After she had done so, he tied her securely to it by running around her three or four times with the clothesline rope. In just a few seconds she was trussed securely, like someone who has been kidnapped, although her mouth was left uncovered. I noticed that the rope was digging into the folds of flesh on her abdomen, but apparently not to such an extent as to cause her pain. I said, "Well, Joe, you've got the young lady securely tied up here. Now, what did you have in mind to do to her?"

"MistaSteveAllen," he said, "you justa watch."

At that he stepped behind the chair, got down on his knees, grabbed the knotted rope behind the young lady in his teeth, and with a mighty yank, stood erect. I suppose he had envisioned that the woman/chair combination would work very much like the wooden table, in that it would remain in a generally horizontal position. Perhaps he had underestimated the woman's weight. For whatever reasons, the chair tilted steeply forward. This meant that the rope cut even more deeply into the lady's middle so that instead of sitting comfortably in a horizontal position, she was pitched forward, no longer supported by the chair at all but just by the rope across her stomach. The discomfort of this became immediately clear because the poor soul began yelling like a stuck pig. I am perfectly aware that none of us should have laughed at this but can report only the fact that it did strike the three hundred people present as hilariously funny.

Something about it must have seemed odd to Joe, too, because for the first time in all the years he had been appearing on my program, he goofed—he dropped the young lady from a height of about three feet. She landed directly in the pile of broken glass. Fortunately she suffered no serious injury from this, but there were tiny cuts and scratches on her knees, her stockings were ruined, and all in all, it was a remarkable spectacle, especially considering that the entire incident took no more than twenty seconds to transpire. It was pure Joe Interleggi all the way.

From my earliest days in network television, in 1951, I've generally preferred to interview unusual, off-beat people rather than the usual talk-show parade of movie actors, singers, and other entertainers. Some of my fellow performers have been wonderful guests, but for giant laughs, I'll take a character from the audience, or from out of the blue, any time.

I've been asked if, when I suddenly walk out into the audience with a microphone, having made no plans whatever, I have a way of telling, just by looking at the faces of the people, which of them will help me get big laughs. The answer is yes. The first thing I do is almost totally rule out young men who are handsome or young women who are beautiful. The closer they are to perfection, the less inherently amusing they are, all other things being equal. Exceptions are made, of course, in the case of a woman who has something strikingly odd about her. If she were, for example, wearing an unusual dress, even an unusually attractive one, perhaps a wild hairdo, or something of the sort, then that would suit my purposes because it would immediately establish an obvious subject about which the audience would be legitimately curious.

I also rarely bother to interview people who appear eminently sane, civilized, well-dressed, and self-assured. It's not that I can't get laughs with them—if you are practiced at that particular art, you can get some sort of laughs talking to anybody at all—but the laughter comes so much more easily if you interview someone wearing a strange hat, a guy with a front tooth missing, a woman with her purse hanging open or her wig slightly askew. Or just someone with a crazy look in the eye.

There might seem to be a possible problem in this selection process, so let's consider the imaginary fellow with the front tooth missing. Would I interview him about his teeth? Not at all. I would ask him perfectly common questions, at least to get the conversation started. What is your name, sir? What do you do for a living? What is your home town? That sort of thing. But while the man is answering my questions he would just *look* funny, whereas somebody who looked like columnist George Will would seem sober, serious—hard to describe to police, shall we say.

One lucky thing I've discovered over the years is that people who look a little odd often *are* a little odd. But to refer to the problem potential, it's vitally important, to me at any rate, *not* to say anything unkind or thoughtless just to get a cheap laugh. Actually I prefer it when the visitors in the studio audience get the laughs themselves, with me simply playing straight for them.

I will on rare occasions verbally assault someone in my audience—although always in a kidding way, not going for the jugular—but only in situations where the other person has started it. In other words, if somebody heckles me or puts me down, then it's perfectly alright to go on the counterattack, keeping in mind, needless to say, that the point of the exercise is to make others laugh.

Although several other talk-show hosts have borrowed this routine, they don't generally get really hearty laughter out of it. I wonder why some of the fellows do it at all, because, like I say, what generally is produced is lightweight, good-natured banter, with rarely any flashes of true wit. If I were on the production staff for one of those shows, I would try to think of some gimmick, some underlying rationale that would justify going out into the audience, since obviously getting screams seldom happens.

There are some ancient radio announcer or game show audience gimmicks that might work for a combination comic and talk show host: Who traveled the farthest to come here tonight? Who's got the rattiest looking pocketbook? Which of you out there can make the best speech telling us why we should elect you president? Something of that sort can provide an interesting framework that might produce its own laughs. But I'm certainly not the only performer who can get laughs ad-libbing with audiences. Not many of the talk-show hosts can, but there are other comedians who do the trick quite well. Jim Brogan would be a good example. He's very fast and witty and says fresh, inventive things. Not just preset, cookie-cutter jokes that he's done before but fresh lines actually based on the feedback he's getting from the audience.

In one of my routines—"Where Are They Now?"—we pretended to show various guests from the past in their homes or workplaces. Count Dracula was one we visited frequently. The characterization was done by the late Gabe Dell. Gabe used to do assorted characters as a regular member of our comedy gang, but Dracula was his masterpiece. First of all, he would make himself look remarkably like the serious actors who used to play Dracula, combining that with a faultless Transylvanian accent. Then, just before he went on camera, Gabe would eat some little heart-shaped cinnamon candies so that when he opened his mouth it was a hideous red color.

Here is a sample of one of the Dracula scripts, most of which were written by Stan Burns, Herb Sargent, Arne Sultan, Marvin Worth, Bill Dana, and Don Hinkley. We gave Gabe the phony name Boris Nadel, the actor who allegedly played Dracula in old movies.

GABE: How do you do, Steve? Welcome to my castle.

STEVE: My goodness, you look exactly the same as you did twenty years ago. How do you keep in shape?

GABE: I work out at Vic Tanney's.

STEVE: Mr. Nadel, where did you get all the ideas for your fantastic makeup?

GABE: From my father. . . . He was a master of makeup.

STEVE: Oh, your father was an actor?

GABE: No, an *actress*. . . . A master of makeup.

STEVE: I see what you mean. You know, I've been a fan of yours ever since I can remember. I'll never forget the scene in *House of Blood*, when they drove a wooden stake through your heart.

GABE: That was nothing. Did you see the one in which they set fire to my stomach?

STEVE: What movie was that in?

GABE: It wasn't a movie. It was a commercial for Pepto-Bismol! I've got to make a buck, you know.

STEVE: I understand that you almost won an Academy Award in 1923. Is that correct?

GABE: Yes. It was my first picture. My remarkable makeup caused a sensation. The sight of me almost frightened people to death. For this character, I had my nostrils spread apart, celluloid discs in my mouth distorted my cheekbones, both my legs were twisted out of shape . . . my eyelids were sliced and all my teeth were sharpened to give me a truly fiendish appearance.

STEVE: Sounds horrifying. What was the name of the picture?

GABE: *Little Women.*

STEVE: Very sweet. Now that you're retired, sir, what do you do with your time?

GABE: Oh, I like to watch TV.

STEVE: Do you watch all the horror shows?

GABE: Just yours, Steef.

STEVE: Mr. Nadel, I think that your movie *Dr. Jekyll and Mr. Hyde* was your greatest achievement.

GABE: Thank you.

STEVE: The most frightening sight in the movie was the scene where you transformed yourself from a man into a werewolf. If it's not asking too much, is it possible for you to show us that famous transformation?

GABE: Not at all. First, I'll need a drink to start me off. (*He takes a foaming drink, goes into wild transformation bit, with red and green lights, snorts, growls, and choking sounds, finally looking like a horrible monster.*)

STEVE: Good Lord, how did you do that?

GABE: (*snaps back to normal*) Do what, Steve? (*sound of scream off stage*)

STEVE: What was that?

GABE: Dinner is ready. (*calls off stage*) Coming, mother! Good night, Steef.

MUSIC: *Playoff*

*   *   *

Is there anything else the professional practitioner of the comic arts should be on the lookout for? Yes. Criticism. I'm not using the word in the intellectual sense, according to which analytical criticism may involve both praise and a negative evaluation, but considering the term in its more common sense. The criticism comedians receive can be deserved or undeserved.

A young performer is unlikely to start out being absolutely brilliant. And, even if he were, he would not be at his best in every outing. From time to time even the greatest artists have had off nights, worked in weak plays or films, been miscast, been ill, or, for whatever reasons, turned in a second-rate performance. If their egos are strong enough to study the criticism they receive at such times, they can learn from it. I do not mean that they should accept every word as gospel, for the simple reason that critics often cancel each other out. I had no idea about this until it first happened to me in 1951, when I began working on network television, for CBS. I would do a particular show, after which fourteen critics would say, in effect, that it was one of the funniest things they ever saw in their life—and seventeen others would say the very same show was terrible. That, as the old saying goes, is what makes horse races. But still, the performer should pay some attention to criticism, especially from the more able critics.

Personally, I've always been more fascinated by criticism that is totally undeserved, the good old bum-rap. Of course it isn't only professional critics who do that sort of thing. All of us are sadly gifted at it. People have even been killed by the state after having been convicted, by due process of law, of crimes later discovered to have had nothing to do with them.

As regards performing comedy on television, the very fact that the audiences are so enormous means that it is a literal impossibility to get a unanimous consensus for or against anything. So even on your best nights, even after your best shows, there will almost certainly be some who will just not have gotten the message, and who will render a negative verdict on whatever you might have presented.

Have I ever experienced an instance of violent opposition to one of my jokes or sketches? Yes. Anyone who has the good fortune to be employed on television, either regularly or occasionally, should be prepared for the fact that someone, somewhere across the nation will be offended by almost anything you might say.

The same thing happens in small clubs, of course, but the performer rarely becomes aware of it. You're ahead of the game if about 75 percent of your audience is laughing, since the sound volume is almost identical to that of instances in which 100 percent are laughing. But when people get angry about something they've seen on television, they write letters about it.

I refer to one such case here, as a more-or-less typical illustration:

Back in the days when Dick Cavett was still doing a conventional ninety-minute talk show, from 11:30 P.M. to 1:00 A.M. each night, opposite the "Tonight Show," he asked me to fill in for him for a week while he vacationed. I did so, and it has subsequently been a source of profound regret that I did not immediately arrange to acquire copies of the videotapes of those shows, since each of them turned out to be as good as I am capable of doing.

When things go that well, of course, the factor of luck is always operative. For example, one of my oldest television comedy routines involves pointing a camera out at whatever street is adjacent to the studio and commenting spontaneously on what the camera reveals. Dick's producers wanted me to do the routine on his show, and we put it to good use every night. The camera was kept on all during the show; a small monitor just to the right of my desk showed me what was in view. Whenever things began to look particularly interesting, I would interrupt the flow of the on-stage action, ask for the outside camera to be punched up, and we were off and running.

One night I noticed that one of those New York Police Department tow trucks had just stopped in front of the theater. As our studio audience was suddenly shown this real-life drama, a man's anguished voice floated out from the balcony saying, "Oh, no," as he recognized his car about to be taken away by the police. Given that stroke of good luck—mine, not the driver's —it didn't much matter what I said because the situation itself was hysterically funny. But we got no complaints about that particular routine.

What made everything hit the fan was the appearance, a couple of nights later, of comedian-writer-producer Bob Einstein. Fans of the old "Smothers Brothers Comedy Hour" may recall Einstein as Officer Judy. He was also producer-performer on John Byner's TV series, "Bizarre," the star of his own "SuperDave Show," and the brother of comedian Albert Brooks. That both brothers are witty and inventive practitioners of the comic arts is not unusual, I suppose, given that their father was a famous radio comic of the 1930s—Parkyakarkas—who worked on the "Eddie Cantor Show." Whenever Bob worked with me, he was never introduced as himself, since he has no act but always appeared as a supposedly real-life personage.

Anyway, in this case, Einstein was introduced as Gil Drabowski, head of the Polish Anti-Defamation Society. The storyline of the ad-lib sketch Einstein and I then performed involved his pretending to be an irate spokesman for Polish-Americans who had come to lodge a public protest against Polish jokes. He threatened to sue various networks and programs and, to substantiate his case, read from a paper several commonly heard Polish jokes to which, he said, he took particular exception.

Few comedy routines I have ever heard have drawn a bigger laugh than this one. The audience was at first embarrassed, since they believed that the man on stage was actually a Mr. Drabowski. But when he began to read jokes—of the typically outrageous sort then heard daily all over the country—they lost all control because of the psychological dynamics of the situation itself. First of all, the jokes were funny, although they were certainly in poor taste. But the idea that an actual leader of an organization protesting jokes would read these same jokes on the air made the situation —well, the point is clear enough.

At one point Einstein (as Drabowski) said, "For example, Mr. Allen, here's an instance of a joke that we Poles find particularly offensive: What does a Polack use for underarm deodorant?"

The straight line itself convulsed the audience. In my response, I naturally did not use the word *Polack*. "Well, Mr. Drabowski," I said. "The only thing that occurs to me is the conventional answer: I give up. What *does* a Polish gentleman use for underarm deodorant?"

"A can of Raid," Einstein replied.

Subsequently, telegrams of complaint began coming in from Polish-American organizations around the country, including one from Chester Grabowski, editor of the *Post Eagle,* a Polish-American newspaper. The "Dick Cavett Show" production office later advised me that several angry phone messages were received as well, including death threats and threats of bodily harm.

The next afternoon, members of Mr. Cavett's production staff told me that Chester Grabowski (the *Post Eagle* editor who had written) intended to come personally to the studio to demand satisfaction. I said, "Well, that's marvelous. When the gentleman gets here, please tell him that I'll be more than happy to have him appear as a guest on the program. That way he can express his views, and any Polish-American who might have been offended by the sketch will be satisfied that their sentiments have been made known."

The Cavett-ABC people agreed to deliver my invitation to Mr. Grabowski in the event that he showed up in the studio.

As viewers will know, programs of this sort are interrupted every few minutes for commercials. It is customary for the performers and production people in the studio to use these brief periods to discuss the progress of the show and to deal with any problems that might have come up in much the same way that a football team discusses strategy and tactics during a time-out period. Two or three times during the course of the program I asked, "Is Mr. Grabowski here yet?"

Eventually it was explained that he had indeed appeared but had declined my invitation to come to the stage.

After the program that evening, Michael Zanella, the producer, came to me and said, "The Polish people decided not to accept your invitation, as you know, but perhaps they'll feel somewhat better about the situation if you spend a few minutes with them in the Green Room (where guests are seated before going on stage) and listen to their point of view."

"I'll be glad to," I said. I went to the Green Room, met Mr. Grabowski and two of his friends, and spent perhaps fifteen minutes in conversation with them. Since matters of taste and opinion are rarely arguable, I naturally took no exception to the emotional response of the three gentlemen to the routine that Einstein had done. When, however, Grabowski said, "We know who's behind all this," and made it very clear that he saw the entire Polish-joke phenomenon in America as an actual Jewish *plot,* I responded by saying that he was very much in error in regard to that aspect of the controversy. I also made it clear that I regretted that he had not chosen to appear on the program. Since my conversation with him was conducted on a gentlemanly basis I found it impossible to understand his later imputations that I had invited him and his friends to appear on the program only to make light of them.

I have subsequently read Mr. Grabowski's account of the incident. He explains his reluctance to appear on the program by saying, in a *Post Eagle* column of August 23, 1971:

> Well, we arrived, but we were not forewarned on the phone that we were going to be welcome on the show. Of course not, they wanted to catch us unprepared, and then try to make us look silly. . . . We did not bite, showing them that the Poles are not the meatheads that their sister-station [sic] depicts weekly on the "All in the Family" show.

Mr. Grabowski's comments called for the following publicly released response:

> It is not at all true that *they* wanted to catch the Polish spokesmen unprepared.
>
> Since I doubt that Mr. Grabowski would claim the power of a mind reader, it therefore follows that he could have had no way of knowing what my motivation was in inviting him and his friends to appear on the program. That motivation, in fact, was simply based on my understanding of the obvious: that it would have been both an act of fair play and also good theater to permit Grabowski and his colleagues to express their views.
>
> Once the Polish spokesmen had taken a position of great seriousness in regard to the question they clearly considered highly controversial, it would have made no sense whatever to "try to make [them] look silly."
>
> The quality of meatheadedness has apparently no correlation with the factor of race or nationality. Assuming that we could arrive at a definition

of the term *meathead*, it would follow that all ethnic groups have their percentage of meatheads, which means there are a few Polish meatheads, just as there are Irish meatheads, Jewish meatheads, Italian meatheads, etc.

Elsewhere in his column, Mr. Grabowski says, "The name used by Einstein was Grabowski." Mr. Grabowski was apparently a victim of what psychologists call the Expectancy Illusion, in which one sees or hears what one expects or fears to see or hear. Neither Einstein nor I had ever heard of Mr. Chester Grabowski before this instance. In any event, Einstein was identified as *Gil Drabowski.*

I take no issue with Grabowski's suggestion that Poles "must band together once and for all . . . in a fight against the media slander of our good image." But I think all decent citizens, Polish or otherwise, will be alarmed by Grabowski's statement that "they only respect one method, that being *force.*" People are injured and killed by instruments of force. . . .

Grabowski has repeatedly referred to Einstein as my straight man. The point is of decidedly minor importance, but the roles were, in fact, reversed. Mr. Einstein is a popular comedian; I served as *his* straightman in this particular instance.

One is naturally dismayed to see anti-Semitism blatantly revealed in Grabowski's newspaper accounts. I suggest that the gentlemen's Polish-American readers, and others, give long and hard thought to his use of the phrase *the Jew Einstein.* . . .

My letter suggested that the offending sketch—which was created by Einstein—would be better understood if considered in the context of a long and eminently successful series of routines he had performed on my television shows during the previous several years. Each of them took the form of a put-on interview in which Einstein purported to be not an entertainer but a real-life individual with an interesting story. On one occasion, for example, he was introduced as an ex-convict who had just served a great many years in prison and who, while incarcerated, had trained a small bird to do an incredible series of tricks. When at last the time came for the bird to go through its paces, it could not even be coaxed from the cage. The sketch finished with a television closeup of Einstein's heavily padded and gloved hand trying, without success, to grasp the bird so that it could be brought forth.

In another instance, Einstein was the World's Strongest Man. He claimed to be able to take almost any sort of punishment; but when I landed an only-moderate punch on his midsection—at his request—he was nevertheless wounded and became rather surly.

Another time he was introduced as a professional football player who had recently left the Detroit Lions. He described the meanness and savagery characteristic of line play—the sort of thing, he said, that the public never becomes aware of. The high point of his account of a recent game came when he said that he had seen a puff of smoke coming from the helmet of an opponent and realized that he had just been struck with a .22 calibre bullet!

On another occasion, Bob appeared on my show as Andy Bernard, the Coyote Man. He claimed to have been abandoned by his parents as an infant and raised in the wild, among friendly coyotes.

In another appearance he was a ping-pong champion.

During the same season that Einstein was doing this series of comedy sketches, he also appeared as Gil Drabowski, Polish-American Attorney. Oddly enough, although my program at that time was seen in many parts of the country, not a single letter of complaint was received. One possible explanation is that the number of viewers watching network television after 11:30 p.m. is greater than those watching daytime TV, although the original program was seen during the evening hours in some parts of the country. Or perhaps at the time of the "Dick Cavett Show" appearance, the Poles had started a fight-back campaign. As regards the four or five Polish jokes that formed the basis of Einstein's sketch, it is important, I think, that Einstein did not create any of them. They were—for better or worse—jokes in common circulation, the origin of which will probably forever remain in obscurity.

Parenthetically, the origin of jokes of the fad type is a question that has long interested me. I relate it to the mysterious origin of dirty jokes. I have met or worked with almost all of the popular American comedians, as well as the several hundred writers who provide their material. I have asked scores of these professional funny people if they personally have ever created any of the dirty stories of the sort that one hears exchanged in offices, factories, and country clubs all over America. In each case, the writer or comedian reported that he or she personally had never written a single such joke, although in most cases the speakers were as ready as the average American to repeat them.

The Polish jokes that caused all this fuss were clearly part of the old American tradition of joke fads, as were, say, the Little Moron jokes of the 1930s. The nation amused itself with the latter for several years, and I suppose they were considered hilarious by everyone but the parents of mentally handicapped children. Then there were the Little Audrey jokes. They all ended with the line "Little Audrey just laughed and laughed because she knew. . . ."

In more recent years, young Americans laughed at the Elephant jokes and the Grape jokes.

And, of course, if we move to an earlier period of our history, there were the Irish jokes, in which Pat and Mike were invariably described as either stupid or drunk. If you find a joke book published before the 1930s, you're certain to read a lot of jokes based on the idea that you can't trust Jews in business dealings, that blacks are shiftless and lazy, that the Scots seem to have no interest but saving money, and that the Italians couldn't seem to complete a sentence in the English language without getting the words all mixed up. One would naturally not deny the right of the Irish, Jews, blacks, Scots, and Italians to take exception to these stories.

A comedy show that deals in social commentary is inevitably going to offend a few viewers. This is not too important, for on a given night when you are performing before thirty million people, you may offend only twelve of them. But often these twelve write angry letters and, unbelievable as it sounds, this sort of thing can throw giant corporations into tremors of fear. "We can't afford to antagonize potential customers" is the way the philosophy is customarily expressed. In a sense, these fears may be justified; I can't deny that the files of many entertainers are bulging with complaints. Let me give some specific examples.

One letter our office received was typed on official-looking stationery. The usual column of names that nobody ever reads ran down the left side of the sheet. "You must realize," the writer lectured, "that not all motorcyclists are delinquents."

I realized it. What had occasioned the protest was a comedy sketch in which I had worn a leather jacket and motorcycle boots as a member of a new vocal quartet, the Four Punks.

In another sketch, we showed the difficulty a homemaker had in opening a bottle of ketchup. This might seem like a harmless subject for humor, but a few days after its broadcast I received a letter from the Glass Container Manufacturers Institute that said, in part:

Dear Mr. Allen,

Though I personally did not see your broadcast of Monday, October 12th, and did not catch up with a kinescope of it until today, a good many of our people did see the live show. To get right to the point, the opinion is general that you were unnecessarily rough on the subject of jars and bottles.

GCMI is a trade association made up of companies which turn out over twenty billion new glass containers every year. It is a business like

broadcasting or any other. Details of the glass container business are out-
lined in the attached industry fact book.

It is our belief that glass containers have many advantages over other
forms of packaging, and we spend a good deal of time, thought, and money
trying to promote these advantages. Your broadcast did the opposite, and
we feel that it may well have hurt us seriously in the highly competitive
packaging industry. . . .

The harm, and we think it considerable, has been done. We did think,
however, that you would want this reaction to your broadcast of October
12, and any comment you may have would be appreciated.

Bush Barnum

Dinah Shore once told me about a sketch with a clever premise done
on her show. As she tells it:

It was cute. The boys dreamed up this idea that cuts of meat—steaks,
chops and so on—be treated as if they were jewelry. Instead of displaying the meat in the usual butcher's showcase, we had it in small glass counters, each piece laid out on black velvet with the price tag attached, just
the way you see things in a jewelry shop. The butcher had one of those
little magnifying glasses—you know, the whole bit. It was a funny idea.

Dinah was right; the sketch was successful, and to a public painfully
aware of high meat prices, it was vastly amusing. But it apparently was
not funny to butchers and meat wholesalers. They protested to Ms. Shore,
to her network and sponsors in no uncertain terms.

When someone passed him cranberries one night on his TV show, Danny
Thomas spurned the offer. "A cranberry," he said, making a sour face, "is
like a pickled mothball." Well, everybody laughed—except, of course, the
thousands of people around the country engaged in the business of growing and selling cranberries.

Some years ago, while watching Jimmy Hoffa, Ducks Corallo, Johnny
Dio, and the rest of their immoral group squirm under the thumb of the
Senate Labor Rackets investigation committee, I decided to use the weapon
of satire in support of Sen. McClellan's campaign. Having long been ap-
palled by the power of organized mobsters in the fields of politics, labor,
boxing, the clothing industry, juke boxes, nightclubs, and the waterfront,
as well as their more historic pursuits in narcotics, gambling, prostitution,
usury, and extortion, I staged a comedy version of the Senate hearings,
aiming barb after barb at Corallo-Hoffa-Dio and company: "I refuse to
incriminate myself on the grounds that it might tend to make me answer,'

the witness said. When I mentioned the name of a certain individual to a squirming villain on the stand he said, "He is no good, he is a detriment to my union, and if I am elected I will kick him out." "Who is this man?" I asked. "Oh," said the witness, "he's my father."

The sketch got very favorable reaction, and we received a nice wire from Sen. McClellan, but a few people around the country disapproved. They thought I was making pointless fun of the committee itself.

Perhaps reiterating a few words about the psychology of humor would not be out of place here. Comedy, as I've said, is about tragedy; Christian tradition lists the seven deadly sins as pride, covetousness, lust, anger, gluttony, envy, and sloth. These are also the raw material of humor. In other words, there's nothing amusing about perfection. Things are funny in some sort of loose relationship as to how far they fall short of the ideal. There may not be laughter in hell, but there couldn't possibly be any in heaven, especially if you accept the description supplied by the fundamentalist sector.

It might be objected that Thomas Aquinas, the leading Christian philosopher, said he could pleasurably contemplate laughing, once he reached heaven, as he considered the plight of those burning in hell, but there is no conflict here. First of all, Aquinas was simply shamefully wrong on the point, as he was in his resounding endorsement of burning heretics alive. The Catholic church reserves the doctrine of infallibility to popes—and even then only on rare occasions. Aquinas was never elected pope. He spoke with authority on many subjects, but humor wasn't one of them.

Comedy sketches generally make a father look like a dolt, portray a fighter as punchy, make an "old maid" seem man-crazy, a motorcycle cop gruff and rude, a drunk the object of laughter, a mother-in-law a meddler, or make some other type selected from life look ridiculous in one way or another. You are perfectly at liberty to protest about all this and to say that there is nothing amusing in any of it; but the only way you could be satisfied is for the networks to cancel all comedy shows.

It would be more rational and rewarding, however, to live with comedy, even when it is aimed in your direction, and to appreciate that humor is a gift of the gods enabling us to multiply magically our sometimes meager fund of material joy.

Do you know what angry people always do when they write to, for example, "Saturday Night Live"? They say the offending joke or sketch wasn't funny. The comedian's writers get thousands of dollars a week and may have been studying humor for perhaps twenty years; but there's always some druggist in Keokuk who can confidently assure them that a particular routine wasn't funny.

Is there a lesson to be learned here? There certainly is. We can smugly assume that we're superior to this hypothetical pharmacist, but the point is we all are the druggist in Keokuk. We all think we're experts on humor. We don't claim to know a thing about architecture, deep sea diving, or playing the zither, but we all pose as authorities when it comes to the genius of Sid Caesar or Jonathan Winters.

Some time ago, Louis Nye and I did a take-off on a pair of crazy tunesmiths, boasting that we had received a medal for a song we wrote during the last war. When we performed the song, it turned out to be a German march.

"But wait a minute," Tom Poston, the straightman, shouted. "That's not an American song. It's German!"

At which Louis showed him the medal we had won—an iron swastika. "What do you think this is?" he snapped. "Chopped liver?"

The line got a hearty laugh, but the next day three prominent columnists took us to task for it. One said, "Nothing will ever be funny about a swastika." The more logical way to express disapproval of this joke would have been to admit that the joke was funny—the audience laughter had established that—but to suggest that the subject matter was too sensitive for many people.

There is an answer even to *this* argument, but at least such criticism is reasonably stated. Parenthetically, I shortly thereafter came across an article in *Newsweek* that reported that a Bavarian entertainer named Ludwig Hoelzel had achieved popularity all over West Germany by doing a satire of Hitler. Certainly all right-minded people must be pleased that Nazis, their philosophy, and their trappings have become objects of ridicule. What we should fear is the mind that still insists on treating such targets only with deadly seriousness.

It's also relevant that the two writers who wrote the swastika joke were Jewish.

In any event, I restate here the apology that I offered several times on Dick Cavett's show the evening after Bob Einstein's appearance. It was not my intention, nor Bob's, to offend anyone. The sketch represents the one instance in which Einstein has dealt with the Polish joke as an article of his trade. In my own capacity as a television humorist, I do not tell such jokes.

Lastly, for whatever the point is worth, I repeatedly tried to arrange for the television production of a program special called the "Polish Comedy Hour." The relevance of that project to the present misunderstanding lies in the fact that the program was designed to be one that Polish-Americans would greatly *enjoy* viewing.

15

Joke and Other Comedy Writing

If you're more interested in writing comedy than performing it on stage, you might start with supplying jokes and one-liners for stand-up comedians who buy material on the open market.

Fledgling jokewriters, however, are unlikely to make a good living at this type of work, since many comedians, even extremely wealthy and successful ones, pay only fifteen or twenty dollars per joke. There *are* times when a comic will give you as much as a couple of hundred dollars for a line; but such instances are rare indeed. So, bearing in mind the product's low street value, even if you sold five jokes to someone at twenty dollars a one-liner, you'd be earning only a modest amount of money.

I personally do not buy jokes on the market; the few times I have accepted material "over the transom," it was really for the purpose of helping the writer. While today's young comics generally create their own material, a number of them also purchase jokes, provided the lines suit their style and stage persona. Some comedians who buy material include Rodney Dangerfield, Phyllis Diller, Tom Dreeson, Bill Maher, Phil Nee, Maureen Murphy, Joan Rivers, Will Shriner, Yakov Smirnoff, and Jimmy Walker.

In addition to tailoring your jokes to a specific comic, you may be able to boost interest in your material if the gags relate to places where the comedian is scheduled to perform, or to a particular group he or she will be entertaining. Thus, if you know a certain comic is set to do a series of shows in Chicago, or perform for a convention of bankers, you might do well to submit, in advance of the engagement, jokes pertaining to that city or to issues of a financial nature.

These days, a common complaint from comics who buy jokes is that much of the material they're sent just isn't funny to them. Another problem is that the submissions often don't suit their individual styles.

There's nothing wrong with writing jokes first and then taking up the question of whom you can submit them to, but most of those who sell jokes regularly write for particular targets. There is such a thing as a Joan Rivers joke, for example. These fall into two general categories—either she is putting down some public figure or she is deprecating herself. People who have mastered the technique of creating jokes will shortly be able to simply create with Joan in mind. And if she doesn't buy the self-insult line, they can still try to sell it to Phyllis Diller, who also does jokes knocking herself.

By the way, although Joan is on the lookout for new themes around which she can build routines, it's possible to obtain from her a list of joke topics that she's especially interested in—rich doctors, cheap dates, being flat-chested and so on.

Then, there are the Rodney Dangerfield "I don't get no respect" jokes. Many of these are compressed minidramas in which Rodney plays the role of the luckless party. "My wife said she wanted to make love in the back seat. While I was driving."

Obviously, while that's a good, strong line, it would have made no sense whatever for George Burns, Bob Hope, Bill Cosby, or Donald Duck. It makes sense just for the character Rodney does.

Yakov Smirnoff bases most of his act on lines about Russia; good news over there is bad news for him. Maureen Murphy often does Marilyn Monroe gags and jokes relating to Australia; and Phil Nee (who won Showtime TV's 1985 Funniest Person in America contest) likes to do material dealing with growing up Chinese in a primarily black/Hispanic neighborhood.

The instruction in all this, then, is to submit your jokes to the right people. It doesn't interest Bernie McGrenahan to know you can write good Steve Martin routines because his way of making people laugh is totally different from Steve's.

As to the technical details of selling jokes to stand-up comics, the first thing you should do is identify and locate the comedy clubs that are within reach. The lucky writers, of course, will be those living in either Los Angeles or New York, although there are hundreds of clubs of this sort now, in cities all over the country, so the matter of personally approaching comics is easier than it ever was before. You meet comedians in the same way you arrange to meet anyone else: you go where they are, approach them, and ask for a moment of their time.

Obviously, you should have in hand a page or so of material. Your name, phone number, and address should be on every page. You should also indicate your present rate per joke.

Naturally a certain amount of intelligence is called for so that you do not approach the comics at the wrong moment. If they're standing at the bar waiting to go on stage, that is clearly not the right time to talk to them. If they've just finished their act and are headed back to the dressing room, or perhaps sitting with friends at a nearby table, your approach is likely to be more effective.

The subject matter of the jokes you write is another important consideration. Comedians who do critical jokes about actual people—Joan Rivers, Don Rickles, Johnny Carson, Dennis Miller, Eddie Murphy, to name just a few—are sometimes criticized for being cruel and insensitive. Naturally the same applies to those who *write* such jokes. And sometimes this is truly the case. But in other situations it's a bum rap. A good deal depends on the comedians having the good sense to know when a given celebrity is fair game and when he's not.

I, too, do an occasional line about a real-life target, but only when that target is enjoying some sort of success or notoriety. My oft-quoted line, done on the first "Night of 100 Stars," would be an instance. Referring to the hoary cliché about concentrations of celebrities, I remarked that "If a bomb fell on this room tonight—it would certainly be good news for Pia Zadora." It was perfectly all right to do that joke at that time because Ms. Zadora's husband was spending vast sums of money in a promotional campaign on her behalf. I don't criticize her for that, but it did, as I say, make her a likely object of interest to comedians generally; I simply happened to do the first Pia Zadora joke, though by no means the last. But after that one instance, I did no more lines about her, because I was beginning to feel a certain amount of sympathy for her.

Another relevant instance would be a line I did after hearing, sometime back, that singer Connie Francis had been arrested after refusing to stop smoking in a no-smoking section of an airplane. That same night, entertaining at a dinner in Los Angeles, I mentioned a number of distinguished performers who were present and then added, "Of course, there's a far greater number of stars who are *not* with us this evening. For example, Connie Francis. Well, actually Connie *was* here, and she intended to come into the ballroom, but she happened to be smoking a cigarette and was unfortunately beaten senseless by Tony Randall."

To understand the point of the joke, of course, one has to know that Tony is almost violently opposed to smoking. But a few weeks after the incident on the airplane, there was a new story to the effect that Ms. Francis had been hospitalized for treatment of severe psychological and emotional problems. That being the case, no comedian in the world would dream of doing jokes about her unfortunate plight.

I think, in this connection, of the many "fat" jokes that comedians did for several years before the death of Orson Welles. Literally scores of comedians were doing such lines. Then, not long before his death, he went from simply being fat to a state of being grossly, almost grotesquely overweight. At that point, the joking stopped. He had become too pathetic a target.

What we're also explaining here, in talking about writing jokes, is methods of ad-libbing funny lines, a remarkable and unusual gift, though not a necessary one. Who cares that Jack Benny never said a witty thing in his personal life? He was still a great and deservedly popular comedian. Jackie Gleason was not witty, but he was a marvelously effective comedy performer. There are scores of ways to get laughs. Joke and comedy writers get theirs by basically doing what I do in my shows—they create spontaneous wit in an ad-lib setting. Jan Murray, Jack Carter, Buddy Hackett, Jonathan Winters, Robin Williams— all of them are very funny just shooting the breeze. But there may be only a score or so comics who are funny that way, whereas there are hundreds of comedy writers who get big laughs in living rooms and offices. It's obvious that these writers must be wittier than comedians, since they have to deliver theatrical merchandise—funny things to say—whereas it is possible to become a successful comedian without ever personally creating a joke.

And, of course, comedy writers are not the only people who are spontaneously, creatively funny in a social setting. All of us know a few people who just seem to be able to come up with a funny or silly comment about almost anything. Sometime back, I had lunch in Washington, D.C., with a couple of friends—conservative columnists John Lofton and Cal Thomas. Both are witty, quick-minded, highly intelligent gentlemen. There were a few points during our conversation, in fact, when the three of us were doing jokes on jokes on jokes.

As we were leaving the restaurant, I said to them, as a simple statement of fact, that there had been more laughs in the preceding hour than if I had spent the same amount of time with two famous comedians who happened to be in town at the same time, even though those entertainers are quite good at what they do. The point is that Lofton and Thomas were funnier, so far as quick, original, witty conversation is concerned.

The perceptive reader will already have realized that in the analysis of comedy, there is a great deal of opinion and far less fact, but this is true of the arts generally. As I've mentioned previously, if I think Richard Pryor is funny and another person doesn't, we're both right, since he's funny to me and not to the other person. Further comparison comes from the fact that no two professional comedians are funny for precisely the same reason. The reasons we laughed at Groucho Marx have very little to do with the reason we laugh at Billy Crystal. Whatever it was about W. C. Fields that made us laugh so heartily has nothing much to do with the reasons we laugh at Paula Poundstone.

Moreover, even gifted practitioners of the art of comedy can be funny only in their own way. Sid Caesar, for example, is the most talented practitioner as regards certain kinds of wild-premise sketch comedy. But Sid would fail if you gave him a Bob Hope string-of-timely-jokes monologue. Joan Rivers is talented at what she does, but she could not make us laugh in the same way that Charlie Chaplin did.

Are some cultures and ethnic groups naturally funnier than others? Yes. In the context of American society, there has been, during the present century, a high representation of Jews, blacks, and Irish in comedy. What these three peoples have in common is a restless submission to dominant authorities, a tendency to *talk* their way out of troubles, and a developed ability to employ humor to deal with the often essentially tragic nature of their social condition.

Necessity, then, may well be the mother of the invention of jokes, as it is of other forms of creativity.

Apart from stand-up comedians, other potential customers for one-liners include radio disk jockeys, and business people or politicians, who often incorporate humor in speeches they are required to make.

Many radio stations around the country have arrangements with special services that provide comedy routines ranging from printed jokes to fully produced, air-ready tapes. The material usually consists of phony phone calls from celebrities, mock commercials, song parodies, sketches, and other pieces with which the DJ can interact. While many of the smaller services are only one-person operations, the major outfits are usually open to buying material from freelance writers.

Two of the bigger services are All-Star Radio (Los Angeles) and American Comedy Network (Bridgeport, Connecticut). Note that neither company buys one-liners. All-Star Radio will accept only conceptual comedy that it can produce on tape. American Comedy Network can use anything from an idea to a taped comedy piece that is appropriate for morning radio shows that play Top 40 music.

When you think you're ready for the big time, there are the TV sitcoms to try. Writing for these, of course, involves considerably more time and effort than creating jokes, short routines, or sketches. Going rates for a thirty-minute sitcom are set by the Writers Guild of America and range from a few thousand to several thousand dollars.

The Writers Guild also publishes, in its monthly newsletters, a changing list of those TV series that accept submissions. For beginners, however, the TV market is difficult to crack. Humorist Larry Gelbart, one of the originators of "M*A*S*H," had this to say, at a Museum of Broadcasting seminar, about networks' and studios' receptivity to material from unknowns:

> Someone they know would have to give it to them. It would not be an unknown agent, an unknown representative. Someone they know could present an idea for an unknown. If they liked it, if they saw some value in it, they would get a bunch of knowns to follow through. They certainly wouldn't entrust much money or time hoping a newcomer could fill a half-hour or hour for them. Networks and studios do look at ideas. What else have they got to do? They don't *pick* many good ones, but they look at a lot.

●   ●   ●

Well, given that I've now written two separate volumes of instruction in the tricks and shticks of comedy, and assuming that the reader has to move along to more substantial works on weightier subjects, we may now arbitrarily conclude our course.

I've argued, in *Dumbth: And 81 Ways to Make Americans Smarter,* that textbooks of any sort should never be thrown away, but referred to, from time to time, as are dictionaries and telephone books. So your task is now to re-study and apply the many lessons given in *How To Be Funny* and *Make 'Em Laugh.*

I will make the one last but quite practical suggestion that, as regards examples given, you now go back and re-read them more analytically than you did at first exposure. They were included, after all, not simply to amuse you, but as instances in which I have practiced what I preached. Always remember that when we use the verb *to be funny* we are not giving relevant instruction but merely using an abstract term that points us in the direction of specifics.

There is always a certain amount of work in studying, no matter what the subject. Whether your purpose is to learn about philosophy, chemistry, motorcycle maintenance, or anything else, you do have to apply yourself to the task. Even as regards the more pleasurable arts—painting, creating music, acting, writing—long periods of concentrated study are a necessary part of the process.

It may be that a study of humor is the only course in the world that is actually fun, even if you flunk.